# American Origins

**L. G. PINE:**

*B.A. London, Barrister-at-Law of the Inner Temple; Fellow, Society of Antiquaries of Scotland, of the chartered Institute of Journalists; Editor of* Burke's Peerage, *of* Burke's Landed Gentry *of Great Britain and of Ireland, of the* International Year Book and Statesmen's Who's Who, *etc.; member Honourable Society of Cymmrodorion, of the Instituto Internacional de Genealogía y Heráldica, corresponding member Collegio Araldico, Rome, and of Instituto Argentino de Ciencias Genealógicas.*

# American Origins

by L. G. PINE

GENEALOGICAL PUBLISHING CO., INC.
BALTIMORE                                    1971

Originally Published
Garden City, New York, 1960


Reprinted
Genealogical Publishing Company
Baltimore, 1967


Genealogical Publishing Company
Baltimore, 1971


Library of Congress Catalog Card Number 67-30524
International Standard Book Number 0-8063-0277-1

# PREFACE

I think it may interest my readers to know how I came to write this book. I certainly feel that they are entitled to some explanation for the production of so large a work. For twenty-five years I have had a connection with genealogy. In 1935 I joined the staff of *Burke's Peerage*. Although I was absent for over six years in the Second World War, I was rarely allowed to forget my connection with Burke. I do not know how many times I filled in forms in the R.A.F. mentioning my prewar occupation. I do remember, though, having landed once on Crete and meeting the R.A.F. officer in command, when he mentioned his name, I said that I knew his family; on his asking how this had happened, I mentioned the entry of his family in *Burke's Peerage*, whereupon he remarked that some of his kinsfolk were very much taken up with genealogy. This sort of incident frequently occurred. In 1946 I resumed my work, becoming then Editor and Manager of the publications, many and various, under the heading of *Burke's Peerage*.

In one sense, however, my connection with genealogy and its allied subjects went back far before 1935. When I was a boy my father had told me the legends and traditions associated with our coat of arms. I became interested in these matters, and it was my knowledge of heraldry which had brought me to Burke when as a graduate of London University I was seeking employment. It is a curious fact that people who are interested in heraldry can and do go on to genealogy, but the opposite I have never known to occur. Genealogists pure and simple rather pride themselves on their ignorance of heraldry.

Before 1939 I had served my apprenticeship with the large genealogical works, *Burke's Peerage* and *Burke's Landed Gentry*. I had been introduced into the intricacies of American genealogy between 1937 and 1939, for at that time an edition of the *Landed Gentry* was produced which contained 1600 American family histories.

I had always been interested in history. It has been my knowledge of history which has enabled me to set the problems of family history in their proper perspective. I had always wanted to be an author. Both the interest and the desire found use and fulfillment from 1946 onward. Nothing had been done about *Burke's Peerage* and *Landed Gentry* during the war years. The revision and reappearance of these was a colossal task. I also dealt with other works—the *Author's and Writer's Who's Who, Who's Who in Music*, etc.—and founded a new reference book, *The International Year Book and Statesmen's Who's Who*. This last necessitated dealing with every country in the world, an experience which was to prove useful later.

During this period I wrote many books. The first, *The Middle Sea* (1950), was a history of the Mediterranean, where I had served in 1943–45, but the others covered the different problems of genealogy, heraldry, and peerage law. *The Story of Heraldry* (1952) told the history of heraldry, for the first time in English. Then came *Trace Your Ancestors*, mainly dealing with the problems of English ancestry. *The Golden Book of the Coronation* tells its own story. *They Came with the Conqueror* was a study of the Normans, and of those who, in Britain or in America, are descended from them. *The Story of the Peerage* gave not only narrative but the legal side of the Peerage as well. *Tales of the British Aristocracy; The Twilight of Monarchy* (a review of the twenty-five monarchies in the world, from Britain to Thailand); *Teach Yourself Heraldry and Genealogy; The Princes of Wales* (an account of the Welsh princes, and the twenty-one Princes of Wales); *A Guide to Titles*—these covered nearly everything of this type of writing in the British Isles.

My international experience was greatly enlarged by a work which I prepared during the years in which these other writings were appearing. This was *Orders of Chivalry and Decorations of Honour of the World*. This required application to every government throughout the world and much arduous work. It is to be published in England this year (1960). It prepared the way, along with my experience on *The International Year Book and Statesmen's Who's Who*, for the present work. I had also become a member of the International Institute of Genealogy and Heraldry, the head office of which is in Madrid, and a corresponding member of genealogical and heraldic societies in Italy, Argentina, etc.

Thus I have arrived by a natural process of development at a position where to write a book on American origins is a logical step. I have done my best in these pages to give the inquirer a chance of beginning his researches in the particular European country from which his family originated. I am aware of the shortcomings of the book: I hope that anyone who has a query will write to me, since only by continued work will subsequent editions be made more useful. But of one thing I am sure: nowhere else has so much genealogical information been brought together in one volume to deal with so many countries.

# CONTENTS

PREFACE         7

INTRODUCTION TO GENEALOGY         23

GENEALOGICAL KNOWLEDGE         25
    *Medieval Records*         27
    *Parish Registers*         28
    *Civil Registers*         30
TRACING RECORDS IN THE UNITED STATES         32
    *Where to Begin*         32
    *Additional Sources*         36
        THE MORMON GENEALOGICAL SOCIETY, 36
        THE LIBRARY OF CONGRESS, 37
        HISTORICAL SOCIETIES, 37
    *Heraldry*         38
    *Quaker Genealogy*         39
    *Books*         39
    *The First Americans*         39
HISTORICAL INTRODUCTION         41
    *The British Isles*         42
    *Scandinavia*         44
    *Germany and Austria*         45
    *The Low Countries*         47
    *Switzerland*         48

*The Latin Countries*                                    48
   FRANCE, 48
   SPAIN, 48
   PORTUGAL, 49
   ITALY, 49
*The Slavonic Countries*                                 50
   GREECE, ALBANIA, BULGARIA,
     RUMANIA, YUGOSLAVIA, 50
   RUSSIA, 50
   POLAND AND LITHUANIA, 51
   LATVIA AND ESTONIA, 51
   CZECHOSLOVAKIA, 52
*Monaco*                                                 52
*Liechtenstein*                                          52


GENEALOGICAL ACCOUNTS                                    53


ACKNOWLEDGMENTS                                          55


ENGLAND                                                  60
*Problems of the American Inquirer*                      60
   ANCIENT FAMILIES, 61
   ORIGINAL ENGLISH PEDIGREES, 63
   THE NORMAN CONQUEST PERIOD, 64
   THE MEDIEVAL PERIOD, 65
   THE REFORMATION AND THE PARISH REGISTERS, 67
*Somerset House*                                         68
*The Census*                                             73
*Wills*                                                  75
   NOTES ON WILLS AND THEIR WHEREABOUTS, 78
*Parish Registers*                                       79
   THE FORTY SHIRES OF ENGLAND, 82
   THE STATE OF THE REGISTERS, 84
*Illusions and Delusions*                                85
   FUNDS HELD IN CHANCERY, 86
   THE DELUSION ABOUT TITLES, 87
   THE COAT OF ARMS, 88
*The College of Arms*                                    90
*Summary*                                                93
*The British Museum*                                     94
*Medieval Records*                                       96
   THE HUNDRED ROLLS, 97
   THE PIPE ROLLS, 97
   INQUISITIONES POST MORTEM, 97

FINES AND RECOVERIES, 98
SIGN MANUAL, 99
RECORDS OF ATTAINDERS, FORFEITURES, AND
    PARDONS, 99
PARLIAMENTARY RECORDS, 99
HERALDIC COLLECTIONS, 99

*The Public Record Office*                            100
*Published Books*                                     102
*Pedigree of the Ancient Saxon Kings*                 106


SCOTLAND                                              108

*Introduction*                                        108
THE IMPORTANCE OF SCOTTISH HISTORY, 108
THE CLAN SYSTEM, 109
THE HERALDIC SYSTEM OF SCOTLAND, 111

*Registration of Births, Marriages,*
*and Deaths*                                          111
PARISH REGISTERS, 112
PRINTED GUIDES, 113
CENSUS RECORDS, 114
TESTAMENTS OR WILLS, 114

*Lyon Office*                                         114
*The Scots Peerage*                                   116
*University Registers*                                118
*Kirk Session Records*                                118
*The Clan System*                                     119
*Scottish Societies*                                  121
*Books and Documents*                                 122
"A GUIDE TO THE PUBLIC RECORDS OF SCOTLAND", 123
"THE SURNAMES OF SCOTLAND", 128
"SCOTTISH FAMILY HISTORY", 128
"RETOURS OF SERVICES OF HEIRS", 129

*The Unpublished Records*                             130
REGISTER OF DEEDS, 130
PARISH REGISTERS, 130
LYON OFFICE RECORDS, 130
ECCLESIASTICAL RECORDS, 130

*Society and Club Publications*                       131
*Cartularies of Religious and Other Houses*           132
*University Records*                                  132
*The Scottish Legal System*                           133


IRELAND                                               134

*Introduction*                                        134
CELTIC FAMILIES, 136

ANGLO-NORMAN FAMILIES, 136
ENGLISH FAMILIES, 137
THE ULSTER FAMILIES, 137

*Northern Ireland*                                            138

THE REGISTRAR-GENERAL, 138
THE PUBLIC RECORD OFFICE, 139
THE ULSTER KING OF ARMS OFFICE, 141
OTHER REGISTERS, 142
THE ULSTER-SCOT HISTORICAL SOCIETY, 142
HOW TO MAKE RESEARCHES IN NORTHERN
   IRELAND, 143

*The Republic of Ireland*                                      144

THE REGISTRAR-GENERAL'S OFFICE, 145
   FORMS OF APPLICATION AND SCALE OF
      CHARGES, 146
THE PUBLIC RECORDS OFFICE, 147
   CENSUS RETURNS, 148
   PAROCHIAL RECORDS—PROTESTANT, 149
   PAROCHIAL RECORDS—CATHOLIC, 152
   PAROCHIAL RECORDS—MISCELLANEOUS, 153
HOW TO PROCEED THUS FAR 153
   WILLS, 154
   INTESTATE ADMINISTRATIONS, 157
   THE REGISTRY OF DEEDS, 157
   COURT RECORDS, 158
   CONVERT ROLLS, 158
   SCALE OF CHARGES AT THE PUBLIC RECORD
      OFFICE, 159
THE GENEALOGICAL OFFICE, DUBLIN CASTLE, 160
   ORIGINAL CELTIC PEDIGREES, 161
   SIR WILLIAM BETHAM'S MANUSCRIPTS, 161
   FUNERAL ENTRIES, 162
   GRANTS OF ARMS, 162
   VISITATIONS, 162
   REGISTERED PEDIGREES, 162
   CITY OF DUBLIN FREEMEN ROLL, 163
   MISCELLANEOUS, 163
   FEES, 163
LIBRARIES, 164
   THE NATIONAL LIBRARY OF IRELAND, 165
   TRINITY COLLEGE, DUBLIN, 165
   THE ROYAL IRISH ACADEMY, 166
   THE ARMAGH LIBRARY, 167
   MASONIC SOURCES, 167
   THE BRITISH MUSEUM LIBRARY, 168
   LAMBETH PALACE LIBRARY, 169
   THE BODLEIAN LIBRARY, 170
   IRISH STATE PAPER OFFICE, 170
PRINTED SOURCES, 170
HISTORICAL MANUSCRIPTS, 172
SOCIETIES, 173

THE IRISH GENEALOGICAL RESEARCH SOCIETY, 173
THE MILITARY HISTORY SOCIETY OF IRELAND, 175
*The Milesian Pedigrees, or Celtic
    Genealogies* 176
*Irish Surnames* 180
*Note on Coats of Arms* 181

WALES 184
*Introduction* 184
*Manuscript Collections* 190
*Welsh Wills—Their Places of Deposit* 194
*The Public Record Office* 194
    EQUITY RECORDS, 195
    COMMON-LAW RECORDS, 195
    GENERAL RECORDS, 196

THE ISLE OF MAN AND THE CHANNEL ISLANDS 197
*The Isle of Man* 197
    REGISTRATION OF BIRTHS, MARRIAGES, AND
        DEATHS, 197
    CUSTODY OF THE REGISTERS, 197
    ECCLESIASTICAL PARISHES, 198
    ARMS, 198
*The Channel Islands* 199
    JERSEY, 199
    GUERNSEY, 200
    ALDERNEY, 201
    SARK, 202

NORWAY 203
*Introduction* 203
*Parish Registers* 203
*Civil Registration* 204
*Census Returns* 204
*Wills* 205
*Public Records* 205
    THE NATIONAL ARCHIVES, 205
    REGIONAL STATE ARCHIVES, 206
*Heraldry* 206
*Genealogical Society* 207
*Newspapers* 207
*Additional Information* 207
*Libraries* 208

SWEDEN                                          209
  *Introduction*                                209
  *The Public Record System*                    209
  *Civil Registration*                          211
  *The National Archives*                        213
  *The Regional Archives*                        215
  *The Armed Forces and Diplomatic Corps*       216
  *Private Archives*                            217
  *Societies for Genealogical Research*         218
  *Heraldry and Nobility*                       222
  *Summary*                                     223
  *Addresses of Archives*                       223

DENMARK                                         225
  *Registration of Births, Marriages, ana*
    *Deaths*                                    225
  *The Public Record Office*                    226
  *Wills*                                       227
  *Heraldry*                                    227
  *Books*                                       228

ICELAND                                         230
  *Introduction*                                230
  *Registration of Births, Marriages, and*
    *Deaths*                                    230
  *Coats of Arms*                               231
  *Wills*                                       231
  *Census*                                      231
  *Icelanders in America*                       232

FINLAND                                         234
  *Introduction*                                234
  *Registration*                                235
  *The Central Archives*                        236
  *Wills*                                       236
  *The Genealogical Society*                    237
  *Coats of Arms*                               238
  *List of Communes*                            239
  *The House of the Nobility*                   239
  *Heraldry*                                    240

GERMANY 242
    *Civil Registration* 242
    *Ecclesiastical Records* 243
    *Central Archives* 243
    *Wills* 244
    *Genealogical Societies* 244
    *German Nobility* 245
    *Heraldry* 245
    *Addresses* 246

AUSTRIA 248
    *Introduction* 248
    *Roman Catholic Church Records* 249
    *Records of the Provinces* 250
    *The Evangelical Church Records* 251
    *The Old Catholic Church* 251
    *The Greek Orthodox Church* 252
    *The Jewish Community* 252
    *Records of Other Communities and for*
      *Undenominational Persons* 253
    *Austrians Resident Abroad* 253
    *Military Personnel* 253
    *Civil Registration* 254
    *Wills* 255
    *Public Records* 255
    *Heraldry* 256

THE NETHERLANDS 257
    *Civil Registration* 257
    *Church Registration* 257
    *Situation of the Archives* 258
    *Wills* 258
    *Societies* 259
    *Heraldry* 259

BELGIUM 261
    *Introduction* 261
    *Parish Registers* 261
    *Civil Registration* 262
    *Wills* 262

General Archives                                        262
PRINTED RECORDS, 264
MODERN RECORDS NOT PRINTED, 264
ANCIENT COLLECTIONS, 264
Societies                                               265

LUXEMBOURG                                              270
Introduction                                            270
Civil Registration                                      270
Parish Registers                                        271
Relevés des Protocoles Notariaux                        271
Coats of Arms                                           272
Heraldic Societies                                      272
Publications                                            273
Roster of Notarized Registrars—Diekirch                274
Roster of Notarized
    Registrars—Luxembourg                               277

FRANCE                                                  284
Ecclesiastical Registers                                284
Wills                                                   285
Heraldry                                                286
The National Archives                                   286
Archives de la Seine                                    288
Les Archives Départementales                            288
Archive Offices                                         288

SPAIN                                                   291
Civil Registration                                      291
Parochial, or Ecclesiastical, Registration             292
Wills                                                   293
Public Record Office                                    294
Heraldry                                                295
Publications                                            296
International Institute                                  297
"General Military Archive of Segovia: Index
    of Personal Documents"                              298

PORTUGAL                                                299
Civil Registration                                      299
Parish Registers                                        300
National Archives                                       300

*Archives in the Direccão-Geral dos Registos
e do Notariado* 302
*Wills* 302

ITALY 303
   *Parish Registers* 303
   *State Registers* 303
   *Census Records* 304
   *Armorial Bearings* 304
   *Wills* 305
   *Public Records and National Archives* 306

SWITZERLAND 307
   *Introduction* 307
   *Wills* 308
   *Heraldry* 308
   *Cantonal Records and Arrangements* 308

MONACO 312

LIECHTENSTEIN 315

POLAND 316
   *Civil Registration* 316
   *Preservation of Civil Registers* 316
   *Ecclesiastical Records* 317
   *Wills* 318
   *Heraldry* 318
   *Central Archives* 318
   *Local Archives* 318

THE FORMER BALTIC STATES 321
   *Estonia* 321
      REGISTRATION OF BIRTHS, MARRIAGES, AND
        DEATHS, 322
      WILLS, 322
      TITLES, 322
   *Latvia* 322
      CIVIL REGISTRATION, 322
      WILLS, 323
      STATE ARCHIVES, 323
      HERALDRY, 323

*Lithuania*                                                        324
   REGISTRATION OF BIRTHS, MARRIAGES, AND
     DEATHS, 324
   WILLS, 324
   PUBLIC RECORDS, 325
   COATS OF ARMS, 325

ALBANIA                                                            327
   *Civil Registration*                               327
   *Religious Records*                                328

BULGARIA                                                           329
   *Civil Registration*                               329
   *Parochial Registration*                           329
   *Wills*                                            330
   *Heraldry*                                         330
   *Additional Note*                                  330

GREECE                                                             331
   *Civil Registration*                               331
   *Church Registers*                                 331
   *Archives of Local and State Communities*          332
   *Wills*                                            332
   *Heraldry*                                         333

RUSSIA                                                             335
   *Registration of Births, Marriages, and*
     *Deaths*                                335
   *Pre-Bolshevik Records*                            337
   *The Nobility*                                     338
   *Wills*                                            340

CZECHOSLOVAKIA                                                     341
   *Civil Registration of Births, Marriages, and*
     *Deaths*                                341
   *Church Registration*                              342
   *Heraldry*                                         343
   *General Note*                                     343

YUGOSLAVIA                                                         345
   *Civil Registration*                               345

*Heraldry*   346
*Wills*   347

HUNGARY   348
   *Civil Registration*   348
   *Parish Registers*   348
   *Wills*   349
   *National Archives*   349
   *Heraldry and Nobility*   350

JEWRY   351
   *Introduction*   351
   *Societies*   352
   *Encyclopedias*   353
   *Other Sources of Information*   354

# Introduction
# to Genealogy

# GENEALOGICAL
# KNOWLEDGE

Genealogy, or the study of family history, is found in all races in varying degrees. Among some peoples, records are kept without writing, by means of some arrangement such as the bead system of the Maoris of New Zealand or simply by traditional narration. Some examples of genealogies which will come to mind are those in the Old Testament, showing descents from Adam, Noah, and others, and in the New Testament, where the genealogy of Christ is given. I cannot in this introduction go through all the features of genealogy in the world. I may refer the reader to an article by me on genealogy in *Collier's Encyclopedia*. Here I am mainly concerned with giving the results of my researches in Europe for the purpose of this present book.

Genealogical knowledge may be divided into two main parts: (1) oral tradition and (2) documentary material. At first, in nearly all countries, genealogies are handed down by word of mouth. This traditional knowledge may be very good. Everything depends on the particular country and its circumstances. In fact, one of the most important of all principles to grasp in studying genealogy is that in every country the genealogical records depend upon the circumstances of the country and upon the way in which records have been kept. Genealogy—the history of families—is only part of the history of the particular country. In its turn, genealogy illuminates the history of the country. It is impossible to understand the wars between England and France, or the struggle for independence by the Scots in medieval times, without recourse to genealogical tables. If there had not been twelve claimants to the throne of Scotland in 1295, Edward I of England could hardly have interfered in the affairs of that country. There would have been no Wallace, no Bruce, and no doubt some dynastic marriage would have united England and Scotland as Castile and Aragon were united. Similarly, the Wars of the Roses in England are completely inexplicable unless one looks at a family tree of York and Lancaster.

There are plenty of cases of oral tradition which has eventually been written down. Thor Heyerdahl's wonderful *Kon-Tiki* deals with the legends of the Pacific islanders which refer to their having come from a land to the east. Many other such traditional stories exist among the Pacific islanders. The Maoris' legends prove that they reached their New Zealand home some 600 to 700 years ago. In Japan the firmly rooted national belief is in the origin of the imperial line some 2600 years ago. The Ethiopians believe their emperor to be the descendant of Solomon and Sheba. Many Arab families boast descent from the Prophet Mohammed, from his contemporaries, or from an earlier period. There are Chinese who descend from Confucius. In Europe, I think there is much truth in the old oral genealogies of the Irish and the Welsh. I see no reason why they should not have been written down at a fairly early period in a fairly reliable form. As a matter of fact, both Irish and Welsh have a few families whose genealogies remount some 1500 years. But the reason for this is precisely because nothing was in writing when the oral genealogies were in their full vigor. Consequently, a descent from Niall of the Nine Hostages, who died about 405 A.D., seems to me quite in order in Irish genealogy. About a century later, when Ireland was becoming Christian, the genealogies of the kings were written down by the monks. The wild features which have made the Milesian tales a byword for fabulous descent owe most of their crudities to the monkish chroniclers. They wished to show that their sovereigns were descended from Biblical heroes, and so they joined the old oral genealogy (usually a mere string of names) onto the genealogies of the Old Testament. But there is no reason to doubt the string of Irish names or that they represent genuine persons.

It is precisely when literature takes a hand that oral tradition is in danger. Moreover, in a society which has always had a literary tradition it is almost impossible for a so-called oral tradition to arise.

This is why, in most cases if not in all, claims to descent from the early centuries of the Christian Era must be rejected except for a few royal lines and for the Celtic races. It remains true, as was observed by the English historian Edward Gibbon, that not even the greatest European families, the Bourbons or Habsburgs, can struggle back into the last age of Rome. The Roman Empire fell, its great families were killed or disappeared. The great families of the invaders took their place. All the time, a thin historical record was maintained by the monks. No records can be found to substantiate the descent of any continental European family from Roman times.

## MEDIEVAL RECORDS

Passing to documentary information, there are roughly three periods in Europe. The "medieval period" is a vague term covering the years 500–1500 A.D. In this vast tract of 1000 years there are exceptions to every rule which can be laid down. It is safe to say that no one is going to trace his family in the Middle Ages unless they were notable as landowners or wealthy, or, of course, were royalty. Yet, in the thirteenth and fourteenth centuries in parts of England, villeins (i.e., serfs) have been mentioned in the manorial records whose pedigrees have been traced for three to five generations. Yet this does not necessarily provide a link with modern persons. Generally, you are very unlikely to be able to trace your family before 1500 unless they were (a) related to royalty, (b) landowners or land tenants, or (c) wealthy townsfolk. This need not deter American inquirers. Probably no one will ever know the number of Americans who have a royal descent from a king of England, but they are very numerous. These descents are legitimate and through the female line. But in other European lands the descents of what one may call ordinary families are very unlikely to be from royalty. The European royal families, as apart from the British, tended to marriage either with royalty or with their nobles. The nobles were often a closed class, whereas in England and Scotland they were not, but intermarried with the gentry, and the latter with the yeomen and commonalty. Hence the vast number of true Americans who have been sired by Edward III some eighteen generations back. In the first half of the sixteenth century we come to a great change.

## PARISH REGISTERS

All over western Europe—in Scandinavia, the Low Countries, France, Italy, the British Isles—in the period 1530–50 parish registers began to be kept. In Spain they are even earlier, in a few cases going back to the end of the fourteenth century. What was the reason for this change? It would be tempting to think that the Council of Trent was responsible. The Council sat from 1545 to 1563, but we have only to notice the date at which parish registers began to be kept in England (1538) to see that the movement preceded the first sitting of the Council. Moreover, the tendency exists as much in Protestant countries, such as Sweden, as in Italy. I think that the real cause of the keeping of parochial records in western Europe in the first half of the sixteenth century is to be found in the growth of literary knowledge. Printing had been invented, books were becoming more common, and there were large sections of learned men outside the clerical profession. There was a growth in historical knowledge and in the desire to know more about the past of one's country. While the Renaissance gave an impetus to this study, the Reformation controversies supplied strong motives for its prosecution. It is from the Reformation period that the study of history dates. The *Magdeburg Centuries,* on the one hand, and the *Annals of Baronius,* on the other, set out the Protestant and Catholic viewpoints. Immediately criticism begins; there begins also a searching and probing. To prove Roman Catholicism wrong, it was necessary to be able to discriminate between the New Testament period and the ages of the early Church and the medieval Church. Controversy gave birth to research and historical study. History is a poor thing without written records, and so it came about in the first half of the sixteenth century that it was the right thing for a country to keep some records even of its lowliest inhabitants. It was natural for such records to be entrusted to the Church, for ecclesiastics had always been the agents in all social and civilizing matters.

But great as is the advance denoted by these parochial records, such information as they afford falls short of what the genealogist wishes to find. There was at first great opposition to the keeping of parish records. That this was a general phenomenon in western Europe can be seen from most of the national entries in this volume, where the date at which the order to keep parochial entries is made is usually followed by a statement that in fact few registers go back to that period.

While an advance in genealogical knowledge was made in the keeping of the parish registers, there were, unfortunately, great losses in valuable materials from earlier periods. The Reformation controversy was conducted with virulence and cruelty. In all countries which became Protestant the monasteries and nunneries were suppressed. When these establishments were abolished many of their records were destroyed. In England alone the loss of the monastic records was very great. It can never be properly estimated, but some idea of it may be gained from the monastic chartularies which remain, a poor remnant.

In countries which remained Catholic, such as Spain, many more records must have been preserved from the Middle Ages than in Protestant lands like Sweden or Scotland. Here again the records have had to run the gantlet of destruction in later periods. While Britain has been remarkably free from civil or internal discords during the last 300 years, continental European lands have suffered terrible upheavals, such as the Napoleonic Wars, the Revolution of 1848, the Franco-German War in 1870 (in France), the war of 1914–18, and the far more destructive war of 1939–45.

Apart from the parochial registers there are other sources of local genealogical information, which herein are listed under each country's article. These are such sources as wills, land transactions, and heraldic information. The keeping of wills varies very much from land to land, in Germany for instance being somewhat haphazard, as against the great care exercised in Britain. Land transactions and the records of courts are of great value, and most western European countries have them.

As regards heraldic knowledge, the beginner has to be very careful. I can only advise him to study some useful work on the subject. It is impossible for me to give anything resembling an account of the origin of heraldry. For this I would refer the reader to the *Encyclopedia Americana,* where an article by myself on heraldry will be found; or to my small work *Teach Yourself Heraldry.* Heraldry is the science and art of armorial bearings; these latter are the hereditary symbols handed down in families or in institutions. To write properly on this vast subject would require an enormous work. After many years study I incline to the position that many of the accepted views on heraldry are simply misconceptions not based on any reliable evidence. I exposed some of these in my other heraldic book, now out of print, *The Story of Heraldry*. In this present work, in the account of Swiss genealogy, I have given, on the most categorical Swiss official statements, proof that heraldic officers do not exist in Switzerland. Yet it is a statement frequently made in England by outstanding writers, that Switzerland as a republic has official heralds.

I have used the expression "western European countries or nations" above because there is a homogeneous quality about the area from Norway to Sicily and from Poland to Ireland. This does not apply to Russia, or the Balkan countries, where heraldry has been copied mainly from the West and where the keeping of records begins later (as we can see in the case of the Russian nobility) than in the West. The state of the records in a country like Bulgaria reminds one of the character in a Shaw play (I think in *Arms and the Man*) who says, "We are the oldest family in the country, we go back quite twenty years." Nowhere does this become more apparent than in the third period of European record keeping.


## CIVIL REGISTERS

With the French Revolution and the growth of the modern state, the keeping of records became directly the concern of the government in each country. (It should be noted that in Iceland the keeping of registers and the holding of a census far antedate the arrangements in either Britain or the United States.) In the eighteenth century there had been a move in England to begin a census, but the ignorance and superstition of the period had prevented it. In the end, the United States, with a census held in 1791, beat the British to it, for it was not until 1801 that the first British census was held. Another generation saw the growth of the movement for offical registration of births, marriages, and deaths. From then on (1837 in England) the move gained ground and the various countries of Europe adopted similar systems. An examination of the various Balkan countries in this book will show the beginning of registration as late as the present century in some cases. France, on the other hand, in the full flush of the Revolution, introduced civil registration wherever she had the power.

From the beginning of the nineteenth century, the thirst for knowledge on the part of the state has grown steadily greater; and in the twentieth century it has assumed proportions far beyond anything that our ancestors would have been able to recognize. It need hardly be said that little of this state information is gathered with any view to the benefit of the individual in a genealogical sense. The individual is only incidental to the activity of bringing in all this knowledge. But as with the records of the Middle Ages which have survived, a huge amount of knowledge about family history can be gleaned from the archives of the state. It is always the more reliable because it is not intended to bolster up family pride.

If we go back over the brief sketch just given, it will be clear that most Europeans will be able to trace themselves for some generations, into the early nineteenth century at least. After that, they are more at the mercy of ecclesiastical records, which were often imperfectly kept and even more imperfectly preserved. Still, many thousands of pedigrees exist which are traced to the eighteenth, seventeenth, and sixteenth centuries. These pedigrees, moreover, are those of ordinary families, not of the great ones of the land.

Equally clear is the conclusion that for the majority of people to trace a pedigree before 1600 is unusual. If it can be traced, it is either (1) connected through some female line with a great medieval family, as so frequently occurs in American pedigrees which stem from Britain; or (2) it comes from an illegitimate source, as with the numerous descendants of the dukes of Burgundy.

It is too much to hope that the dry considerations which I have set out above will guide the too ardent researcher, anxious for the glories of his family. Nonetheless, they are correct considerations based on much experience.

# TRACING RECORDS
# IN THE
# UNITED STATES

## WHERE TO BEGIN

One very important consideration for anyone who wishes to trace his ancestry in Europe is who was the first ancestor in America. Suppose an American has his line of ancestry in the United States back to 1850 and beyond that has only the evidence of his name (e.g., Williams) that his ancestor came to America from Wales. How is he to bridge the gap between 1850 and the date of immigration? Obviously, it is important to have your data and your line in America from the immigrant ancestor before you attempt to trace that ancestor in Europe.

I feel very hesitant in dealing with this part of the subject. It is true that my experience with American pedigrees is very considerable. It began in 1937, and over the next two years I was responsible for the preparation of the 1939 *Burke's Landed Gentry,* which contained 1600 American pedigrees in the form of an American Supplement. Since 1946, when I returned from war service, I have dealt with several thousands of American genealogical and heraldic inquiries. In the great majority of cases these came from Americans who at least had their American lines all prepared and ready with the further question of the European or specifically British or Irish ancestor to be traced. I have never worked on tracing American ancestry in America. I am therefore dependent on following the schemes of American writers on the subject, to whom I give in the appropriate place the most explicit reference.

In the first place, I have found of the greatest interest a delightful book called *Searching for Your Ancestors; the Why and How of Genealogy,* by Gilbert Harry Doane, Director of University Libraries, University of Wisconsin. This was published in 1937 (second printing 1952, by the University of Minnesota Press, Minneapolis, and by Oxford University Press, London). The manner in which this book is written reminded me of my own work for British genealogical researchers, *Trace Your Ancestors* (Evans Bros., Ltd., London). The author obviously has vast genealogical knowledge and has been able to write in an easy manner. He gives all the explanations which are necessary and includes many salutary warnings. There is an extensive bibliography and some useful appendices, particularly on Census Records and on Lists, Registers, Rolls, and Rosters of Revolutionary War Soldiers.

Perhaps the feature in Mr. Doane's book which interested me most, as an English genealogist, was the scheme of research which he outlined for his readers. I should certainly advise anyone who wished to trace his genealogy to obtain as much oral information as possible from his older relatives. I should hardly, however, put that type of information at the beginning. As can be seen from the English section of this book, I advise using Somerset House for information of a parent's marriage or birth certificate. However, I do realize that while England is a small, compact country with a highly centralized government, the United States is composed of fifty states, each with laws and arrangements that can differ from the others' very much. The size of the United States may render the successful prosecution of inquiries in writing much more difficult than in England. This being said, I can see the reason for Mr. Doane's method. He advises (1) the obtaining of as much information as possible from older members of the family and (2) turning out the family papers, particularly using the old family Bible. Then he recommends going to (3) books and libraries, including the many excellent publications of genealogical societies in America; (4) the town records—"There were practically no general laws requiring the registration of births, marriages, and deaths before 1850"; (5) inscriptions in cemeteries—in England these are known as M.I.s (monumental inscriptions) and are certainly useful; (6) wills—here again, there are many more repositories of wills in

America than in England; (7) church records; (8) the census returns from 1790 to 1880. America was thus eleven years ahead of Britain in having a census and fifty years ahead in keeping records. The first census in the United States was meant probably to discover the military strength of the nation. The returns for some of the states which were covered by the 1790 census were destroyed when the British burned the Capitol at Washington during the War of 1812. These last returns were for the states of Delaware, Georgia, Kentucky, New Jersey, Tennessee, and Virginia. The American census returns do not (unlike the British) give names (except for the head of the family) or dates of birth.

Mr. Doane has a chapter devoted to the Society of the Daughters of the American Revolution, in which he points out the exacting requirements of the Society in establishing a genealogy. Altogether this is a very useful book, and I am particularly appreciative of the fact that Mr. Doane warns his readers against the easy identification of an American immigrant ancestor with someone of the same name mentioned in an English record of the seventeenth century.

From Mr. Doane's work I pass to a more recently published book, by James S. Sweet, 1958. It is called *Genealogy and Local History: An Archival and Bibliographical Guide* ($5.00, published by Genealogical Associates, 1204 Monroe Street, Evanston, Illinois). It is a Multigraph production and includes much valuable information, particularly a section headed "Where to Write for Birth and Death Records." This gives the addresses required for these vital statistics, with prices of certificates and the date at which records begin in the respective state. Alabama to Wyoming is dealt with in this manner, in addition to the U.S. territories, the Canal Zone, etc.; and births and deaths occurring outside U.S. territory. "Marriage Records" is the heading of another section.

From sources such as those referred to and from others which I will mention later, I deduce a system of research into American records similar to that shown for European countries in the present work. One great difference, however, between the United States and European countries is that each state of the Union is sovereign and, among other sovereign rights, keeps its own records of the births, marriages, and deaths of its citizens. It therefore follows that an American inquirer may have to search through the annals of a half dozen American states if his family has moved much. The age of these state records varies, but 1875 is fairly early for Maryland. Naturally, the states which arose out of the original thirteen American colonies will have more records and older records than will Montana, for example. Records of birth, marriage, and death were ordered to be kept from the middle of the nineteenth century (1848 in New Jersey), but the older records of the New England states go back to long before the date of state concern for vital statistics. These older records—from the seventeenth century—are often in the registers of religious bodies, and as no Church has ever been established in America, the custody of Church records is frequently a matter of considerable difficulty.

In fact, the tracing of ancestry inside the United States is largely a matter of knowing when the family arrived in America. Up to the Revolution, in 1776, the bulk of the settlers in what is now the United States were from the British Isles, and of these the majority were from England and Wales. After the severance with Britain, the number of British immigrants declined, and the influx of persons from continental Europe began. The main flood did not come until after the Civil War (1860–65); then enormous numbers came in from all parts of Europe to open up the huge country of the West.

Therefore, in tracing inside the United States it appears to me that 1880 is a crucial date. If your ancestors were in America before 1880, then I think you begin with the National Archives. The period from 1880 to the present can be handled through the state archives. The address of the National Archives is:

*United States National Archives and Records Service*
*Eighth Street and Pennsylvania Avenue NW*
*Washington 25, D.C.*

You can then begin to trace your ancestors back through the census returns, which were compiled every ten years between 1790 and 1880. As already mentioned, the American census is eleven years older than its British counterpart, and its returns have been kept, whereas in Britain the returns (except, of course, for the total figures of population) were not preserved until 1841. In addition to this valuable aid, the National Archives contains much immensely useful material, such as files of pension applications, army records, and also passport applications from 1791–1905.

I think, however, that the American whose ancestors are more newly arrived in the United States may find the National Archives of even greater value. The following categories must prove of great help:

*Homestead applications, 1862–1950*

*Passenger lists for ships which arrived at various ports. For instance, in the case of Baltimore the lists cover the century 1820–1919. Each passenger's country of origin is given.*

*Naturalization records. These are found in the records of the courts of the District of Columbia from 1802–1926.*

I would advise anyone who is trying to work out his ancestral line in the United States, before crossing the Atlantic to continue the work, to get both Doane's and Sweet's books. There is very useful information in both without which the inquirer will be lost.

My purpose is, of course, to deal with inquiries outside America; hence my diffidence and reliance on others who know the United States when I have tried to handle the home side of the problem. However, I have acquired by constant research into American genealogical problems additional information which I hope will be of service. It is particularly in the field of bibliography that I can be helpful.

## ADDITIONAL SOURCES

### The Mormon Genealogical Society, Salt Lake City

Some years ago in London, at the Society of Genealogists, I met a representative of the Church of the Latter-day Saints who was in Europe on a special mission. He was engaged in making microfilms of all the original records of Europe which had a genealogical bearing. How far he succeeded in this stupendous task I do not know. I had understood that the parish records in England were not made accessible for microfilming. I believe that considerable record sections throughout Europe were microfilmed; and this being so, the microfilm library at Salt Lake City will probably in due course become the finest genealogical microfilm collection in the New World. However, the aim of this great work is religious, not genealogical. The Mormons are interested in their forebears from the standpoint of religion; something akin to the passage in the New Testament

(First Epistle to the Corinthians, 15:29) where the writer speaks of those who are baptized on behalf of the dead. Nonetheless, though the primary aim of this collection is not to assist genealogical research, it will be advisable to inquire at Salt Lake City whether the record has been microfilmed, and if so, whether it is available.

Microfilm material of American records is also to be found in the archives of many states of the Union.

### The Library of Congress

This is the greatest book collection in the United States. As with the British Museum Library, it is necessary for copyright material to be deposited there. But apart from this magnificent national collection, full use should be made of the vast library service of the United States. In a great many genealogical cases which have come my way I have been informed of the research which has been done through the records of the New York Public Library and the Boston Public Library.

### Historical Societies

There are a very large number of these in the United States. As I write I have before me the *Directory of the Historical Societies and Agencies in the United States and Canada,* 1959. This is published by the American Association for State and Local History and covers every state. There are fifty pages listing the societies and agencies. Then comes a list of Canadian associations, ranged under the provinces of British Columbia, Manitoba, New Brunswick, Nova Scotia, Ontario, and Quebec. In each case the name of the society is given, with full address, name of secretary, wherever possible the type of material handled, and the name and period of appearance of any publication of the society. There is also an index to the work under the headings: (1) Church—Affiliated Agencies, (2) Ethnic and Racial Agencies, (3) Genealogical Societies, (4) Medical Societies (these, like all the others, are concerned with history), (5) Military Societies, (6) National and Regional Associations and Conferences, (7) Professional and Occupational Societies, (8) Railroad Societies, and (9) Topical and Special Interest Groups.

Some of these societies, though placed under a particular state, are concerned with a much larger area. In particular, this is the case with the New England Historic Genealogical Society.

Connected with the latter is another feature of great interest, which should come under the heading of heraldry.

## HERALDRY

There is a great interest in heraldry in America. To meet this a Committee on Heraldry was set up in 1864 by the New England Historic Genealogical Society. The Committee has published seven Rolls of Arms, the earliest in 1928, the latest in 1958. The object of the Roll has been to register and reproduce only arms borne rightfully in America. The canons for the rightful bearing of arms are (1) whether the bearer bore them without protest in the country of origin, or (2) whether they were used at an early date by an immigrant to America, or (3) whether the arms were granted or confirmed by some authority in the British Isles, e.g., the College of Arms, Lyon Office, or Genealogical Office, Dublin Castle. However, while adhering to these canons the Committee has found it necessary to widen the scope of origin of the arms it deals with. In the 1958 Roll it is pointed out that "approximately one third of the arms registered are of Continental origin, from 9 different countries. Of the 14 States from which arms have been contributed in this Part, only two are of New England."

More important, perhaps, from the average American's point of view, than the registration of arms by the Committee is the statement that "the Committee carefully lists in files, arms assumed by an individual." The Society does not sanction "the publication of these assumed arms, nor do they form any part of the Roll."

"An applicant need not be descended from the person who bore the arms which he wishes to have registered." I quote the last sentence because it is obvious that there are many Americans who cannot prove a descent from an armigerous ancestor but who want a coat of arms. It is difficult to see how anyone in such a position can or ought to be prevented from making a coat of arms for himself. It would, however, be much more in order if such arms when assumed could be formally recorded with some learned body in America.

## QUAKER GENEALOGY

In the New World as in the Old, Quaker records have been kept with an amazing precision and attention to detail. For the United States, I would strongly recommend *The Encyclopedia of American Quaker Genealogy,* by Dr. William Wade Hinshaw.

## BOOKS

*The Distinguished Families of America* was first published in 1939 as a 500-page supplement to *Burke's Landed Gentry.* It was called the American Supplement, and the 1600 families were of those Americans whose ancestors came from Britain or Ireland. After the war (in 1947) some copies of this supplement were brought out, apart from the main (British) *Landed Gentry,* under the title *The Distinguished Families of America.* This work, under either title, is one of the very few in English which gives reliable American genealogies without straining after an English or Scottish connection unwarranted by anything except a similarity of name.

Another work which is valuable on the same grounds is *Prominent Families of America,* by A. M. Burke. He was of the same family as the Burkes who produced the well-known *Peerage* and *Landed Gentry.* His work just mentioned was written about 1912 and was intended to be in several volumes. Only Volume I was published. In this work American pedigrees were included which were of non-British strain, for instance the Roosevelts.

## THE FIRST AMERICANS

There will always be, I hope, an interest in the red Indians, by whom the vast North American continent was first sparsely peopled. They were tough enough to prove too much for the Vikings who settled or tried to settle down on the northeastern coasts some 500 years before Columbus. They resisted with stern courage the progress westward of an ever growing mass of whites. As late as 1875 they were capable of winning a battle against the U. S. Army, and the frontier was only closed officially in 1890. Today these earliest Americans live on their reservations, but inevitably they must have mingled their blood with that of their white conquerors. One outstanding instance is that of Pocahontas, daughter of Powhatan, an Indian chief in Virginia, whose short life lasted from about 1595 to 1617. She saved the life of the famous Captain John Smith, one of the leaders in the colony of Jamestown. She married an Englishman, Captain John Rolfe, in 1614. With her husband she went to England, where she was treated by King James I as a sister sovereign. She died in 1616 and was buried at Gravesend in Kent, England. Princess Pocahontas had time, however, to leave descendants, and several notable families in New England (and old England) trace their ancestry from her.

Between the U. S. Government and the different Indian tribes, many treaties were made, and in these it often happened that clauses were included providing for various benefits to be allowed to members of the tribe. In order to deal properly with these provisions, the U. S. Government often had rolls of the particular tribe. These sometimes go back to 1840, while many more date from after the Civil War (1865). These records are preserved in the U. S. National Archives, Washington 25, D.C. There is thus a certain amount of Indian genealogical information available.

# HISTORICAL

# INTRODUCTION

Anyone who seeks to conduct researches into European genealogy will need to know something about the alignments in the various European countries. Germany and Italy as political unities are not 100 years old. The fact that they were composed of separate states has, of course, a considerable influence on their records. In Germany there is not the centralization of records which there is in England. Then again, at present Germany is divided into two separate states. Anyone seeking modern German records will find himself dealing in a minor degree with the same problem which afflicts the researcher into medieval matters. A glance into a book of European history will usually show a map of Europe in the twelfth century. Leaving the British Isles out of account, the map is politically almost unimaginable. France is divided into two. The eastern portion from the borders of Flanders to the Mediterranean is the kingdom of France, ruled in at least a nominal sense by the King of France in Paris. The western part of France comprises Normandy, Brittany, Maine, Anjou, Poitou, Gascony, and other areas; most of which is held by the King of England. Crossing the Pyrenees, we have the kingdoms of Navarre, Aragon, León, and Castile. Alongside these is the kingdom of Portugal, but nearly half the Iberian Peninsula is still under the Moors, the Almoravid kingdom. Italy is divided between the Holy Roman Empire (which controlled the North—Lombardy and Tuscany), the Papal States around Rome, and the Norman kingdom of Sicily and southern Italy. The Holy Roman Empire occupied a great part of Germany-Franconia, Swabia, and Bavaria. There was a powerful duchy, or semi-kingdom, of Burgundy stretching from what is now the Mediterranean coast of France almost to the North Sea and taking in eventually the area of Belgium and Holland. Other states shown are Saxony, Brandenburg, Thuringia, Lausitz, Meissen, Bohemia, Moravia, Austria, and the kingdom of Hungary, stretching away to the East, where the princes of Russia were still independent of the Tatars, and to the Byzantine Empire.

Two hundred years later, the European map shows the British Isles ruled from England, except for the independent kingdom of Scotland; the kingdoms of Norway, Sweden, and Denmark in their present form; France a larger kingdom, but with Guyenne in the West still a duchy under the English king; and on the east France loses much territory to the Holy Roman Empire, which now stretches from the North Sea to the Mediterranean. In the Iberian Peninsula, Portugal has taken its modern shape, there are the kingdoms of León and Castile and of Aragon, while the Moorish kingdom of Granada is merely clinging to the South. Italy, apart from the North, has the Papal States and the kingdom of Naples and of Sicily. The Byzantine Empire is now much reduced in size, while a group of barbarous states—Serbia, Bulgaria, Wallachia, and others—divide the Balkan Peninsula north of Greece. There are the kingdoms of Bohemia, Poland, and Hungary. Russia is largely under the Tatar Empire. The grand duchy of Lithuania is as large as Poland, while the Teutonic Order rules what is now Prussia.

I have taken the above facts from the maps in the *Shorter Cambridge Medieval History* (Cambridge University Press, 1952), but any student will easily find a historical atlas which shows the changes in the make-up of Europe over the last 1000 or 800 years. Following is a series of historical notes briefly to explain the position in each group of countries.

## THE BRITISH ISLES

The great distinction here is between Saxon and Celt. These names are somewhat arbitrary, but they are convenient for differentiating the main constituents of the British Isles. The highlands of Scotland, Wales, Cornwall, the Isle of Man, and Ireland constitute the Celtic fringe; to these must be added the land of Brittany, the ancient name of which was Armorica and to which many of the Britons fled after the Saxons had invaded Britain.

In the fifth century the Angles, Saxons, and Jutes from Frisia and Germany and Denmark invaded Britain. They conquered the country as far as the mountains of Wales, the peninsula of Cornwall, and the lowlands of Scotland. In England seven kingdoms arose, the well-known Heptarchy—Kent, Sussex, Essex, Mercia, Northumberland, Wessex, and other smaller territories. These kingdoms were never united until the Viking invasions forced some sort of union upon them; even then great parts of northern and eastern England became Danish. Finally, in the beginning of the eleventh century, all England came under the rule of the Danish kings for some twenty-five years. The English line was restored from 1042 to 1066, but the final conquest of England was achieved by the Normans, who were themselves kinsmen of the Vikings. Thus the history of England—Saxon or English, Viking, then Norman, blended into the modern Englishman—makes the pattern of English genealogy.

The Anglo-Norman product of the Norman conquest of England determined also the course of Welsh and Irish history. Genealogically speaking, the Celtic influences in England can be completely disregarded. In Wales and Ireland Celtic influences in genealogical matters persist to this day, but greatly under the influence of English conquest. Both in Wales and Ireland the result of the English conquests was to destroy the old Celtic laws. An English pattern was imposed upon the Irish and Welsh, and consequently the study of their genealogical systems must constantly take into account the history of each country. Otherwise, it is impossible to understand how the amalgam of Celtic and Saxon came about.

In Scotland we deal with a mingling of Celtic and Saxon, or English, influences of a quite different type. An apt quotation illustrates the position. "Scotland is in the main made up of five formerly separate realms, three of which spoke Celtic languages in historic times, while the other two were founded by more recent Teutonic conquerors who did not exterminate the subjugated Celtic peoples in their territories. Generalizing broadly: in the west lay the kingdom of the Gaelic-speaking Scots, and to the east and northeast that of the Picts, while the western Isles (and for a long time the far north) were under Norse rule. In the southwest was a kingdom of the Welsh-speaking Britons, and the southeast was ruled by English-speaking Angles." (Iain Moncreiffe, "Landed Gentry of Scotland. A Genealogical Introduction," in *Burke's Landed Gentry,* 1952.)

In 850 Kenneth MacAlpin, King of Scots, united his realm of Dalriada with that of the Picts. By 1018 King Malcolm had united English Lothian (i.e., southeast Scotland) with his Picto-Scottish kingdom. British Strathclyde was also soon brought in. It was not, however, until the end of the fifteenth century that the Orkneys and Shetlands came under the rule of the Scottish king and Scotland reached her present political boundaries. Long before this the English language had spread over the whole of lowland Scotland, for Scots is only a variant of English. In the Highlands the Gaels maintained their own language and tribal system. After the suppression of the 1745 Rebellion, the old clan system was broken up by new laws. The clan system which is now with us is a modern adaptation of the old system. There are some very notable differences, especially in such matters as the patterns of various tartans. Old illustrations before 1745 show tartans different from those now in use in the same clan. The reason is that the weaving of the tartans was stopped for over a generation by law, and many of the exact patterns were lost.

From the above sketch the reader can see that Scottish genealogy has strong Celtic and English elements, plus a Norse factor to be considered.

## SCANDINAVIA

The three countries of Denmark, Norway, and Sweden have much in common, not only as regards language but by the entanglements of their history. For many centuries, however, they were separate kingdoms. Very little was known about them in the Roman Empire, even to writers such as Tacitus and Pliny. Curiously enough, a slight lifting of the curtain of darkness over Scandinavia occurs through the old English poem *Beowulf.* This was written down in the eighth century, but the events referred to occurred much earlier. There are references in this poem to all three countries. It is probable that the Danes moved into Denmark from Sweden after the ancestors of the English had moved over to England. The Viking invasions came from Scandinavia, particularly from Norway and Denmark. Under Canute (1016–35) the three kingdoms of Denmark, Norway, and England were united, but this did not outlast his reign. With the settlement of England by the Normans, the Danes were compelled to forgo their attempts to conquer England. Henceforth, the battle was to dominate the Baltic area. In 1397 the Union of Kalmar was effected, with one sovereign for Denmark, Norway, and Sweden. In the case of Sweden, this union lasted until the sixteenth century, when Gustavus Vasa became King of Sweden in 1523. With Norway, the union with Denmark lasted until 1814, when the country was united with Sweden. Norway's union with Sweden was dissolved in 1905. All three countries shared in the trading expansion which occurred through the discoveries of the fifteenth and sixteenth centuries. Iceland had been united with Norway in the thirteenth century and therefore came under the Union of Kalmar. It remained a Danish possession until 1944, when it became an independent republic. The languages of Scandinavia are closely akin, and they are also of the same family as the Germanic tongues, which includes German, English, Frisian, and Gothic. An understanding of the fluctuations of power between the three Scandinavian kingdoms is useful in studying their records.

Finland has been an independent state only since 1917. It was originally conquered, civilized, and converted to Christianity from Sweden in the twelfth century. It became a grand duchy under Gustavus Vasa about 1528. It was a bone of contention between Sweden and Russia for centuries, until in 1809 the grand duchy of Finland came under Russian rule. The Finnish language belongs to what is called the Finno-Ugrian group, which includes Lapp, Estonian, Hungarian, and others.

## GERMANY AND AUSTRIA

The history of Germany and its divisions is a vast subject, beginning with the appointment of Julius Caesar as Roman governor in Gaul (59 B.C.). Caesar conquered the tribes as far as the Rhine and even crossed the river into Germany. During the period of the Roman Empire the importance of Germany consisted in the periodic discharge of hordes of tribes onto the borders of the Empire. At length, in the fifth century, the Germanic effort prevailed and the

German hordes overran the whole Roman Empire. It is this fact which underlies the statement often made in genealogy that the ancient royal and noble houses of Europe are all of Teutonic stock.

Under the rule of Charlemagne, the great Frankish emperor who became Holy Roman Emperor in 800 A.D. (see below), Germany was conquered and made Christian. Thereafter Germany passed under the rule of the Franconian dynasty (Henry the Fowler, or Henry I, 919). Germany was, however, divided into great duchies, like that of Bavaria, where the Crown did not always have full control. The great feudatories of Germany elected their kings and gave them little real power. The elected king often wished to become Holy Roman Emperor. (The many details of this very romantic title ought to be read in the classic work on the subject—*The Holy Roman Empire,* by Lord Bryce.) From 1438 until the dissolution of the Empire in 1806, the Emperors, with two exceptions, were of the house of Habsburg. This race ruled Austria and welded it into a great power, the Austro-Hungarian Empire, which lasted until 1918.

The theory of the Holy Roman Empire was that the Pope had revived the title (forfeited by the heretical Greek Emperor at Constantinople) for the benefit of Charlemagne in 800. The Emperor was elected. Once the Imperial Crown was offered to Edward III of England, and at another time to Alfonso X of Castile. The electors of the Empire were the great princes who formed it, hence the Elector of Hanover, who eventually became King of England.

The countries of Europe have been very much affected by dynastic marriages. The Austrian family of the Habsburgs were to become rulers of the Low Countries (Holland and Belgium) and of Spain. Right up to 1477 (when Charles the Bold, the last Duke of Burgundy, died) there was the powerful "Middle Kingdom" of Burgundy stretching from Switzerland to the North Sea. On Charles' death the French king Louis XI secured his dominions, apart from the Low Countries. These passed to Charles' daughter, Mary. She married the Archduke of Austria, Maximilian. In 1493 he succeeded his father as Holy Roman Emperor. The son of Maximilian and Mary, Philip the Handsome, married Joanna, the daughter of Ferdinand and Isabella, King and Queen of Spain. The child of this marriage was Charles V, born in 1500. He ruled Spain, Milan, Germany, and the Low Countries. The northern portion of the last named became the Republic of the Netherlands after a long war, but the southern portion (i.e., Belgium) remained under the rule of the King of Spain. It should be mentioned that the Habsburgs had divided in the time of Emperor Charles V into two branches. The Spanish branch had vast dominions (including almost all of Latin America except Brazil) and also ruled the Spanish Netherlands. The Austrian Habsburgs ruled the great area of Austria-Hungary and other central and eastern European areas. The Peace of Utrecht (1713) closed the war of the Spanish Succession. By it, the Spanish Netherlands became the Austrian Netherlands (Belgium) when the Great Powers agreed that Charles VI of Austria should become sovereign of Belgium. He also ruled Naples, Milan, and Sardinia. The last was ceded to the Duke of Savoy in exchange for Sicily.

These brief notes will do something to explain references to the Spanish and Austrian Netherlands, which must at first sight seem very strange.

## THE LOW COUNTRIES

These are the three present Benelux countries in the western European union—Holland, Belgium, and Luxembourg. Holland and Belgium are the Low Countries, the Netherlands, where for several centuries, the wars of western Europe tended to be fought. In 1437 the Duke of Burgundy, Philip the Good, became sovereign. His son was Charles the Bold (see above). (Very useful for the tangled history of the Netherlands is *The Rise of the Dutch Republic,* by the American historian J. L. Motley.) Along with Holland and Belgium, Luxembourg was the prize of contending dynasties. Up to 1437 Luxembourg was ruled by the Counts of Luxembourg derived from Conrad, who died in 1086; but it became a duchy in the fourteenth century. In 1437 it passed to the Habsburgs, but in 1443 was seized by Duke Philip the Good of Burgundy. It was regained by the Habsburgs, passing to the Spanish line in 1555. It remained Spanish territory until at the Peace of Utrecht (1713) it went to the Austrian Habsburgs. After the French Revolution the grand duchy of Luxembourg passed back and forth between Holland and Belgium until at last, in 1890, on the death of King William III without male issue, the duchy went to a distant male cousin of the House of Nassau.

## SWITZERLAND

This country is composed of twenty-two states, or cantons, which were once part of the Holy Roman Empire. As far back as 1291 some of the communities—Uri, Schwyz, and Nidwalden—formed an Everlasting League against the Austrian Habsburgs. They defeated the Austrian chivalry at Mortgarten in 1315. This caused the growth of the Swiss confederacy, which further increased with its other great victories—Sempach in 1386 over the Austrians, Grandson in 1476, Morat and Nancy, also in 1476, over Charles the Bold of Burgundy. In 1499 practical independence of the Empire was gained, which was formally recognized in 1648 by the Treaty of Westphalia.

Switzerland is partly a Latin country, though the bulk of the inhabitants are German-speaking.

## THE LATIN COUNTRIES

### France

France has been for so many centuries one of the foremost countries of Europe that we are apt to forget how gradual has been its growth to its present boundaries. Normandy became a feudal fief held by the invading Vikings in the tenth century. It was united under the same sovereign as England by the Norman Conquest in 1066. In 1154 nearly half of France was under the rule of the English king. It was not for another 400 years that the English were expelled from France. Indeed, as late as 1558 they retained a footing in Calais. After the departure of the English from the bulk of their territories in France (in 1461) the French sought to extend their boundaries eastward and gained various provinces which are now included in France.

### Spain

Fortunately for the genealogical inquirer, the union of Spain took place over 450 years ago. Ferdinand of Aragon and Isabella of Castile were married and the two crowns united. In 1492 they drove the Moors from Granada and ruled over all Spain. The Spaniards then began their expansion into the New World, where they controlled for three centuries all the land (except Brazil) from Florida to Cape Horn. At the same time Spain was drawn into numerous European conflicts because the only son of Ferdinand and Isabella died and so the throne of Spain passed to the grandson of Ferdinand and Isabella, Charles V, Emperor of the Holy Roman Empire. It was in this way that the Habsburg family came to rule in Austria and Spain through its two branches.

### Portugal

Despite the might of Spain in the sixteenth century, her rule did not extend over the whole of the Iberian Peninsula, except for a period of sixty years known as the Spanish Captivity. One small part of the peninsula was the kingdom of Portugal. This was founded by Crusaders who came from the sea to aid the King of León (in the North of Spain). In 1128 the founder of Portugal, Affonso Henriques, won his first victory. He reigned for fifty-seven years, and before his death in 1185 the sovereignty of Portugal had been recognized by León and by the Holy See at Rome. Lisbon had become the capital of Portugal and the new country had begun its 800 years of history. (A fascinating account of the origins and growth of Portugal is by W. J. Barnes, entitled *Portugal—Gateway to Greatness.*)

### Italy

Between the fall of the Roman Empire and the year 1870, Italy had no position as a nation or a political entity. It was a battle-ground of the nations. Part of it was held by the Holy Roman Empire. Another large part formed the Papal States, right across central Italy. Several republics arose in the peninsula—Genoa, Venice, Florence. The Venetians built up a considerable maritime empire right around to the Aegean. The French and the Germans and Austrians disputed rule over the North of Italy. By the time of the French Revolution, the North of Italy was under Austrian rule, and despite the campaigns of Napoleon, so she remained after 1815. The dukes of Savoy became kings of Sardinia and of Piedmont. At last, after many struggles, all Italy was united in 1870 when the Papal States were the last obstacle to Italian unity. Throughout

Italian history numerous small states had flourished from Milan to Naples. To deal with their history requires far more space than can be allotted here.

## THE SLAVONIC COUNTRIES

### Greece, Albania, Bulgaria, Rumania, Yugoslavia

For 1000 years after the Western Roman Empire had broken up, the Eastern Roman Empire continued, with its center at Constantinople. This was known more often as the Greek, or Byzantine, Empire. It gradually lost ground to the Moslem races—the Saracens and Turks—and in 1453 Constantinople was captured by the latter. Within a short time they conquered the Balkan Peninsula and threatened Europe right up to Vienna. For 300 to 400 years the Turks ruled in the Balkans. In 1821 the Greeks rebelled and secured independence for Greece.

Albania became independent in 1912 after 445 years under Turkish domination.

Bulgaria became fully independent in 1908 after a limited independence from 1878.

Between 1859 and 1878 Rumania secured freedom from the Turks.

Yugoslavia is the union of the six republics of Serbia, Croatia, Slovenia, Bosnia and Herzegovina, Macedonia, and Montenegro, all of which shook off the Turkish yoke within the last century.

The late emergence of these countries goes far to explain the difficulties in connection with their records and the late date at which much of their record system begins. In the case of Greece, some long pedigrees exist, but, as can be seen under the Greek section, these occur only when the Greek families in question were subjects of Venice. The Venetian Republic for a long time held valuable territories in the Greek world, notably Cyprus, a fact which readers of Shakespeare's *Othello* will remember.

### Russia

Here we deal with a very great country whose history cannot be summarized in a few paragraphs. The founder of the Russian state was a Viking, Rurik. Christianity and civilization came from

Byzantium, or Constantinople. In the thirteenth century the Tatar hordes from central Asia overran Russia, conquering and destroying. The princes of Moscow, by subservience to the Tatars, maintained their own position until in the fifteenth and sixteenth centuries they rebelled against the Tatars. From that time, the Czars of Moscow expanded their power until, in the seventeenth and eighteenth centuries, Russia became one of the great powers. The Czars took the title of the Caesars of Constantinople and regarded themselves as the successors of Byzantium; hence the double-headed eagle on the Russian arms. Here again we see the comparatively late origin of the organized Russian state, and the difficulty in tracing pedigrees for any length of time comparable with the best efforts in Germany or France.

### Poland and Lithuania

These countries were united in 1385, Lithuania being a grand duchy. In 1572 the ancient Jagellon dynasty of Poland ended and was replaced by the system of elective monarchy. Poland went through an unruly period, 1572–1795, ending in her disappearance from the map of Europe until 1918. Poland was partitioned among Russia, Germany, and Austria, but when these three empires crashed in 1918, Poland and Lithuania both secured their independence. The close connection of these two countries in the past can be gauged from the greatest poem of Poland. This is the famous *Pan Tadeusz,* by Adam Mickiewicz. The full title of this epic is: *The Last Foray in Lithuania: A Story of Life among Polish Gentlefolk in the Years 1811 and 1812.*

### Latvia and Estonia

Two other countries which also became independent in 1918–1920 were Latvia and Estonia. Neither of these countries had any real independence before this period, and as we know, it has been short-lived. The Latvians are akin to the Lithuanians. They have been ruled in turn by the Germans, Poles, Swedes, and Russians. The Estonians were dominated by German landowners, a fact which explains some of the references in the section on that country. Russia controlled Estonia from 1721 and has again since the 1939 war, with the brief interlude of independence after 1918.

The small peoples of the eastern Baltic region were for centuries under the heel of conquerors—Swedes, Germans, and others—who were able to feel a glow of righteousness at converting pagans whose lands were worth annexing.

### Czechoslovakia

Czechoslovakia as an independent state originated with the breakup of the Austro-Hungarian Empire. It is the national state of the Czechs and Slovaks and consists of Bohemia, Moravia, and parts of Silesia and Slovakia. These areas are of ancient history in Europe, for example, the Kingdom of Bohemia, which was submerged in the religious wars of the seventeenth century.

## MONACO

Monaco owes its separate political independence to a series of curious incidents. The area formerly belonged to the Holy Roman Empire. It was ceded to the Republic of Genoa by the emperor Henry VI. A leading Genoese family, the Grimaldis, gained possession of Monaco in 1297; since then this family has ruled this little state.

## LIECHTENSTEIN

Liechtenstein is another small country which originated from the Holy Roman Empire, finally gaining its independence when the Empire ended in 1806.

# Genealogical
# Accounts

# ACKNOWLEDGMENTS

ALBANIA
Mr. Alfred Andoni.

AUSTRIA
Dr. Hanns Jäger-Sunstenau.
Prince Charles Schwarzenberg.

BELGIUM
M. Léon Robin, Ministère des Affairs Etrangères et du Commerce Extérieur.
M. le Secrétaire, L'Association de la Noblesse du Royaume de Belgique.
M. E. Sabbe, Cabinet de l'Archiviste Général.
M. le Président, Le Conseil Héraldique.
M. George M. de Milliano

BULGARIA
Mr. J. A. D. Stewart-Robinson, Commercial Secretary, British Legation, Sofia.

CZECHOSLOVAKIA
Miss V. Basetlikova, Public Relations Officer, Embassy of the Czechoslovak Republic, London.
Mr. J. Louda, University Library, Olomouc.

DENMARK
Dr. h. c. Ole Rostock.
Afdelingsbibliotekar, Sven Houmøller Danmarks Adels Aarbog, Redaktionem.

De kgl. ordeners. Albert Fabritius, Dr. Phil. (Author of *Haandbog i Slaegtsforskning*).

ESTONIA

Mr. Eesti Saatkond, Estonian Minister, Estonian Legation, London.

FINLAND

Mr. George Luther, Chief of Section, Central Statistical Office of Finland.

Mr. Toristen G. Arninoff, Riddarhuset (Genealogist at the House of the Nobility).

FRANCE

M. le Baron Pierre Durye, Conservateur aux Archives Nationales.

M. Jacques Meurgey de Tupigny, Président Société Française d'Héraldique et de Sigillographie.

GERMANY

Herr Karl-Egbert Schultze, Papenhuder Strasse 36, Hamburg 22.

Dr. Ottfried Neubecker, Der Herold, Verein für Heraldik, Westfälische Strasse 38, Berlin-Halensee.

The Embassy of the Federal Republic of Germany, London.

GREECE

Mr. P. Couvelis, Director General, National Statistical Service of Greece.

HUNGARY

The Director, Hungarian News and Information Service, 167 Kensington High Street, London W.8.

Professor Geza Grosschmid, Duquesne University, Pittsburgh, Pennsylvania.

ICELAND

Mr. Eirikur Benedikz, Counselor of Embassy, Icelandic Embassy, London.

IRELAND

Mr. Gerard Slevin, Chief Herald of Ireland, Dublin Castle.

Mr. R. J. Hayes, National Library of Ireland.

Miss K. Darwin, The Deputy Keeper, Public Record Office, Belfast.

Miss Margaret C. Griffith, The Deputy Keeper, Public Record Office of Ireland, Dublin.

The Registrar-General, General Register Office, Belfast.

The Registrar-General's Office, Customs House, Dublin.

Mr. Eric Montgomery, Information Service, Stormont Castle, Belfast.

Miss I. Embleton, Secretary, Ulster-Scot Historical Society, Belfast.

The Rev. J. B. Pim.

ISLE OF MAN

Government Office, Isle of Man.

CHANNEL ISLANDS

Registrar-General's Office, Greffe, Guernsey:

The Deputy Greffier of the States, States' Greffe, Jersey.

The Rev. J. S. Norman, Acting Dean, Jersey.

JEWRY

The Secretary, The Board of Deputies of British Jews, Woburn House, Upper Woburn Place, London W.C.1.

The Librarian, The American Jewish Committee, 165 East Fifty-sixth Street, New York 22, New York.

The Librarian Editor, American Jewish Historical Society, 3080 Broadway, New York 27, New York.

The Administrative Secretary, Conference on Jewish Social Studies, Inc., 1841 Broadway, New York 23, New York.

The Secretary, Commission on Research, Yivo Institute for Jewish Research, 1048 Fifth Avenue, New York 28, New York.

LATVIA

H. E. the Latvian Minister, Latvian Legation, London.

LIECHTENSTEIN

The Chancellery of the Liechtenstein Government.

LITHUANIA

H. E. the Lithuanian Minister, Lithuanian Legation, London.

LUXEMBOURG

M. Jean-Robert Schleich de Bossé.

M. Robert Matagne, Conseil Héraldique du Luxembourg.

M. Léon Zettinger, Archiviste de la Ville de Luxembourg.

M. Antoine May, Conservateur aux Archives du Gouvernement.

M. Emile Erpelding, 23 Rue de Rochefort, Luxembourg-Beggen.

MONACO

M. le Commissaire Général au Tourisme et à l'Information, Principauté de Monaco.

M. Louis Aureglia.

M. Auguste Settimo.

M. Jean-Charles Rey.

THE NETHERLANDS

Prof. Dr. Ph. J. Idenburg, Director General of Statistics, The Netherlands Central Bureau of Statistics, The Hague.

Mr. C. M. R. Davidson, Secretary, Koninklijk Nederlandsch Genootschap voor Geslacht en Wapenkunde

Jkr. Mr. C. C. Van Valkenburg, President, Central Bureau voor Genealogie.

NORWAY

Mr. Gunvald Bøe, Archivist, Riksarkivet, Oslo.

Mr. Anthon Busch, Secretary, Norsk Slektshistorisk Forening (The Norwegian Genealogical Association).

Mr. Bjørnulf Bendiksen, Chief, Demographic Division, Statistisk Sentralbyra (Central Bureau of Statistics), Norway.

Mr. A. Wessel Nyhagen, Secretary, Universitetsbiblioteket i Oslo.

POLAND

The Press and Information Office, Polish Cultural Institute, 81 Portland Place, London W.1.

PORTUGAL

The Director Arquivo Nacional da Tôrre do Tombo.

The Director, Presidência do Conselho, Instituto Nacional de Estatística.

El Marquês de São Payo.

RUSSIA

Mr. Nicolas Ikonnikov.

Mr. Second Secretary Spartak.

Mr. I. Baglov.

Press Service, Soviet News, London.

SCOTLAND

Mrs. M. Nancy Browne, Scots Ancestry Research Society.

SPAIN

Señor Faustino Menendez-Pidal, Instituto Internacional de Genealogía y Heráldica, Madrid.

Señor Vincente de Cadenas, El Secretario General, Instituto Internacional de Genealogía y Heráldica, Madrid.

El Jefe del Servicio, Lo Instituto Nacional de Estadística.

SWEDEN

Mr. Gunnar Scheffer, Chamberlain de la Cour de S. M. le Roi de Suède et Directeur du Service Héraldique de l'Etat Suédois.

Prof. Bengt Hildebrand, Svenskt Biografiskt Personhistoriska Institutet.

Capt. L. Zielfelt, Secretary, Genealogiska Föreningen.

Mrs. Elsa Dalstrom-Soderburg, Secretary, Föreningen för Släktforskning.

Docenten Bertil Broome, Secretary, Personhistoriska Samfundet.

SWITZERLAND

Le Service Fédéral de l'Etat Civil.

M. A. Hohl, Cultural Section, Swiss Embassy.

Dr. H. E. v. Fels, Schweiz Heraldische Gesellschaft.

M. Alfred J. Bolzern, Secretary, Swiss Registrars' Federation.

WALES

Mr. E. D. Jones, Librarian, The National Library of Wales.

YUGOSLAVIA

M. P. Stevčić, Editor in Chief, Information Service of Yugoslavia.

# ENGLAND

## PROBLEMS OF THE
## AMERICAN INQUIRER

An American who wishes to trace his ancestry in England
faces immediately one difficulty: who was the first immigrant ancestor into America and where in England did he
come from?

Most Americans who have traced their ancestry in the United
States do know the first ancestor in England who sailed from England to America in the seventeenth, eighteenth, or nineteenth centuries. But, and it is a very big but, they by no means always know
the place whence he originated. How can they overcome this first
and great difficulty? Well, in many cases they will not be able to
overcome it, and that is a fact that must be faced. If their ancestor's
name was an unusual one, such as Gorges or Grosvenor, it may well
be that they will be able to search the pedigrees of the noble family
of that name in England and, in so doing, find in a more or less
obscure branch a person who clearly was their ancestor and whom
they may so claim by the identification of the name and the Christian
names. But it has to be observed that this problem of tracing the
place of origin of the immigrant ancestor is one which must in
many cases lead to disappointment. We will assume that a man
called John Horton sailed from Plymouth in 1630 and went to
settle in the American colonies. We have a record in the lists of
settlers and of those that sailed from England for America which
gives us John Horton's name, but of course it does not tell us his
birthplace, and in consequence of that omission we dare not assume

that he was born in Plymouth, which was only his port of embarkation, but we are thrown back on the possibility that he may have come from anywhere in half a dozen counties in southwestern England.

Otherwise, leaving aside this one difficulty for the moment, about which I will say something more later on, the problems of research into family history are the same for an American as for an Englishman, with this difference—that a tenth-generation American begins with his ancestor ten generations back, whereas an Englishman begins with his father. The American, so to speak, has to telescope his ancestry over those ten generations and feel that John Winthrop, for example, stands in the same position as if he were his father. I make this statement because in what follows I shall always counsel the inquirer to work backward and not forward. There are many people who do attempt to work forward, but they are by no means successful and in fact they make a tremendous mess of it.

### Ancient Families

Most of us who wish to trace our genealogy do persuade ourselves that we have distinguished ancestors. In my many years of experience with *Burke's,* I have not found many people willing to be delighted at the prospect, or perhaps I ought to say hindsight, of descent from a laborer, a shepherd, or a blacksmith. They would prefer to have descent from a king or a great nobleman although in many instances they know quite well that such descent can be obtained in one way only and that is by having a bastard as one's ancestor. Now, one thing needs saying very clearly, and that is that in the nature of the case only a few people in England can trace their ancestry for a very long period. Some Englishmen will tell you that they are descended from the Romans. One story of descent from the Romans did at one time in the early nineteenth century find its way into genealogical publications. This was the alleged pedigree of the bonny house of Coultart. About the year 1840 this extraordinary family was represented by a respectable banker who lived at Ashton-under-Lyme and who was sold what is colloquially known as a pup by two genealogists. They persuaded the banker that he was descended in a direct male line from one Coultartas, a lieutenant in the army of the Roman governor of Britain, Agricola, and who had been left behind in Scotland after his general had retired; he apparently settled down with the daughter of one of the Scottish chiefs. It need hardly be said that this fabulous story was purely and simply a fabrication and proceeded from the Roman lieutenant down to the Ashton-under-Lyme banker with additions of a similarly fictitious nature in each generation. This tale was actually produced, as I have said, in some works of reference, but the exposure which it received from eminent scholars was sufficient to show that tales of descent from the Romans could not be entertained by Englishmen. Why is this? The Romans occupied Britain for four hundred years, and during that time many of them settled in the country and intermarried with the original British inhabitants. Now, in the fifth century—the classic date is 410 or 411 A.D.—when the Roman Empire in the West was collapsing and the Saxon tribes from across the North Sea were beginning to invade Britain, the Roman province of Britain was gradually pulled to pieces and destroyed by a wholesale conquest on the part of the Angles, Saxons, and Jutes. As a result, 180 years later, in 597 A.D., when Britain again became open to contact with Europe, there was no longer anything resembling the Roman province, but there was an entirely new entity, a country called England, or Angleland. This country was divided into a number of warring kingdoms. They are known as the Heptarchy, and from time to time one of them would obtain control over the others and would become the boss, or overlord, state. But apart from these political bodies there was the country of England and there was the language known as English, which had been brought into the country by the rude tribes who had overthrown Roman civilization in Britain. Now there is no very clear evidence as to what happened to the original British inhabitants. When I was a child at school, I was taught that the Britons who were not killed by the Saxons fled away to the West and shut themselves off in the wilder country of Wales, Cornwall, or Cumberland or went over the sea to Brittany. Modern research, however, takes a different view and is of the opinion that many of the British inhabitants survived the English conquest, though they were in a decidedly inferior position. Even if this is so, we cannot say of any one particular person who is of English descent that he or she has also some Roman blood, because the written records which survived from the period of the English conquest are so scanty that they do not enable us to reach any conclusion.

### Original English Pedigrees

What was the attitude of the English invaders of Britain on the subject of pedigrees? Did they attach any importance to them? Yes, they were very interested in descent and regarded the descent of their king and great nobles as being of vital importance. Most of the kingdoms which were set up in England by the Saxons had as their ruling royal family a house which claimed descent from Woden, who was the high god of these ancient people. Consequently, pedigrees and descent were certainly a matter of interest to our Saxon ancestors, but they did not record them in any style which is likely to be very helpful to a modern inquirer. They contented themselves in making poems about their ancestors and in chanting or reciting these at their feasts, where they were apt to drink and eat far too much.

There is an interesting example of a pedigree of a royal line which is given in the *Anglo-Saxon Chronicle* and which tells us about King Ethelwulf, who was the father of King Alfred the Great. Ethelwulf's ancestry is given right back through his certainly known ancestors into the realm of unchecked fable. In a document written in all probability by a monk we have the genuine names of the royal line of Wessex, then of the god Woden and his ancestors, after which the monk has tacked on an additional genealogy, which would show Ethelwulf to be descended from Adam and through Noah. The chronicler very cleverly observes of one person in the genealogy, whose name he gives as Sceaf, that he was the son of Noah and was born in Noah's ark.

On pages 106–7 I give a full note showing this curious pedigree in its entirety, and it will interest my readers to reflect that this pedigree is essentially that of the present Queen of Great Britain, Elizabeth II; she descends from Egbert, King of the West Saxons, and he is the Egbert mentioned as the second person in the pedigree.

Two points strike one about this pedigree. First of all, it is the pedigree of a royal line. Secondly, it is a bald narrative pedigree with names only and without any attempt at dates. If, then, the lines of the Saxon kings were recorded in this fashion, what likelihood is there that the pedigrees of lesser folk, even the great nobles, would be recorded with any greater detail? As a matter of fact, we have only to look at what has been collected on this subject. W. G.

Searle in 1899 produced a book entitled *Anglo-Saxon Bishops, Kings and Nobles; the Succession of the Bishops and the Pedigrees of the Kings and Nobles*. This work shows quite clearly that there are hardly any cases of English pedigrees before the Norman Conquest (1066–72) where a pedigree of more than three generations can be collected from the existing records. This does not mean that the ancient English were not interested in pedigrees, but only serves to show that they did not care to record those pedigrees in any very careful fashion.

Very few persons now living in England can trace their descent from the pre-Conquest period. There are three cases where I would be certain of this descent. Those cases are Arden and Swinton and Berkeley. It is possible that Wilberforce could be added to the list. It will be clear that these descents are in the male line and are great rarities.

Consequently, an American inquirer who has been provided by some rather doubtful agency with a pedigree purporting to return to a very early period in Saxon England can cheerfully assume that such a pedigree is not worth the paper on which it has been printed. He had better scrap it and begin the other way around.

### The Norman Conquest Period (1066–72)

After the English had dwelt 600 years in England they were conquered by the Normans, who were of the same race as themselves and the Vikings, who had descended on the shores of England in the eighth, ninth, and tenth centuries. With the Norman Conquest the natural development of England was diverted into a foreign channel. It was not until some 400 years after the Norman Conquest that the English genius again found its natural form of expression in English poetry in the time of Geoffrey Chaucer.

With the coming of the Normans a great change took place with regard to record keeping. The Normans professed to pay great respect to birth and nobility, perhaps because very few of them really possessed either of these qualities. They were much more concerned with holding what they had conquered and with raising enough money to maintain the king's forces and the government of the country. They could not do this without records, and therefore, as soon as he had pacified his new possessions, William the Conqueror determined to have a complete record of his realm of England. This record was taken with great care and forms the basis of English social study; it is also the first rough and ready census of this country and contains a good deal of genealogical information. The genealogical material was not included in Domesday Book for any purpose of tracing ancestry. The object was to set out how the land in England was held and what the value of that land was. In so doing, the Domesday commissioners had to record to whom the land had belonged on the date of the death of Edward the Confessor, that is, the fifth of January 1066. They then went on to give the name of the Norman successor, for in the great majority of cases the Saxon lord was dispossessed or killed and a Norman put in his place. From Domesday Book social historians have been able to form a good idea of the population of England at the time of the Conquest. The population could not have exceeded about one and a half million, and as far as Domesday Book is concerned the great bulk of this one and a half million might as well have been cattle and swine, because they were mentioned along with the animals on the property as being so many laborers or serfs. The only persons to be mentioned by name were the landowners, and they are given in order that the state may have clear knowledge of whom it is to take notice as the owner of the land. There were about 5500 knight's fees in England after the Norman Conquest. A knight's fee was, of course, not connected in any way with money. The term "fee" was used of land which was considered sufficient to maintain a knight, that is, an armed horseman with a small following. Such a holding was perhaps three hundred to four hundred acres, and we read in the medieval records of knights having five, six, ten, or more fees, and there are cases of half a knight's fee. But it should, of course, be clearly understood that in many cases the holder of a knight's fee did not himself go to war. He sent his substitute. The king or other overlord who had given the fee was not concerned with the identity of the person who answered his summons to war. All that he wanted was to have an armed man on horseback and a certain following who would serve in his army.

### The Medieval Period

The Domesday Book, which was compiled in 1086, lasted as a record of the landowners of the country until a century later, when, under Henry II, the great-grandson of William the Conqueror, a new survey was made. In the interim period there had appeared a series of records which were to become increasingly important during the next four hundred years. These were the Feet of Fines and the Pipe Rolls. These records were concerned with land and with taxation. When they are explained to a modern Englishman he has every sympathy with ancestors who lived several centuries ago. He begins to realize that it was not only a socialist government which taxed him heavily, or a government during a vast world war, but that his forebears five or six or seven hundred years ago were equally miserable over the taxes which they had to pay. But while we may feel some sympathy for our ancestors in dealing with the modes of tax exaction in the reigns of the Norman kings, we must also realize that these tax records are of the greatest value in tracing genealogy. I shall not go into their nature in the present section, but when I am working backward and showing how each set of records contributes to the over-all picture, I shall explain these various items.

For the present, suffice it to say that in the period between the reign of Henry II (1154–89) and the end of the Wars of the Roses in 1485 the basis of medieval society gradually extended. Not only are we able to trace many of the families of the nobles and of the smaller landowners but we are also able to make a beginning with the pedigrees of people who were prominent in the cities. One such case is that of the family of Farrow. This family is traced in the late fifteenth century to Norwich and can be traced much earlier in the county of Norfolk. In fact, some very good scholars consider that the family of Farrow is of the same descent as that of Ferrers. The house of Ferrers was without doubt a Norman family and is found at the time of the Conquest.

An even more extraordinarily interesting case is that of the ancestry of Lord Nuffield. Lord Nuffield's family name is Morris, and he began his working life by keeping a repair shop for bicycles. Now, this was in Oxfordshire, and for eleven generations the Morrises have lived in the same county of Oxfordshire and worked on the land which they rented but never owned. This takes them back in a direct line without any break to the reign of Elizabeth I, to 1586. This is not the end of the story. There is every reason to believe that the original Morris can be found living at a place called Swarford in 1278. This family of Morris, then spelled Morice, can be traced down to 1524. From 1524 to 1586 is not a long time and many great authorities think that the Morris of Swarford is the ancestor of the Morris of Kiddington, the line which produced Lord Nuffield.

In fact, during the Middle Ages we even get some cases for a few generations of the pedigrees of the poor villeins. I mentioned a little earlier that at the time of the Norman Conquest the laborers, who were tied with the land and who were sold with it just like animals, were so little regarded that their names were never noted down. Charles Kingsley in his famous story *Hereward the Wake* remarks of Martin Lightfoot that no one knew when he died, because no one took notice of such footpad churls in those days. Well, evidently by the time of Edward III the poor churls had begun to acquire names, and the industry of a scholarly lady, Miss M. K. Dale, has traced in the records of the county of Bedfordshire the pedigrees for several generations of the poor laborers. These people whom Miss Dale has traced are mentioned in connection with their lord and master, Sir Nigel Loring. He has given his name to the brave and wonderful knight of the romance by Sir Arthur Conan Doyle.

In this way we see that, even in the depths of the Middle Ages, men and women were beginning to acquire not only a name but also some degree of character and sturdy individuality. But it is not until the sixteenth century that national records begin to take in everyone.

### The Reformation and the Parish Registers

With the break between the Pope at Rome and the King of England in the reign of Henry VIII (1509–47), there came a great change in the outlook of the whole people of England. In the course of sixty years the English people changed as they have never changed at any time until the twentieth century. The Bible was translated into English, and even those who could not read were able to have the Bible read to them in every church in the land. There was a great increase in schools and many more students went to the universities. The services of the Church were conducted in English. The theater was founded and the drama became extremely popular. Writing of all kinds flourished, and there was a very great output of pamphlets, which served the function of many of the newspapers of today.

It was not unnatural that those who were concerned with the

government of the country should seek to have better records about the people. It is interesting that about the same time that parish records were instituted in England they also began in Spain. There seems to have been a general movement in the sixteenth century to give more information about people. Perhaps it was because European governments had become so much more centralized. Some say that Thomas Cromwell, who introduced the keeping of parish registers into England, was influenced by what he had seen in the Low Countries. Some even say that he was trying to introduce a police state into England. All this seems a little farfetched, but whatever Cromwell's motives, he was responsible for ordering in 1538 that in each parish there should be kept records of baptism, marriage, and burial. The order was tardily obeyed and, unfortunately for the genealogical inquirer, only a few of the parish records in England go back as far as 1538. By 1600 most parishes had begun to keep the records. It is probable that before the date at which parish records begin there were details kept, not as ordered in a stout volume, but in a more evanescent form, and that these earlier records have long since perished.

It is easy to see how great is the value of these parish records to the research worker, yet owing to the difficulties of the government in the seventeenth and eighteenth centuries in enforcing its laws—difficulties such as the bad roads and the lack of any effective police force—the parish registers were often kept and preserved in a very defective condition. Consequently, it is not until we have adequate provisions for record keeping that the whole of the people are at last covered, and we can say that we can find information about anybody.

## SOMERSET HOUSE

It was in 1837 that records of births, marriages, and deaths registered in England and Wales were ordered to be kept by act of Parliament. Even then it took about twenty years for the system to catch on, and I have found instances much later than 1857 where a birth has not been recorded, but of course it is possible to find exceptions to every rule.

It is at this point that, having given a brief résumé of the main periods in English record keeping, I shall now reverse and begin to work backward, beginning with your father—I am addressing myself to you, reader—and show how, working from your own date of birth, you can trace your ancestry through the records, beginning with those of Somerset House.

What is Somerset House registration? In England, by an act of Parliament, records of birth, marriage, and death have been kept by the Registrar-General from July 1, 1837. From that date the state took the important control in the keeping of what are known as vital statistics. How are you to begin? Bear in mind what I said above, that I shall deal with an American inquirer just as I would deal with an English inquirer, and assume that you begin by tracing the particulars of your father's family. I have met Americans of English descent who are only second- or third-generation citizens of the United States. On the other hand, most American inquirers will probably have their ancestry in the United States for several generations. However, it will be valuable to set out the procedure for dealing with the basis of a pedigree. What was your father's date of birth? The seventeenth of November, or the tenth of December, yes. But can you immediately give the year? Do you know, was it 1882 or 1884? If you don't know this then the information can be obtained for a few shillings (seven shillings equal roughly one dollar) from Somerset House. By the way, it may interest you to know why this building, which stands in London overlooking the Strand on one side and the Thames Embankment on the other, is called Somerset House. It is named after an infamous character, the Duke of Somerset, who held the office of Lord Protector in the early days of his nephew Edward VI (1547–53). Somerset reached enormous wealth and power but lost it all when his enemies turned the young king against him. He was sent to the block, and so little did his nephew care about him that he sent a messenger to inquire if the Duke had been executed while the wretched man was still awaiting his death. It is a fact that the Duke of Somerset had obtained the land on which to build his palace from the people, and it is a curious irony that Somerset House should have become the headquarters of the taxgatherers of England. It is for this reason that an enormous quantity of public records are found there, for, as I have explained, public records do tend to be concerned with taxation.

For the sake of example I shall assume that you are looking for a man called John Grosvenor, your father; and that you are not quite sure of the date of his birth. You do know, of course, that his approximate date of birth is 1883; you also know his Christian names and perhaps his place of birth and his occupation. Now, if you can go to Somerset House, you can pay one shilling and sixpence and you can make the search yourself. You are allowed for this not very large sum to search the registers of a five-year period. Once you have gone into the galleries and looked at the books you will by diligence find your John Grosvenor. I say diligence because you may have to look through twenty volumes. The register books are arranged in quarters, and if you know that your father was born between 1880 and 1884 inclusive, you will have to begin in the 1880 quarters, but you may not find him until you reach the last quarter of 1884. Once you have found John Grosvenor, you put down on the form the necessary references from the register and go down again to see the officials. You will then be asked to pay two shillings and sixpence, for which you will be given a copy of the birth certificate; you usually have to wait twenty-four hours before you can call to collect the certificate.

If you are unable to go to Somerset House you can write to:

> *The Registrar-General*
> *Somerset House*
> *The Strand*
> *London*

The charge is then seven shillings and sixpence for the search and certificate. There are enormous numbers of people who make these inquiries, and there have been a great many more since England went in for a considerable amount of socialism and since the Welfare State was set up. In many cases the marriage certificate or a birth certificate is required before a pension can be obtained.

If, then, you have found your John Grosvenor, born on November 17, 1882, his birth certificate will give you the names of his parents. Therefore you will know the names of your grandfather, and also his occupation and where he lived, and the names of his wife, including her maiden surname. Having obtained this, you will now want to obtain particulars about your grandparents, and so you will want to go on to get their marriage certificate. There is one difficulty, and that is that in periods before the present century, families were much larger than they are now, and your father was not necessarily the eldest child of his parents. I remember one case where I had to work through a period of fifteen years before I found the marriage certificate of the grandparents of the man in question. The reason for this was that the father of my inquirer, so far from being the eldest child, was well down the list, and his parents had been married for fourteen years before he was born. Still, if a man was born in 1882, it should be possible to find not only the marriage certificate of his parents but also the birth certificate of his father. This birth certificate will give the names and particulars of the inquirer's great-grandparents, and so a rudimentary pedigree is established of three generations. It may well be that there is a record at Somerset House of the marriage of the great-grandparents, but I ought to advise you that in the case of anybody born in 1882 you are not likely to be able to go back at Somerset House beyond about 1850, when that person's grandparents would have been married.

Presently I will mention some of the other valuable records kept at Somerset House, but I would like here to state that births or deaths at sea dating back to the first of July 1837 are also kept in the General Register Office. This is a very valuable provision, because sometimes an ancestor was born or died at sea. In all the cases which I give you, I have myself made an investigation and have proved the point at issue.

Then, in addition, there are records of births, deaths, and marriages which have been kept by British consuls from 1849 in regard to British subjects abroad; army records, dealing not only with the soldiers but with their families and going back sometimes to 1761. I remember one case in which a soldier was traced through his regimental records right back to the beginning of the war against France in the French Revolution, about 1793. I also remember a case where an officer was traced as having fought with his regiment in North America during the American War of Independence. Just to complete the record, I ought to mention that there are returns of Royal Air Force personnel which begin in 1920. Somerset House itself issues some notes for the guidance of visitors, and these can easily be obtained by writing to the Registrar-General.

There are some records which are preserved in Somerset House that go back before 1837. These are concerned with religious denominations other than the Church of England and go back, in a few cases, to about 1550. These records deal with religious bodies such as the Baptists, Independents, Presbyterians, Quakers, and

Wesleyan Methodists. These records are extremely valuable, and to them can be added registers of marriages, births, and baptisms which go back to the seventeenth century and which were formerly kept at Greenwich Hospital, Chelsea Hospital, and the Foundling Hospital.

I would suggest that in any case in which the inquirer thinks that his ancestor may have belonged to some religious body outside the Church of England, he should write in the first instance to Somerset House to make inquiries as to what records concerning that religious body may be held there.

It will be as well for the inquirer to know the current fees at Somerset House. They are as follows:

> For a particular search in the indices of registers for a period of five consecutive years, three shillings and ninepence.
>
> For each certificate of birth, marriage, death, etc., three shillings and ninepence.
>
> For each short birth certificate, ninepence.

It should be noted that the search fee is one shilling and sixpence if the applicant goes to the General Register Office himself and makes the search. If he applies in writing for the certificate, the fees are seven shillings and sixpence. It is also worth noting that an all-out search can be made for a sum of about thirty shillings. This all-out search will cover the whole period of Somerset House registers.

Any correspondence about the various documents mentioned should be addressed to the Registrar-General. The public search rooms are open between 9:30 A.M. and 4:30 P.M. On Saturdays the rooms close at 12:30 P.M.; the rooms are closed on Sundays and public holidays.

The American inquirer is not likely to have much call for the records of Somerset House, because the majority of Americans of British descent will find that their ancestors went to America probably more than 200 years ago. However, there will be times when they will need to consult some of the records at Somerset House, so I have given the information.

There is one very important point. Suppose you have found that your ancestor—shall we say your great-grandfather—was married about 1850 and that, therefore, the record of his marriage is kept at Somerset House. Your next step is to find out more about him, especially the date and place of his birth. This will be found through the parish registers, which I shall explain in a section below. But how are you to bridge the gap between 1850 and the parish registers if you do not know the place from which your ancestor came? By this I mean that if your great-grandfather was married in 1850 and if the record of this marriage is found, as it will be, at Somerset House, it may only say that his marriage took place at Manchester or Bristol, both of which were important cities at the time, but it does not follow that your great-grandfather was born in Bristol or Manchester. You probably realize that in England there was a great deal of movement of the population between the end of the eighteenth century and the beginning of the reign of Queen Victoria in 1837. The reason for this was partly the Industrial Revolution and partly the coming of railways. The Industrial Revolution called for more people in certain parts where industry was being set up. Consequently, people left their villages in Yorkshire or Cheshire or Lancashire and went to some growing industrial town. Then again, the coming of the railways meant that a boy who was born and brought up on a farm in Somerset or Devon could often make his way to Bristol or London. There he may have married but did not return to his native place, and there would be nothing at Somerset House—supposing he was married in 1850—which would show his place of origin.

## THE CENSUS

To bridge the gap between Somerset House records and the parish registers, we find it very useful to consult the census. What was the census? The census was first undertaken in England in 1801. The word itself is Latin in origin, and the censor in ancient Rome was a person employed by the state to keep up the roll of citizens and to take off that roll any person whose conduct was considered to be unworthy. Hence our word "censorious" and also the use of the word "censor" to mean a person who expunges items from a book or record. Now, there are various references to a census, in the sense of taking a numbering, in the early books of the Old Testament (and also in the New Testament), but the most important of these is in the first Book of Chronicles, chapter 21. There is the verse "Satan stood up against Israel and provoked David to number Israel." In consequence, a pestilence came upon the Israelites until David repented.

There is even today among many peoples in Africa and Asia a strong objection to a census because they think that by so numbering the people some kind of evil influence will descend upon them. This idea finds its expression in the passage quoted above from the Old Testament, and in consequence of this notion, when an attempt was made in the middle of the eighteenth century to take the number of British people, it was rejected in Parliament in England because it was considered that to take a census was to risk incurring the wrath of God. Some fifty years later, in 1801, the people had apparently become less worried and perhaps the French Revolution and the war with Napoleon which was then just beginning had made them realize that there were worse calamities than finding out how many people lived in England.

So the first census was held in 1801. Unfortunately, it was not until 1841 that the enumerators thought of preserving the record of the census. Between 1801 and 1841, all that they did was to keep a record of the number of the people; so they found out that in 1801 there were 12 million persons in England and Wales. But in 1841 they did keep the records, and these records are preserved in the Public Record Office. I shall give a full description of this below, but for the moment I want to talk about the census returns which are kept there. This census of 1841 does give us a survey of the whole of England and Wales, and it is most useful if we have any idea of the place where the persons whom we are tracing were living at that date. I stress the last sentence because in the 1841 returns people were asked to state only if they had been born in the city or county where they then lived. By 1851 a much greater advance had taken place. In 1851 each person had to say in the census returns where he or she had been born. If you know that your great-grandparents were married in 1850, it is fairly reasonable to suppose that the addresses given for them in 1850 were fairly permanent. Particularly, this would be the case with your great-grandfather, and you would imagine that his address at the time of his marriage about 1850 would be his address for the census return in 1851. If such is the case and you can turn this up in the 1851 census, it means that you will find out where he was born and from that you will be able to trace his date of birth and particulars of his father and mother.

Census returns are, of course, taken in the United Kingdom every ten years except during times such as the Second World War. Consequently, no census returns were made in 1941, when they should have been made. In 1931 there was a census, but there was not another census until 1951. The returns from 1861 to the present date are kept at Somerset House (see above). It is not possible to consult them personally. You can, however, go into Somerset House or, of course, write to the place and state what you want in the census from 1861 to the present. The officials then look it up for you and send you the information. This usually costs about ten shillings. The reason why you cannot consult these records yourself is that they are considered to relate to living persons, and although this is somewhat out of date for people who were recorded in 1861 and 1871, the British Government does not take chances and, for that reason, you cannot consult these documents yourself.

But the documents of 1841 and 1851 are for your inspection for a very small charge, of not more than a few shillings, at the Public Record Office, in Chancery Lane, London. You are allowed to look at the actual returns, and they are, of course, invaluable. This is the bridge between the parish registers and the more modern records of Somerset House.

Other records which are kept at Somerset House concern another great section with which the inquirer ought to make himself acquainted as soon as possible, namely, wills.

## WILLS

At Somerset House there are rich collections of wills. In England there are records of wills from Anglo-Saxon times. In the beginning of organized society in England, the keeping of wills, or rather the making of them, was a matter in which the Church had a great deal to say. It was considered essential that a man who was approaching his end should make a will if he had anything to leave. Consequently, the proving of wills and the keeping of the documents was from early times in England a matter for the Church. Right up until 1857 wills had to be proved in the ecclesiastical courts. In 1858, however, a law was passed by which the Probate Court was set up and wills were proved therein. This was, of course, one of the ordinary courts of the realm and had nothing to do with the Church.

From 1858 wills have been proved in the Probate Court and have been stored at Somerset House in a department called the Principal Probate Registry. It should be possible for you to secure copies there of the wills of your father, grandfather, and great-grandfather—supposing, of course, that all these were born and lived in England. It is possible to obtain photostat copies of wills, and these do not cost very much; even a large will costs no more than about ten shillings and sixpence.

I would like to explain before we go any further the position with regard to wills from early days. As I have mentioned, we possess wills which date back to Saxon times, and after the Norman Conquest of 1066 the forms of willmaking were retained and such matters were dealt with in the Church courts. It came about in England that there was, during the Middle Ages, no trust law as we know it today. But in place of the trust there was something called "the use," which was indeed the forerunner of our law of trust. Under this usage of the use, a man could leave his property in trust with a friend for the benefit of his family or his heirs. The reason for this was that freehold property could not be devised, and therefore great hardships were likely to arise if a man died while his children were still minors. At last, in 1540, in the reign of Henry VIII, the Statute of Wills allowed that in a written will two thirds of the land which a man owned could be devised.

The importance of the ecclesiastical jurisdiction in connection with wills is shown when we consider a will dealing with property in more than one county or district. In such a case the ecclesiastical court in the area may not have been able to deal with the will because it did not have jurisdiction over the area adjacent to its own. Then the will had to be proved, not in the Archdeacon's Court, for example at Wells in Somerset, but in what is known as the Prerogative Court of the Archbishop of Canterbury or York. The Canterbury Court is usually referred to in documents as the P.C.C.

Consequently, when the property mentioned in the will was in more than one archdeaconry, then the will had to be proved in the Prerogative Court of Canterbury. Very often it will state at the bottom of a will that after probate had been begun in the Archdeacon's Court, it had been found that the property was in more than one jurisdiction and so the will had been transferred to the P.C.C.

Now, all these wills which had been proved in the P.C.C. have been placed in Somerset House, and so you will understand that at Somerset House there are not only wills from 1858 to the present day—say, just over a hundred years ago—but also wills which go back into the Middle Ages.

If you want to consult one of these wills at Somerset House, you can either make the search yourself or arrange for one of the officials there to make the search for you. If you can go yourself, it is better, but if you are working from across the Atlantic, obviously you will have to write and state what you want. You will then be informed of the moderate costs involved. Anyone who calls at the Principal Probate Registry at Somerset House will be asked to pay one shilling on admittance. You are then allowed to look through the records of a five-year period to find the particular will you are seeking. The volumes in which you search are large, hand-written volumes; the writing is excellent and there is no difficulty about reading it. If you find the record of the will which you seek, you then ask to have the actual will brought upstairs. The wills are bound in books, and you may come across cases where the writing has yellowed and also where there is a difficulty in following the handwriting. One of the regulations at Somerset House is that you can take notes about a will but you must not make full copies. If you want that, you must ask the official to have copies made for you and you can, of course, have photostats.

One great difficulty does present itself when searching for wills in England; that is, that apart from the two classes I have mentioned, namely those from 1858 and those in the P.C.C. before 1858, there are many places in England and Wales where wills may be stored. There are something like twenty-three provincial storage places for wills. At the end of this section on English genealogy I am including the most up-to-date information I can obtain with regard to the various depositories, but there are great difficulties, because during the 1939–45 war many of these valuable documents were moved.

By the way, you may well wonder whether many British records were lost during the last war. We did lose some, notably at Exeter, where there were many West Country records, and again in Yorkshire. Otherwise we came out of the war very well in this respect.

Why should you bother about wills? Well, I think I can explain that to you by taking an example. I was once asked to trace the pedigree of a family named Matthews. I got back through eight or more generations and then I found Richard Matthews of Norwich, who was a carpenter by trade and whose marriage took place in the year 1686. The family with whom I was concerned thought, on the other hand, that they descended from a line of baronets (this is a hereditary title). I found that these baronets were entered in some records in the year 1633, and I wanted to know whether the first of the baronets, namely Philip Matthews, was the eldest son of a certain Joachim Matthews of London. Now, to trace this, I had to get the will of Joachim Matthews at Somerset House. I obtained the will and it was a very lengthy document. Seven children were mentioned, two daughters and five sons. None of the children was over seventeen, and I traced out several of them of whom I had previous knowledge. As a consequence of my work, I was able to show as conclusively as is possible in this kind of work that the line of the Matthews of Norwich was not connected with that of the baronets who bore the same surname.

In days gone by, wills were much more informative than they are today. A man often began by giving thanks to God in his will and commending his soul to his Creator. He then went into great detail about his property, his intentions, and his family. Again and again in wills a member of the family is mentioned who in subsequent years has dropped out of the record. In very many pedigrees in England the only mention of certain names in families is in the will, and one reads in pedigrees simply this laconic notice: "mentioned in his father's will 1590." The importance of such an entry to a transatlantic inquirer is obvious. That William Hooke or John Mordaunt who is mentioned in a will of 1580 may be the very missing link that you are seeking as the beginner of your pedigree.

I would therefore advise that as many wills as possible be obtained. It is not very expensive for you to have a complete search of Somerset House records in this respect. You can get a record of every will in a certain family, and the staff at Somerset House will undoubtedly work out the whole thing for you and will show whether a name is likely to be connected with the line in which you are interested.

### Notes on Wills and Their Whereabouts

There is fortunately a work on this difficult subject, to which reference should be made by those who are going deeply into the subject of their ancestors' wills. This is *Wills and Their Whereabouts,* compiled, mostly from original sources, by B. G. Bouwens; the second edition has been prepared with alterations and corrections by Miss Helen Thacker. It is published by the Society of Genealogists, 37 Harrington Gardens, South Kensington, London S.W.1., price 12/6. This work contains, first, some notes about wills and testamentary procedure, an index of existing and past jurisdictions, and then a list of the various registries. These are:

1. Bangor. A note to the second edition states that records have been transferred to the National Library of Wales, Aberystwyth (see Welsh section).

2. Birmingham Registry. Some records have been transferred to County Record Office, Bedford.

3. Blandford Registry. All records transferred to Winchester Registry.

4. Bodmin.

5. Bristol.

6. Canterbury. All transferred to County Hall, Maidstone.

7. Carlisle.

8. Carmarthen. All transferred to National Library of Wales.

9. Chester. Welsh records taken to National Library. Non-Welsh records transferred to County Record Office, Chester.

10. Durham.

11. Exeter.

12. Gloucester.

13. Ipswich.

14. Lancaster.

15. Leicester. All records transferred to County Record Office, Leicester.

16. Lewes.

17. Lincoln.

18. Llandaff. All records transferred to National Library of Wales.

19. London Principal Probate Registry. Act books and original wills and administrations of deaneries of Shoreham and Croydon transferred to County Hall, Maidstone. Registers of wills, bound with those of the Peculiar of Arches, London, remain at P.P.R.

20. Norwich.

21. Nottingham.

22. Peterborough.

23. Shrewsbury. All records transferred to National Library of Wales.

24. Winchester. Records of Episcopal Consistory for Archdeaconry of Chichester, Peculiars of the Dean of Chichester, Pagham, and Tarring, transferred to County Record Office, Chichester.

25. York.

It should be stressed that the above information is accurate only at the time of writing, as there are many changes in the place of keeping of the above records.

## PARISH REGISTERS

We shall be coming back to the interrelation of the various departments of research later on, but now I want to introduce you to a most important series of records. These are the parish registers, and let me tell you straightway that they go back, in theory at least, to 1538. There are misguided people who will tell you that there were parish registers before 1538, but this is not true. In 1538 the monasteries had been suppressed only a few years, and no doubt a certain amount of record keeping had gone on, because, whatever they may not have done, the monks were interested in keeping chronicles and various notes. At the same time the chief minister of Henry VIII was Thomas Cromwell, who had served as a mercenary soldier in the Low Countries. When Cromwell returned to England he took service with the famous Cardinal Wolsey, but although true to Wolsey until the latter's end, Cromwell did not share in his fall. He had a recommendation to Henry VIII and he was taken into the King's confidence. In return, Cromwell suggested a vigorous prosecution of the suppression of the monasteries, and a great deal of money and landed property came to the King because of this. Then Cromwell thought that it was time that a record system was set up. He was not thinking of the aims of people like ourselves, but of keeping tabs on the people of England and of knowing more about them through these parish registers. So in 1538 Cromwell, as the King's minister, issued instructions that a book and a coffer with two locks should be provided in each parish in England and Wales, and that on every Sunday, in the presence of the churchwardens, the parson was to write in this book the records of all the baptisms, marriages, and burials of the preceding week. There was a great deal of opposition at first to the keeping of these records. Cromwell was not popular and the people of the time regarded the keeping of the registers as an unwarrantable attempt to interfere with their liberties, and it was thought that all this information would lead to greater taxation. In consequence, the parish registers were not popular, and as a reflection of this, they were not kept in many cases until long after 1538. There were various attempts to make the keeping of the registers a more serious matter, but it was left in the end to the individual conduct of the vicar or rector of the parish. But all in all, the parish registers are a very valuable source of information. It sometimes makes one feel very nervous when visiting a parish church in England and perhaps on meeting the vicar for him to say, "Our registers go back to 1660. Would you like to see them?" He then produces from a safe some beautifully written books which go back for three hundred years. These books contain information which is literally priceless to those who are seeking for it. They cannot get it anywhere else, at least not in such a useful form.

As I have explained, in years gone by few people moved very far in England but were mainly concerned in being born, married, and buried in the one place where they lived, and so it comes about that ten or eleven generations of a family can be found in a particular parish. Now, this is very useful indeed to an inquirer like yourself, who perhaps has an ancestor who went to America in 1700. Well, if you know the parish in which he lived, you can get in touch with the vicar and find out a great deal about the history of your family, because it is quite likely that they lived there before 1700. If you get this information you will very likely go back another three or four generations, and even if they did not live in that particular parish, they very likely lived not far away, and so you have only to start looking on a map and finding out places within a radius of five or ten miles distant.

How would you begin to deal with the question of approaching the registers? I will take here, as I always do, a particular case and suggest that we start with a small place such as Porlock or Ashbrittle in Somerset; you would have a fair example of tracing your ancestry, because many families who have subsequently lived in London or one of our great cities or have emigrated to the United States began in some little place.

Although England is a small country and thickly populated, there are many areas where it is very lonely and where a small place has stayed much the same with regard to the numbers of people for many generations. At Ashbrittle, for example, there are even now only about two hundred people, and yet it has a big church and several big houses and is only five miles from Wellington, which is the seat of a famous school.

I can understand how puzzling it must be to an American inquirer when he comes to deal with small places in England. England is only three quarters of an island, and yet between Northumberland or Cumberland on the border of Scotland and Cornwall or Devon on the southwest coast there is an enormous difference. There can be few countries in the world where in so small a space there is such vast diversity of scenery and also of characteristics among the people. All down the northeast side of England, from Northumberland to Norfolk, there is a different type among the people from what you would find in England south of the Thames. This is because the northeastern side of England was the area settled by the

Norsemen, the Vikings. Then again, in the western part of England, and especially the part which borders on Wales, you get a considerable amount of Celtic admixture, because many of the older British inhabitants of England still lived on in that part of the country.

### The Forty Shires of England

Americans very frequently make mistakes and write about Kentshire, Surreyshire, and so on. I am afraid that English nomenclature can only be accepted. You must get to learn it in time if you are looking in English records. Only some counties in England have the ending "-shire," for instance Lincolnshire, but nobody would talk about Norfolkshire, although Norfolk is a county. The word "shire" comes from an old English word meaning a division, and according to tradition, Alfred the Great divided England into forty shires. Whether or not this is true, it is undoubtedly a very old division in England. The word "county," on the other hand, came in after the Norman Conquest; the area of a county was the jurisdiction of a count, or, as the English came to call him, an earl.

By the way, two counties in England have very curious divisions. Yorkshire, which is the largest English county, is divided into three administrative divisions, which are very ancient. They are the North Riding, the East Riding, and the West Riding. The word "Riding" was brought in by the Norsemen and the name has stuck. Again, in Sussex there are six divisions, which mean very little now but which meant a great deal in former days. These are the "Rapes" which divided Sussex into six areas. As you may well come across these puzzling terms, I am mentioning them to you now. Again, there is a curious division in Northamptonshire, and on the edge of Huntingdonshire, where you have the Soke of Peterborough. This was an ancient Saxon name given to the territory and it has remained.

I strongly advise you if you are looking for English ancestry to get a good gazetteer of Great Britain and Ireland. A good one is that by Messrs. Bartholomew; you may not always find the modern details in this, quite what you would want from the point of view of an economic study, but as a guide to the places in England, and indeed in the British Isles, it is invaluable. It has hundreds of pages giving names and particulars of places, and it tells you how many miles from the nearest town each place is. If you remember what I said just now about looking in neighboring parishes, you will realize how important this information is in a gazetteer. Then again, you must have a series of maps of England, and while all good atlases contain maps of England, you will find that you need much larger maps than would be usual in a collection of world maps. In *Bartholomew's Gazetteer* there are detailed maps of every part of the British Isles. Or you could get a map of the area in which you are interested from the British Ordnance Survey, which is published by Her Majesty's Stationery Office. These maps give an immense amount of detail.

Now, I have been referring to parishes. How do you go about finding a parish? Well, there are fourteen thousand parishes, that is to say, church divisions, in the Church of England. Fortunately, there is a very useful book called *Crockford's Clerical Directory.* This book is published by the Oxford University Press at Warwick House, Amen Court, London. It gives a list of all the incumbents in the Church of England. Incumbents are the rectors or vicars— or, if you like, the priests or ministers—of the fourteen thousand parishes. They are people whose names and addresses appear in *Crockford's Clerical Directory.* You will also find the dates given for the foundation of the more ancient churches, so that if you have to look for a baptismal entry in a parish register, you would consult this directory and there you would find the dates of the churches in, shall we say, Leeds, which is a big city, but you would know that if the church was founded after the date when you should find the record of the baptism, there is no need for you to waste your time writing to the incumbent of that church.

If you are going to do an extensive genealogical research in England, I suggest that you get a copy of *Crockford's Clerical Directory.* This is not a cheap book but costs, now, nine guineas. On the other hand, the information which it contains will be most helpful to you. I advise you, however, as a general rule not to write to the vicar or rector of a parish by name, but to address your letter to The Reverend the Vicar, and then follow it with the address at which he lives. If you write to the Reverend John Smith, you may find that he has left and gone to another parish, and if so, your letter will be sent on to him and so cause delay.

When you are writing to an incumbent, always be sure to offer to pay for any trouble to which he is put by your request. I know that you cannot send him stamps as a person living in England can, but send him a few cents, which he can readily change at his bank and so not be out of pocket in answering your letter. The English clergy are as a rule very badly paid, and they do find it difficult to meet expenses on items such as postage and stationery. The fees for searches by the clergy are not very large and do not usually exceed one pound, unless, of course, you are asking them to search their registers for a period of thirty or forty years. In some cases an incumbent will ask you to make a gift to some charity or fund in his parish. It would be a good idea to do it. Quite apart from the good cause which he is pleading, you will, by giving something, make a friend and you may well have to ask him to do something else for you.

### The State of the Registers

This is a matter which has often been deplored by genealogists. I give the following quotation from *The Times* of November 26, 1956. "It is rare indeed to find the early registers in a good state, though occasionally the miracle does happen. More often damp and decay have done their evil work and obliterated many entries for ever. Sometimes the books seem to have been given as playthings to the incumbents' children."

Many registers have been destroyed, and there was a period in the troubles between King Charles I and his Parliament, around 1645, when very few records were kept at all. However, much has been done to repair this loss as far as can be and to prevent it from spreading. There was a company, named Messrs. Phillimore of Chancery Lane in London, which printed a large number of parish registers. The greatest work in connection with parish registers has been done by the Society of Genealogists. This society has a national index of parish-register copies, which can be bought for three shillings and sixpence. In one of the sections below, I will give a full account of the Society, with its address, and you can refer to that and it will be very helpful to you. There is also a catalogue of copies of parish registers which the Society possesses; the price is five shillings.

It is no use denying that there are many snags in the examination of parish registers. I very often receive correspondence from various parts of the world in which I am asked to give some light in genealogical darkness. The reason is that the inquirer has looked in the parish registers and has obtained a certain amount of information and then has come to a dead stop, shall we say in 1740. Now, in the course of this chapter I shall give you the benefit of the various answers which I have worked out for my correspondents. But for the moment I would like to confine myself to dealing with the parish registers and their troubles. For one thing, only a few go back to 1538, although you can never tell, because a little while ago I was shown a magnificently kept series of records which did actually go back for four hundred years, and this was at St. Giles in the Fields, in London. As this was a fashionable area for a very long time, you can imagine the enormous number of names and of well-known families which were represented in these four hundred years of priceless records. Another problem is the old style of handwriting, though this does improve after 1650. For the past three hundred years there has not been much difficulty in reading the handwriting of the documents, but before that time there was an awful lot of trouble in deciphering documents because the writing of the Tudor period was in what is known as court hand, which seems to us to have been anything but courtly. At any rate, we have to learn it. Then again, as I mentioned just now, between 1645 and 1659 not very much was done in the matter of keeping any records in parishes. The reason for this was that the Parliamentary party in the Civil War in England, when they were in power, tried to turn out all the Church of England clergy and put in clergy of their own way of thinking. As a result, there was very little done to keep up the church system until after the restoration of Charles II in 1660.

Something which is very irritating is to find the entry of a baptism, or rather, of a marriage, in which no particulars are given of the parentage of the parties. This is due entirely to the negligence of the local clergyman. Nothing can be more annoying, because it means that you are stopped at the very point where you are most interested.

## ILLUSIONS AND DELUSIONS

I think that this is not a bad stage to deal with certain troubles which undoubtedly do afflict the inquirers in America who want to look into their British antecedents. By the way, this applies not only to Americans but also to Australians and Canadians. One of the most frequent causes of trouble is funds held in Chancery.

### Funds Held in Chancery

I had a letter once from an American lady who told me that her grandfather bore a strong resemblance to Queen Mary. I have no reason to suppose that this lady had not been acting in good faith, but she went on to talk about the resemblance between her grandfather and Queen Mary and to imply that he was one of the royal family who had run away and gone to America. I hope that I need not say that this story is nonsense, but I receive other legends and tales that are not very much less fantastic than this curious myth. And among the foremost of these is the story of millions and millions of pounds lying waiting in coffers in England, just waiting for someone to come and claim the money. I can assure anybody who reads this book and is interested that there is nothing in this story whatever.

As I write, I have before me a document called *Dormant Funds in Court*. This document is issued by the Supreme Court Pay Office, Royal Courts of Justice, London W.C.2. In this leaflet we are told that there is a list of accounts for which money is held under the control of the Supreme Court. It is expressly stated that a large majority of these funds are very small in their amount. Half of the sums of money do not exceed one hundred and fifty pounds and only about one twentieth exceed one thousand pounds. Every five years in the *London Gazette,* which is an official document issued by Her Majesty's Stationery Office, a list of accounts which have such funds outstanding is published. In this document the Supreme Court Pay Office particularly makes mention of the stories about huge sums running into millions held in the name of Page, Hyde, Drake, Mullins, Everingham, Hobbs, and Edwards. The document is very careful to add that these things are imaginary and, of course, the whole of the facts with regard to money held in Chancery is far more prosaic than romantic. My advice is that if you think that you have money waiting in England for you, you should think again and think very resolutely and then abandon the idea.

If, on the other hand, by some chance it should come about that there is some possibility of truth in the idea of money in England, then you had better write to the following address:

*The Chief Accountant*
*Supreme Court Pay Office*
*Royal Courts of Justice*
*London W.C.2*

You must quote the correct title of the matter and you must sign this, and in due course it must be stamped with what is known as a Judicator Fee Stamp, which costs half a crown. However, if you will write in the first instance and make your position quite clear, then you will be informed what to do about the stamp and how it can be obtained.

I would like to quote one item from the document I have referred to because it so clearly has been inserted only because of troublesome correspondence with which the authorities have been vexed.

"This [that is, the amount of the fund and particulars of the Order of the Court related to it] is usually the only information which can be furnished, as the Supreme Court Pay Office is solely an Office of Accounts and has no record of the origin or details of the various suits, or of the circumstances under which the fund has been directed or allowed to remain in court, neither has it any information enabling it to reply to inquiries as to descent or relationship."

### The Delusion about Titles

Almost as many letters reach me regarding people who say that one of their ancestors should have been a lord, or at least could have had some title, and that he gave up the title in favor of his brother and went away to America. Let me tell you, with all the emphasis that my connection with *Burke's Peerage* for twenty-five years can give, that this story is completely without foundation. In English peerage law it is not permissible to give up a title in favor of someone else. That sort of thing has happened on the continent of Europe, but it simply does not take place in English law. It is certainly true that a man who has inherited a title can for various reasons not use it. Sometimes he is poor and therefore finds a peerage dignity of no value to him but rather a handicap. Sometimes, although he has plenty of money, he does not want to use the title. But he cannot give it up and pass it over to his younger brother or his best friend. Therefore, all these stories about great-uncle Zedekiah or great-grandfather Aaron who should have been Lord Knights-bridge are so much balderdash. Forget that.

Just as there is a vast amount of nonsense about titles, there is a residuum of truth in the idea that the holder of a title may be wandering about different parts of the world not knowing that he is a peer of Great Britain. The Earl of Egmont some thirty years ago was a Canadian rancher. Sir Frederick Hay was a Melbourne (Australia) grocer and did not know of his succession to a baronetcy until it was found out that two of his uncles had lived and died in Australia without being aware of their succession to the baronetcy. I believe that the heir to the old earldom of Traquair is living in the United States. I am certain that the heir to the barony of Gardner is an Indian or Anglo-Indian peasant living in poverty in India. Therefore, you may have this much in your family legend, that perhaps at some time there was a peerage in your family, and it may well be that a cousin whom you have never liked is the heir to the title. But generally speaking we had better eschew all claims to title, and you will be much happier and can then spend your money on proper research into your family. I remember another case, in which an American lady wrote to me and for a long time argued with me that one of her ancestors had been a peer. At last, after a good deal of research, I did find out that one of her ancestors was a nobleman and that with truly noble morals he had begotten an illegitimate son, who was packed off to the American colonies. When I communicated my discovery to the good lady in question, I must say she received it with a marvelous spirit, but from that day to this I have never known her to express any interest in family history.

## The Coat of Arms

The last illusion that I want to deal with at the moment concerns coats of arms. I shall below give an account of the College of Arms, which is responsible for all matters of heraldry in England and Wales. There is a current delusion that for every name there is a coat of arms. This is not true. There are perfectly respectable names, and thousands of them, where no coat of arms exists. Many of these names are quite unusual; equally, there are common names, such as Smith, where there are something like eighty coats of arms in existence for persons with the name of Smith. An amusing book was written in the late Victorian period called the *Heraldry of Smith*.

Now, if a name like Smith has something like eighty examples of the coat of arms, it is not surprising that the idea of a coat of arms per family name is completely erroneous. It simply is not true, and you must reconcile yourself to the possibility that your family name has no coat of arms attached to it. Moreover, if you do have a name which bore a coat of arms in the past and in connection with an English family, it by no means follows that you are entitled to use that coat of arms. Many Americans simply look in a book like *Burke's General Armory,* and because they have the name of Grosvenor and they find Grosvenor in the *Armory,* they conclude that they are entitled to the coat of arms of Grosvenor. They are not necessarily entitled to those arms; in fact, the presumption is all the other way. There are agencies in the United States the like of which have been driven out of business in England but which do give promises of supplying coats of arms to those who send them five or ten dollars. In some advertisements which have appeared in the United States, I have known of cases where a description of the coat of arms has been offered for five dollars, a picture for ten dollars, and a pedigree for twenty-five dollars.

Needless to say, there is no value in an offer of this nature. There are only three ways in which a citizen of the United States can acquire a coat of arms legitimately:

(1) To apply to the College of Arms in London for a grant of arms. Many Americans have done this and are doing so. To apply to the London College, it is necessary for the American to be of English or of Welsh descent. For an American of Scottish or Irish descent, the procedure is quite different.

(2) To prove his descent from an armigerous person. This can be done, in many cases, by an American who finds his family was in the past seated in England. As we shall see, we shall find in many cases that his family had a coat of arms which was legitimately borne. If, therefore, an American inquirer can prove his descent from such a person, he will be entitled to arms because according to the rule of English heraldry all the descendants of the original grantee are entitled to use the arms in question.

(3) To apply to the Committee on Heraldry of the New England Genealogical Society. Address applications to:

> *Dr. Harold Bowditch*
> *44 Harvard Avenue*
> *Brookline 46, Massachusetts*

This excellent society has spent many years in investigating claims to arms by American citizens. It will register such arms only if it is satisfied that they are borne by correct usage from the original owners.

One of the worst faults in genealogy is the tacit permission given by many authorities to an American inquirer, which permit him to use the arms of a family of the same name as his own. Thus, Americans have acquired the idea that there is for every name a corresponding coat of arms. Nothing, as I have tried to point out, could be further from the truth.

While we are dealing with the subject of coats of arms it will be just as well to explain the College of Arms to the inquirer.

## THE COLLEGE OF ARMS

The popular name for this institution is Heralds' College. The correct term, which is used by the Officers of the College, is the College of Arms. The College of Arms is on Queen Victoria Street, London E.C.4. The head of the College is the Earl Marshal. He is one of the last of the great hereditary officers of state, who used to function in the Middle Ages. The Earl Marshal is the Duke of Norfolk, and the office of Earl Marshal has been held, at first intermittently, in his family from the time of Richard III (1483–85). For about two hundred years after that time, the dukes of Norfolk, who are the heads of the house of Howard, used to find themselves in alternating periods of court favor and periods of disgrace and real danger. The Duke of Norfolk in the reign of Queen Elizabeth I lost his head, literally as well as metaphorically, for the sake of Mary, Queen of Scots. But in the reigns of Charles I and Charles II the office of Earl Marshal was finally settled in the family of the Howards, the dukes of Norfolk. Under the rule of the Earl Marshal comes the management of the College of Arms.

The Officers of the College under the Earl Marshal are thirteen in number. They are divided into three categories. These are Kings, Heralds, and Pursuivants. The three Kings of Arms bear picturesque titles—Garter, Clarenceux, and Norroy. Garter derives his name from the Order of the Garter, the most distinguished order of chivalry in Britain. Clarenceux is so called from the dukes of Clarence in the Plantagenet period. "Norroy" is a contraction from the "North King," that is, the "Roy du Nord." Norroy is so called because he has jurisdiction over matters heraldic north of the river Trent. Clarenceux deals with matters south of the Trent. The province of Garter is to deal specifically with peers, baronets, and knights and also to act as second in command to the Earl Marshal in all important matters.

The six Heralds are known as Windsor, Somerset, Lancaster, Chester, York, and Richmond. The four Pursuivants bear very beautiful medieval names—Blue Mantle, Rouge Dragon, Rouge Croix, and Portcullis. The word "pursuivant" means a follower, or junior herald.

Quite apart from the picturesque functions which you will associate with the Heralds, they also keep large quantities of records. No doubt from very early times they kept records, but it was not their primary duty so to do. In former days the Heralds had many duties to perform, such as the conduct of embassies and the management of the funerals of great men and women. But it was not until the reign of Henry VIII (1509–47) that the systematic keeping of records by the Heralds began. The reason for this was that, in 1529–30, King Henry VIII ordered the Heralds of the College of Arms to conduct what was known as a visitation.

These visitations were tours of different counties of England and Wales in which the arms of various persons and institutions were recorded. Not only did the Heralds record the arms but they took down a statement of pedigree from the owner of the arms. These statements did not usually go back much before the great-grandfather of the man who made the statement, but as the visitations were continued from generation to generation, many more details of pedigree were added.

The visitations continued from 1529–30 to 1686. During this period it is very interesting to trace the manner in which the Heralds would visit various counties, such as Devonshire or Yorkshire, and would enter in details of pedigree as well as arms, generation by generation. To take one case, the family of Hooke in Gloucestershire is found in every one of the Heralds' visitations of that county. Many other cases occur like this, but on the other hand, there are many instances where a family is mentioned only once in a visitation; for example, the Mountaines of Westow are mentioned only in the one visitation of Yorkshire, namely in 1666, when Sir William Dugdale conducted the visitation of that county.

Gradually throughout the period of 160 years in which they were made, a great deal of information was accumulated in the visitations. The original books used by the Heralds, which contain not only written matter but drawings of the arms also, are held in the College of Arms. The inquirer cannot take these volumes down and search in them himself. He will have to be content to make an inquiry of the Heralds, who will make the searches for him.

Many of the Heralds' visitations have been printed, by various persons, and consequently there are many printed visitations available in large libraries. The Harleian Society made a very large number of copies of Visitation Pedigrees, and these copies are to be found not only in the British Museum but in many other large libraries as well.

The Visitation Pedigrees are a body of information on heraldry and genealogy which is almost unique in Europe. Quite apart from the very large amount of information which the Heralds hold in the College, there are other sources of record there. Among these are a very large number of notes and private corrections made by Heralds in former days. Then there are, of course, large books with the pedigrees of peers, baronets, and many other folk.

The procedure in order to obtain information at the College of Arms is, if you can go there, to inquire of the Duty Officer. He will be one of the Heralds or Pursuivants who will be on duty for two weeks at a time. He is expected to deal with any inquiry which comes into the College during his period of duty, and if you go there and make a request he will deal with it. Requests at the College of Arms fall into two classes. First there is the general request of someone called Whitbread or Martineau, who wants to know if arms are recorded for him at the College. A general search of this nature is usually at the rate of three to five guineas, but it is generally unproductive. The reason is that it would be very difficult for anyone to be sure that arms registered in 1850 really belong to someone else of the same name who comes there in 1960.

If, however, the general search is unproductive, then it may well be that you may wish to have a further search. This may cost anything from twenty-five to two hundred pounds, and many of those who have had searches undertaken for them at the College have paid out much more than two hundred pounds. This is because it has been necessary to search in documents of a remote period where there are many difficulties.

If you cannot go to the College, then you would write to:

> *The Secretary to the Earl Marshal*
> *The College of Arms*
> *Queen Victoria Street*
> *London E.C.4*

Or you could write to the Registrar of the College, with the same address as above. Your inquiry will then be given to an Officer, who will deal with the matter.

It is essential for the inquirer to understand that he will not be allowed to search in the College of Arms in the same way that he can search in Somerset House, the Public Record Office, or the British Museum. The records kept at the College are regarded by the Heralds as their own property. The Heralds are officers of the Queen's Household, and they interpret their functions to mean that they alone are able to use the records which they have built up. These records, however, concern a much wider field than the granting of arms. It has been said, and I think rightly, that there is no man or woman of note in English history concerning whom the College of Arms has no information.

You are therefore in the position that if you want to make inquiries with the College of Arms you have simply got to let one of the Officers conduct the search for you.


## SUMMARY

Now, before we go further, let us recapitulate what we have already gone through. In the first place, we dealt with Somerset House, and with tracing records there, back from the present day to the early nineteenth century. We also pointed out that there are records there dating back to an earlier period and giving details of denominations other than the Church of England.

We also stated that there were at Somerset House a very large number of wills, and that census records from 1861 onward were kept there.

Then we dealt with the Public Record Office to some slight extent because we mentioned the census, but a further account of the Public Record Office in Chancery Lane will come later.

We explained the position with regard to the parish registers and the dispersion of these records all over England and Wales. We went through various delusions, and also gave an account of the College of Arms and of the procedure for consulting its records.

All this adds up to tracing a person from 1960 back to 1837 through the records of birth, marriage, and death at Somerset House. By means of the 1841 and 1851 census at the Public Record Office, we bridge the gap between 1837 and the parish registers.

The parish registers, as we saw, may take us back to 1538, though we are going to be lucky to reach that date and may have to be content with tracing into the seventeenth and not the sixteenth century. Then we enlisted the aid of wills, which often brought to light members of our family of whom otherwise we might have heard nothing.

## THE BRITISH MUSEUM

It would be advisable, I think, to describe next the greatest collection of books in the world—in the British Museum Library, in Bloomsbury, London W.C.1.

The American visitor to London has this great advantage, that Somerset House and the Public Record Office are almost within the proverbial stone's throw, while the College of Arms is a six-minute taxi ride from Somerset House and the British Museum is possibly ten minutes from the Public Record Office. Thus, if our inquirer exhausts one source he can easily go on to the next in the same day, and in fact many Americans do conduct a very extensive research in the course of a few days in London, always assuming they know where to look.

The British Museum was founded in 1759, and it is a curious thing that it was founded in consequence of a successful lottery. It started off by including several very fine private collections, such as those of Sir Hans Sloane.

From the beginning it was laid down by act of the British Parliament that copies of all books published in Britain were to go to the British Museum Library. This law was not carried out as it should have been for a long time, but fortunately, early in the nineteenth century some very energetic librarians at the British Museum made the law effective.

Something like six million books are held in the British Museum Library. I do not know how many thousand books there are on the open shelves, but there is enough material there to occupy the normal reader for a lifetime. All published books go to the Museum, but many private books which do not come within the scope of the law are sent to the Museum by their authors or publishers because they want to be sure that one copy at least will be accessible to the researcher and the reader.

It would be obvious to anyone that at the British Museum a vast treasure house exists for the genealogical and heraldic searcher. Quite apart from the enormous number of printed books, there are also a great number of manuscripts.

Access to the British Museum is easy, and access to the Library is not difficult. It is, of course, futile going to the Museum and hoping to walk into the Library without obtaining a ticket, but the authorities are very reasonable about the granting of tickets and will do everything in their power to assist the genuine inquirer. The merely frivolous or curious will be warned off or discouraged, but the true searcher will get all the help he or she needs. That help is given free.

To make use of the British Museum you must know how to use the catalogue. As you might expect, this runs into hundreds of volumes. Under the heading of "Christ" alone a huge folio volume is filled with entries. One of the most unpleasant penances is to be given a reference to a book in the British Museum catalogue by an author called Brown or Smith. If you do not know his initials, then you may have to search your way through sixty or seventy folio pages, each filled with printed slips pasted into it.

However, I am going to assume that you know the books and the authors, with their initials, whom you want to consult. You will go into the reading room with your ticket, and I think you will find it impossible not to be impressed with the enormous wealth of human knowledge displayed before you. It was Mr. H. G. Wells who described the British Museum Library as a "cell of the world's brain."

The reading room of the Museum is open every day from nine till five, including Saturdays.* When you go in you will want to look in

* On Wednesdays and Fridays until 9:30 P.M.

the catalogue for the author you are seeking. You will then take a slip, many of which are lying in enclosures in front of you while you look in the catalogue. The directions are very clear as to the way in which the slip should be completed. Having completed the it with the particulars given in the catalogue, you take the slip around to a little window, where one of the Museum attendants is sitting. You give it to him, and in about one and a half to two hours the book is brought to you. It is rather tedious and somewhat awkward for a busy person to wait so long without anything to do, but in fact you can be looking things up from the books on the open shelves. Alternatively, you can put in your slips and mark them with the date of the next day, or any day you like, so as to waste no time. If you do this the books will be reserved for you and you will be able to come in the next day and get the books at nine o'clock.

It is no use going to the British Museum Library unless you know what books you want. You will then waste no time there getting out their names and going straight to the information you need.

By the way, there are two very useful books which will give you innumerable clues as to the sources of pedigrees. One of these books is *The Genealogist's Guide,* by Marshall, which was published in 1893. This gives many thousands of family names and, following these names, places where pedigrees for them may be found. In addition to this, there is a more modern work, called *The Genealogical Guide,* and this was produced only a few years ago. This brings up to date whatever there is in Marshall. Armed with these two books, you can get a great deal of information from the British Museum, because the pedigree references given in the books will enable you to lose no time in what you are searching for. I may say that the references in both books give not only the book where the pedigree is found but also the page, and if there are several volumes to the book, then it will state which volume and give the page.

## MEDIEVAL RECORDS

Now, all this information will be of use to you in tracing out various items of your ancestry, but there are still a large number of items of information which you require, and more especially for the American inquirer, because his inquiries will usually begin much further back than those of the average Englishman. The American inquirer will not want to begin in the nineteenth, but in the eighteenth or more probably in the seventeenth century. Consequently, he has need of information concerning records of the 1700s backward, and especially he wants to know the meaning of the many medieval records in which England is so rich.

I shall propose in the next paragraphs to describe these records and to explain where they can be found and what it is likely the inquirer will trace through them.

It is, of course, always possible not to do the tracing yourself, but to pay someone else to do it; but if you do, and if you are going to search in the records of the Middle Ages, then you must be prepared to spend some hundreds of pounds. It is much more interesting to do it yourself, and while there are many Americans who suffer from one or more of the delusions I listed before, there are many Americans whose knowledge of genealogical research is really outstanding.

### The Hundred Rolls

These constituted a survey of the rights and revenues of the Crown under Edward I, and they are very valuable in giving evidence as to names of families, because there are no fewer than 70,000 persons mentioned in the indices of names for the Hundred Rolls.

### The Pipe Rolls

These are the great Rolls of the Exchequer, otherwise called the Pipe Rolls. They contain accounts of the revenues of the Crown, put under counties and made out each year. These revenues were of various kinds and consisted of all the different charges on which a payment had to be made to the Crown. These Pipe Rolls begin in the reign of Henry I (1100–35) but do not form a continuous series until the second year of the reign of King Henry II (1154–89). The Pipe Rolls continue until the beginning of the reign of William IV (1830–37).

### Inquisitiones post Mortem

These were inquiries which were made into the extent of property held by a person who had died, and they were very important because until the charges had been paid on the property of the deceased the heir could not succeed. Indeed, these inquisitions were somewhat similar to the death duties which are such a bane to anyone who has property in England. The procedure was that on the death of an important tenant of the Crown an officer called an escheator was appointed, and he took all the property under Crown control. He then assembled a jury to find out (1) the land held by the deceased, (2) the rents or services by which this land was held, and (3) who the heir was and whether the heir was of full age. Many pedigrees contain notes that such and such a person— John, the son of Roger—was of full age, followed by the date when this was established at an I.P.M. The jury was required to give its finding on oath, and the Crown acted on those findings. This was very important to the Crown, because if the heir was under age he would then become a ward of the Crown and the revenues of the estate would go to the Crown. The Inquisitiones go down to 1645 in the reign of Charles I (1625–49). Feudal tenures were abolished in 1660 at the restoration of the monarchy, but we still have Inquisitiones post Mortem taken by a coroner in cases of suicide, murder, manslaughter, and so on.

### Fines and Recoveries

These are very useful records which go back to a distant period in England. The records have been regularly preserved from the time of Richard I (1189–99). The Committee of Public Records, referring to them, said, "The utility of these records to all persons desirous of tracing property and pedigree is unquestionable." These records contain proceedings which were adopted to convey estates and to free them from various burdens, and in most cases they involved the payment of a sum to the Crown. An interesting case in which a fine and a recovery occur is that of Roger Stafford, who was the heir to the barony of Stafford and who was about to proceed to that title in the reign of Charles I in 1640. Roger Stafford was a man who, although of noble birth, had very little education and had been badly brought up. Charles I did not think him too suitable for the House of Lords, and by means of various persuasions Roger was induced to surrender his peerage into the hand of the King. There was a payment of money for this purpose and the peerage was then promptly granted to Sir William Howard.

### Sign Manual

Very often there are references to a person's having changed his name and arms by Sign Manual. This is an expensive matter and refers to a warrant signed by the sovereign and which authorizes the change in question. Signet bills are also documents which receive the sovereign's signature. There are many instances of such documents in British history, going back to Richard II and continuing to the present day.

### Records of Attainders, Forfeitures, and Pardons

It would be advisable for the inquirer to understand what is involved in the terms given above. A peerage can be attainted; this means that the holder has been found guilty of high treason and for that reason is deprived of his peerage. There have not been cases of attainder for a long time, but they occur frequently until the eighteenth century and they ought to be understood. Forfeiture applies, of course, to land which has been forfeited to the Crown. Pardons need little explanation.

### Parliamentary Records

Here we come to the Rolls of Parliament, which are extremely valuable and which contain an account of the statutes. They also contain lists of persons to whom a writ was issued to attend Parliament. These rolls are complete from the early days of Edward I and are very useful in giving details of persons who were called to Parliament, either in the House of Lords or the House of Commons. A full history of Parliament is now being prepared and will gradually be issued. The journals of Parliament commence for the House of Lords in 1509, the first year of Henry VIII, and for the House of Commons in 1547, the first year of Edward VI. These journals contain a great deal of information of value.

### Heraldic Collections

These have been to some extent dealt with under the heading of the College of Arms, but there are so many details in connection with heraldry which affect the study of genealogy that it will be very desirable to say a few more things about the heraldic collections. The visitations are to be found in many instances in manuscripts and in printed books outside the College of Arms. One work in particular which is useful is by R. Sims. It gives an index to the pedigrees and arms contained in the Heralds' visitations in the British Museum. A great deal of this can also be found in the Public Record Office, and in many cases original documents are found outside the College of Arms which one would normally expect to find inside the College.

There is an enormous amount of information in the College of Arms, but this, as has already been explained, is not accessible directly to the inquirer. However, a considerable body of material on the peerage does exist in various libraries, and a great deal of it will be found in the Public Record Office and in the British Museum. A section on printed books is given at the close of this account. It will suffice to say here that for several centuries the Heralds have been required to keep the pedigrees of peers and baronets, and they have unique opportunities of arranging to do this, for when new peers are created the Heralds write to them and ask them for information.

## THE PUBLIC RECORD OFFICE

*A Guide to the Manuscripts Preserved in the Public Record Office,* by M. S. Giuseppi, an Assistant Keeper of the Records, 1923, is a work of extreme value as giving an explanation not only of what is to be found in the Public Record Office but also of what the records mean. It is impossible to give more than a selection of the records which will be useful to a genealogical inquirer, but it should be noted that the author gives considerable detail on the origin of the law courts in England which have been treated above.

Included in the genealogical riches of this vast repository are the Close Rolls. These extend from the time of King John (1199–1216) to 1903, and there are over 20,000 of them; they are letters and documents addressed to individuals from the sovereign. They were folded, or closed up; hence the name. Patent Rolls, on the other hand, were open for all to see. As an example of what may be found in these records, I might mention that particulars of naturalization are often found among the Close Rolls.

The Inquisitiones post Mortem, to which reference has been

made above, are given here in nearly 2000 files from Henry II to Charles II.

Every court which has existed in England that has been a court of the Crown (as distinct from a court held by a baron or Corporation), and whose records have been preserved, is to be found described in this work. For example, the records of the Court of Star Chamber, which was so famous in English history for 150 years, are found here. It would need a volume as large as the whole of the present work to describe all these records in detail, but Mr. Giuseppi particularly notes that "the records of this Court consist of Bills, Answers, Depositions, and other proceedings of great historical and genealogical interest."

To you, reader, as an inquirer, I may mention that full particulars are given of the various prisons, such as the King's Bench Prison, the Fleet Prison, and the Marshalsea. There are proceedings of the Court of Bankruptcy and such items as special collections (such as the Hundred Rolls) and collections of seals, which are, of course, very interesting to anyone who thinks that he can identify the arms of his family.

The first volume of Giuseppi's work is devoted to legal records, and the second volume to the state papers and records of public departments.

In a great deal of the information which is noticed in the second volume, genealogical details occupy a much less important place. Obviously, they will only come in as incidentals in such things as the records of the Admiralty or of the Colonial Office. The essence of this part of the contents of the Public Record Office is that documents come into the office regularly from the various departments of the British Government, and so we are dealing with state records far more than with individual matters. For instance, the Ministry of Munitions was created in 1915 in the First World War and did not exist after 1924. Many of the records of this First World War ministry were transferred to the P.R.O. A permit from the Treasury is necessary for their inspection, but judging by Giuseppi's account, not very much relating to individuals would come out of this source.

On the other hand, the records of the National Debt Office give details of annuities which were obtained 200 years ago and of compensation when the slave trade was suppressed early in the nineteenth century. Here in this latter class there are certificates of deaths as well as of marriages, and many individuals are mentioned.

The records of the War Office go back a very long way, some of them even into the seventeenth century, and in fact before the Office was actually known as the War Office and when it was styled the Board of Ordnance. The records of this last board date from 1570. From the point of view of the genealogical inquirer, the most important records of the War Office are those which give details of the soldier's service. In many cases a full account of the military career 150 years ago can be found in this source. Also under this heading come instances of marriages and baptisms at army establishments.

Simply to show the immense amount of information which has steadily gone into the P.R.O. since its foundation, I may mention that there is a box with the reference number W.O. 29 and which contains a deed in which there was an identification of the body of the Prince Imperial who was killed by the Zulus in South Africa in 1879. He was the great-nephew of the famous Napoleon.

These volumes of Giuseppi's can be obtained from Her Majesty's Stationery Office.


## PUBLISHED BOOKS

Here we are launched on a vast sea of information, and the inquirer will probably appreciate some help in this respect. One of the books to which I have referred, namely, *Sims' Guide,* or *Manual for the Genealogist,* contains large numbers of lists giving pedigrees under various counties. This is useful but has, of course, been enormously supplemented by other sources since Sims' book was produced. I am referring to *The Genealogist's Guide* and to *The Genealogical Guide,* which bring the story very much up to date. Still, it would be advisable, for anyone who has the chance, to look into Sims' references, because many of these may have dropped out of later accounts. There are numerous books which deal with the various aspects of titles, heraldry, and family history, and I think the best advice I can give to anyone would be that they visit the Society of Genealogists, which is situated at 37 Harrington Gardens, South Kensington, London S.W.7. This society has something like 35,000 to 40,000 volumes and is able to give a clue to many who seek help and who will then be able to go to the British Museum and obtain other books on the subject. The first thing to do is to find out the name of the county or district in England with which you are likely to be concerned; then you will find at the Society the various documents and books relating to that county set out under the heading of Bedfordshire, Somersetshire, Northumberland, or whatever the area might be. This is useful, and in addition there is a large library of family histories and also of sections dealing with reference books concerning peerage, heraldry, and such separate items as the East India Company and the law, medicine, the Church, and many other occupations and professions. Many old books exist which are still useful, as they may contain references which have since been lost. When one is on the subject of reference books, it is practically impossible to enumerate all the sources which can be used. Among printed books, for instance, there are pollbooks, which give records of those who had the right to vote at an election, and there are also directories. These are very useful because they deal with an area as it was 120 or even 150 years ago. Not long ago I saw a small directory of Bristol which had been produced about 1800. It was very useful in connection with a family whose history was traced to that city, but it would have been equally useful for many other families.

With regard to peerage books, a valuable work is the *Complete Peerage,* which runs to fourteen (the latter part of the work has been financed by Lord Nuffield). This record, as the name implies, gives account in print of every peerage which has ever existed in the British Isles, but it gives only an account of the actual peerage holders and does not give their family histories, nor does it necessarily mention their younger brothers or sisters. There are many other peerage works; many of these old peerages, like Banks' book on dormant baronies, are supplementary to the more modern accounts such as the *Complete Peerage.* The number of old peerage books is really too many to be mentioned, but if you come across any, do not disdain them, because all of them contain material which is useful to some family history.

*Burke's Peerage* must be mentioned because it has since 1826 been providing as detailed as possible an account of peerage families and their titles and ancestry. This is the value of the book, that it does give pedigrees. *Debrett's Peerage* does not give pedigrees but is concerned with biographies. There is also *Dodd's Peerage,* which is again purely biographical, and *Kelly's Handbook to the Titled, Landed and Distinguished Classes.* This work gives notes on the lives of the persons in the categories of the title. *Who's Who* is useful, especially an old edition, as it will give you the names of people who have dropped out of current reference books because of death. On the other hand, from the same company which produces *Who's Who,* you can get *Who Was Who,* which is a collection of the biographical notices from various dates, taken from the old issues of *Who's Who.*

There are twelve volumes of *The Ancestor,* which was a magazine produced in the early years of this century and which was bound and can be obtained in sets at a reasonable price. It contains very well-written articles on many ancient and very interesting families, and there is a great deal of genealogical and heraldic information in its pages.

With regard to coats of arms, we have a very considerable literature. This may be summed up in the following account. *Burke's General Armory* contains particulars of some 80,000 coats of arms in the British Isles. *Fairbairn's Book of Crests* is in two volumes and gives particulars, as the name suggests, of crests with the names of the families to whom they belong, and also illustrations. For some reason, which I have not been able to discover, this book commands a very great price, but however useful it may be to artists, engravers, and heraldic stationers, it is absolutely useless to a person who is really studying heraldry.

The works of the late A. C. Fox-Davies on heraldry are useful provided that one is aware of his shortcomings. Fox-Davies really knew nothing about the history of heraldry and so could hardly write about it, and his remarks as to medieval heraldry ought to be forgotten as soon as read. When it comes to modern heraldry and its practice and the rules for delineating coats of arms, Fox-Davies comes into his own and his books are extremely useful to all who are engaged in the study of heraldry. He wrote several books, such as *The Complete Guide to Heraldry* and also a large book in two volumes, *Armorial Families.* This book gives a mass of particulars about families and their arms which it is very difficult to obtain elsewhere. Then there are small books about the College of Arms, of which perhaps the most useful are Planche's *Pursuivant of Arms* and Wagner's *Records and Collections of the College of Arms.* Genealogical books have a habit of going out of print and of becoming scarce, but if you are studying these subjects you will be able to refer to such books.

With regard to the professions, there are certain volumes published most years which give information about professional people. In England the legal profession is divided into two branches, the Bar and solicitors. Details of barristers and solicitors are given each year in the *Law List*. Doctors come under the *Medical Directory*, and in each of these cases information can often be obtained by writing to the offices of the company concerned. The *Law List* is published by Messrs. Stevens, Chancery Lane, London. The *Medical Directory* is published by Messrs. Churchill, Paddington, London. With reference to the Church, the Established Church has its records dealt with by *Crockford's Clerical Directory;* in this book biographies of all clergymen of the Established Church are given. Unfortunately, there are some clergymen who will not give particulars and whose names do not appear in, or who drop out of, *Crockford's*. Military, naval, and air force officers are found mentioned in their respective lists, which are issued by the three services concerned at regular intervals. That is, such officers are mentioned while they remain on the regular list. Chartered accountants, surveyors, veterinary surgeons, and opticians, to mention no others, have particulars of their careers given in books which deal with their own particular profession. Then there are useful records dealing with schools and universities. There are a large number of records of public schools where the name of the boy is entered and the name of his father, with his profession and address. The same thing happens with universities. In England until the nineteenth century, the only universities were Oxford and Cambridge. Since then there has been a very great growth in the number of universities, and there are now some twelve in the country, while other schools are on the way to becoming universities. In the case of a student entering a university, particulars of his parentage will be given in the record. Similarly, students of the Inns of Court must have their names put down with their parents' particulars, and this again is of great help to a genealogist.

So far I have been working through various sources and have endeavored to give you as much information as possible to assist you in tracing your ancestry. I hope you will be successful, and I hope that you will enjoy the search. I do suggest that, whatever you find in England concerning your ancestry, you should not be ashamed of it, no matter what it is. We cannot alter the texture of our ancestry, and whatever our ancestors were like, we can be sure that they resembled us or we resemble them, and even if their characteristics are not reproduced in us, we may reflect that they are probably lying dormant and will come to light in our children or grandchildren. This being the case, we should accept philosophically whatever is found in the records.

The next point I should like to make is that these notes are given you as a means of getting started with your genealogy and that you must not expect to find everything given here. There is a great deal which you will find out for yourself, but with the items I have given, you will be able to trace your ancestry and to work out a great deal on your own. I wish you good luck.

## PEDIGREE OF THE ANCIENT SAXON KINGS, FROM WHOM HER MAJESTY QUEEN ELIZABETH II IS DESCENDED

855. In this year the heathen for the first time wintered in Sheppey. And the same year king Ethelwulf granted the tenth part of his land over all his kingdom by charter for the glory of God and his own eternal salvation. And the same year he proceeded to Rome in great state, and remained there twelve months, and then made his way towards home. And Charles, king of the Franks, gave him his daughter as queen, after that he came to his people, and they were glad thereof. And two years after he came from the Franks he died, and his body lies at Winchester, and he reigned eighteen years and a half. And that Ethelwulf was the son of Egbert, the son of Ealhmund, the son of Eafa, the son of Eoppa, the son of Ingeld: Ingeld was the brother of Ine, king of Wessex, who afterwards went to St. Peter's (Rome) and there gave up his life afterwards; and they were the sons of Cenred, and Cenred was the son of Ceolwald, the son of Cutha, the son of Cuthwine, the son of Cealwin, the son of Cynric, the son of Cerdic, the son of Elesa, the son of Esla, the son of Gewis, the son of Wig, the son of Freawine, the son of Frithugar, the son of Brand, the son of Baeldaeg, the son of Woden, the son of Frithuwald, the son of Frea-

wine, Frealaf,* the son of Frithuwulf, the son of Finn, the son of Godwulf, the son of Geat, the son of Taetwa, the son of Beaw, the son of Sceldwea, the son of Heremod, the son of Itermon, the son of Hrathra, who was born in the ark: Noah, Lamech, Methusaleh, Enoch, Jared, Mahalaleel, Cainan, Enos, Seth, Adam, the first man, and our father who is Christ. Amen.†

* The above part of the pedigree is not clear. Apparently an additional name slipped into the ancient manuscript. Also, the Sceaf mentioned earlier, on page 63, occurs in another version of the royal pedigree.

† From *The Anglo-Saxon Chronicle* (Everyman's Library, 1953), page 66.

# SCOTLAND

## INTRODUCTION

There are many differences between English and Scottish genealogy. If these are not realized, the inquirer who is of Scottish origin will experience many setbacks. Even now, after two and a half centuries of union with England to form Great Britain, Scottish records are often quite distinct.

For one thing, most records in Scotland begin later than their opposite numbers in England. The reason for this is the turmoil of Scottish history; for centuries Scotland was ravaged by contending nations.

### The Importance of Scottish History

In every country it is true that the genealogy cannot be understood without a study of the history. This is particularly so with Scotland. The outsider is under the impression that every Scotsman belongs to a clan. He thinks that the "Mac" is the distinctive sign of the Scotsman. In fact, of course, it is an indication of a Highland family. The first step in Scottish genealogy is to understand that the Highland and Lowland Scot belong to different peoples. First of all, the Celts were driven back into the Highlands by the coming of Germanic peoples exactly similar to those who overran the Roman province of southern Britain. The Highlanders, as they came to be called, were of a different make-up in every respect from the Lowlanders. Their mode of keeping records was entirely different. In the Lowlands, clans are found especially along the border between England and Scotland, but in these cases they seem to have adopted a system from their Celtic neighbors. In any event, these Lowland clans are very different from the Highlanders. Then, in addition, the Lowlanders themselves are quite a mixed people, and for ages part of southern Scotland, such as the Lothians, formed part of northern England. Edinburgh is "Edwin's Burgh," and Northumberland for centuries included land north of the Tweed.

The first King of Scots, Kenneth MacAlpin, united these different peoples in a nominal rule. Hardly had this occurred when great parts of the Scottish islands were taken over by the Norsemen. For something like five or six hundred years they continued to control the Orkneys, the Shetlands, and parts of the Hebrides.

As the Norse control slackened, a semi-independent kingdom grew up in the Western Isles. This was the domain of the Lord of the Isles, and so independent did he become that in the reign of Edward IV of England (1461–83) a treaty was made between Edward and the then Lord of the Isles as between two independent kings. They were to divide Scotland between them. Eventually, by the end of the fifteenth century, the King of Scots succeeded in securing control of the whole of the Western Isles. Today the title Lord of the Isles is one of those borne by the Prince of Wales.

As if these troubles were not enough, Scotland had to struggle with England for hundreds of years, and this very largely prevented the keeping of proper records.

### The Clan System

This will be explained in greater detail later in this chapter, but something of it must be understood at the beginning. Most people assume that everyone bearing the name of a clan is descended from the same stock. This is not true, for in Highland history people were accustomed to assume the name of the chief under whose protection they had placed themselves. All MacDonalds are not descended from the original Donald who founded the line. Highland chieftains do claim and have a descent over many generations from a person who founded their family and whose name they bear. This person is known in technical language as the eponymous, or name chief. Figures of this type are found all over the world, for example, among the tribes of Israel in the Bible and with the ancient

Greeks, and also among the Japanese. The founder is a real person, but modern people who bear his name are not necessarily descended from him.

There is an extensive trade in supplying tartans and all sorts of Highland ornaments for Americans who visit Scotland, but unless the American inquirer wishes to be taken in, he should be very careful as to the facts about a clan or tartan which is offered to him. Some of the clan names which are seen nowadays never existed in the Middle Ages, or even in the sixteenth century.

The one clan which has a greater blood connection than any other is that of the MacGregors. They were engaged in so many raids upon their neighbors that at last some of the Lowland gentlemen decided to teach them a lesson. In the ensuing battle, however, the lesson went the other way. The MacGregors were completely victorious, and there was a terrible slaughter. As a result, over three hundred widows and orphans, wearing over their own clothes some bloodstained garments of their husbands or fathers, went in solemn procession to King James VI of Scotland. They begged him to take revenge for them on the MacGregors. The King, who was soon to become James I of England (1603), ordered the MacGregors to be outlawed. They were not to use their own names at all. This ban was in force for nearly two hundred years, but when it was repealed, those who avowed themselves Mac-Gregors numbered nearly eight hundred. Obviously, they must have belonged to the same connection; no one would have tried to remain a MacGregor unless he had really been one, for they were outside the law and every man's hand was against them. For nearly two hundred years the lives of members of the clan had been almost unendurable, and it was not until the end of the eighteenth century that the British Parliament did away with the law against the MacGregors, at the same time that they relaxed the laws against the wearing of Highland dress. These laws had been brought into being by reason of the Rebellion of 1745, in which the Highlanders had supported the last attempt of the exiled Stuarts to regain the throne.

The best plan for anyone who wants to understand the clan territorial layout is to get a map which will show Scotland divided into clans. Up in the extreme North, for instance, there will be the Mackays, while the Mackenzies will be in the western Highlands. The Campbells will be in Argyllshire and, on the other hand, there will be cases of clans on the borders, such as the Johnstons. Then again, in the Western Isles, off the coast of Scotland, you will find the Macleods on the islands of Lewis, Harris, and others. Useful small books on this subject are published by Messrs. W. and A. K. Johnston of Edinburgh; for instance, *Scottish Clans and Their Tartans*. Also very useful is another book published by the same company, *Scottish Tartans, with Historical Sketches of the Clans and Families of Scotland*. However, we shall go into details of the clan system later on, but these items are given as a beginning.

### The Heraldic System of Scotland

As we have pointed out, the clan system mentioned above does enable many people of Scottish descent to feel they have ancient ancestry by their association with the line of the clan chief, even though their own actual descent can be traced only for about four or five generations. So there is also another feature of Scottish genealogy which is very interesting and has great advantages for the inquirer. This is the heraldic system.

This also will be explained in detail further on, but for the moment it is sufficient to mention that in Scotland, even today, heraldry is part of the law of the land. It is therefore illegal for a Scotsman to use a coat of arms which does not belong to him. He can, in fact, be brought before the Court of the Lord Lyon, which is part of the Court of Session in Edinburgh. The result of this is that not only is Scottish heraldry very well regulated and managed but there is a large amount of record as to the relationship between branches of families. For instance, if anyone's name is Cameron, it is useless to pretend that his family is connected with the well-known Cameron of Lochiel unless he really can show a blood connection. The mere use of arms which bear a resemblance to those of a chief is not only misleading but, unless it can be proved by showing a descent, the user will find himself fined for using arms to which he is not entitled.

## REGISTRATION OF BIRTHS, MARRIAGES, AND DEATHS

Now, in Scotland as in England the inquirer must begin with the precise details of his father's birth registration certificate and the marriage of his grandparents, and so on. In England this information, as we know, is obtained from Somerset House. In Scotland the compulsory registration of births, marriages, and deaths was introduced later than in England. It was introduced even later in Ireland; but why the act of 1837 in England which established the records at Somerset House was not at once extended to Scotland and Ireland is not quite clear. However, the compulsory registration began in 1855, and the place where the records are kept is the General Registry Office of Births, Marriages, and Deaths in Edinburgh. Application is made to H. M. Registrar General, and application can be made, of course, in person in Edinburgh or by writing. The scale of fees is much the same as in England. It is not necessary to say very much about this side of the inquiry, as it is all so straightforward and really means that there is a century of modern records preserved at Edinburgh. It must, of course, be understood that in many cases this type of modern record will not help the American inquirer very much, and he is more likely to be concerned with something before 1855. On the other hand, many of the people of Scottish descent who settled in the United States went there much later than the English settlers. I think it is true to say that before 1783 comparatively few people of Scottish descent had settled in New England. The reason for this is not difficult to understand. Until the breakdown of the Scottish clan system in the Highlands—that is, the breakdown of the clans as warlike bodies—there was not the inducement for Scotsmen to settle in what was part of an English empire. Therefore, the inquirer is likely to find that it is about 1800 that his difficulties begin, and here Scotland is able to offer useful information in a more accessible form than in England.

### Parish Registers

There is a very remarkable phenomenon here. In Scotland all the ancient parish registers are kept in the same building, that is, in H. M. Register House. This is very convenient for the inquirer, but because of the events of the last twenty years it could have been disastrous. Had a bomb fallen on the Register House, the whole of the parish registers might have gone just as in Ireland the commotions among the Irish themselves after the departure of the British led to the destruction of the Irish records.

In general, the parish registers of Scotland do not go back as far as those of England, and in most cases they do not extend much before 1700. However, it is possible to obtain extracts from them certified in just the same way as those from the state records which began in 1855. I do not know whether it is necessary to say that the parish registers of Scotland are those of the Presbyterian Church, known as the Kirk, which is the Established Church of Scotland, just as the English Church is the Episcopal Church in England.

As to the number of the parish registers and the dates which they cover, there is an official volume which gives the figures, and therefore the inquirer will be able to find out, by sending a note to the Register House, where such a parish was and the dates which the registers cover. As to locating the parishes, the remarks which I made above with regard to a gazetteer are extremely important. *Bartholomew's Gazetteer of the British Isles* will be found invaluable to all inquirers who are laboring to find out where their ancestors came from. Many of these places in Scotland are very small and very little will have changed in them for many generations. Also, it is very easy to make mistakes in the names, and every effort should be made to check these names against the gazetteer before writing officially for information. If a mistake has been made and such a name as Torpichen, for instance, is rendered as Torpicwith or something like that, you may get a note back from the Register House saying that they do not know the name of this place or where it is. Incidentally, while we are on the subject of a gazetteer it may be advisable for the inquirer to know something of Scottish history, and here a very useful book, which is now to be obtained secondhand or in libraries, is Andrew Lang's *History of Scotland*. This has the merit of being readable as well as accurate, and anyone who takes the trouble to study it is going to avoid a lot of muddling with reference to his Scottish ancestry. Scottish history, like Scottish genealogy, is not easy, and there are many complicated features in it, which is why a useful book like this on Scottish history will help. There are also smaller books, published by firms like Johnston, which give a sort of synopsis of the history of Scotland. A shorter book which is very useful is Brown's *History of Scotland,* which was published before the 1939 war and is still in print. This is a one-volume work and very easy to read.

### Printed Guides

One which is very useful is *Scottish Family History* (1930). This gives an account of the Scottish public records and also has a list of families with reference to pedigrees and records. There is also a book by M. Livingstone called *Guide to the Public Records of Scotland Deposited in the General Register House.* These books are not easy to come by; but if anyone is going to visit Edinburgh, as many Americans in search of their Scottish ancestors do, then it would be a good idea to study these works which can be seen in the Register House, or if the inquirer is in London he can look them up at the Society of Genealogists, 37 Harrington Gardens, South Kensington, London S.W.7.

### Census Records

Here there are available a number of records on the same lines as in England which are very useful, especially in bridging the gap between compulsory registration in 1855 and the earlier parish records. These records of the census are available for 1841, 1851, 1861, and 1871. Forms of application and the rules as to how search can be conducted in the census returns can be obtained from the Registrar General, The New Register House, Edinburgh.

### Testaments or Wills

These were proved before the counterpart of the English Courts Ecclesiastical, that is, they were proved before the Commissariat Courts; these can be listed as follows and the dates are of those of the earliest entries.

| | | | |
|---|---|---|---|
| 1514 | Edinburgh | 1661 | The Isles |
| 1715 | Aberdeen | 1663 | Kirkcudbright |
| 1674 | Argyll | 1595 | Lanark |
| 1576 | Brechin | 1561 | Lauder |
| 1661 | Caithness | 1684 | Moray |
| 1637 | Dumfries | 1644 | Orkney and Zetland |
| 1539 | Dunblane and Perth | 1681 | Peebles |
| 1867 | Dunkeld | 1802 | Ross |
| 1547 | Glasgow | 1549 | St. Andrews |
| 1564 | Hamilton and Campsie | 1607 | Stirling |
| 1630 | Inverness | 1700 | Wigtown |

These wills have been calendared (i.e., arranged in order of date) and the calendars printed.

## LYON OFFICE

Here we come to a very important office in connection with Scottish genealogy, for, as I have mentioned above, it is impossible to separate genealogy from heraldry in Scotland. The position is best explained in this way. In Scotland, owing to the many wars and disturbances in older days, it was not very easy to conduct tours of inspection of coats of arms as was done in England. Consequently, there are no visitations in Scotland as in England. Instead of this the Scots decided in 1672 to pass an act of Parliament which would deal with the subject of heraldry. This act was, of course, one of the Scots Parliament before it was united with that of England. Under this law the user of arms in Scotland had three months' grace in which to record his arms with the Lord Lyon, but after that his arms were illegal if he did not have them registered, or, as the Scottish phrase has it, matriculated.

Who was the Lord Lyon, and how did this matter come into his hands? He was the equivalent of the Garter King of Arms in England (see page 90), or perhaps it would be truer to say he more nearly resembled the Earl Marshal, owing to his great position in Scotland. At any rate, from a very early period in the fourteenth century, if not earlier, the Lord Lyon was responsible for matters of heraldry in Scotland and also to a certain extent for record keeping. In fact, many Scottish scholars think that the Lord Lyon is the representative of the old Sennachie, who used to chant the pedigrees of the Scottish kings at their coronations at Scone. Be that as it may, there is no doubt that from the medieval period onward, the Lord Lyon was, and is today, the head of the whole Scottish heraldic system. After 1672 his position was enhanced, as he had the power of law behind him and, being a judge in his own court, he was able to bring offenders against the law before the court and to fine or even imprison them if they did not carry out his orders. Exactly the same position prevails today, and in the hands of an energetic Lyon there is no doubt that the law would be enforced, and in fact, quite recently has been, with fines. This law of 1672 was reaffirmed, or confirmed, by an act of 1867 which went through the British Parliament at Westminster. This last act laid down the scale of fees, which, although it has been altered, is a very useful thing, as it gives the only legal list of fees and does not allow officials to charge what they like.

Indeed, nothing could be better than the system used in the Lyon Office, because the inquirer knows exactly where he is. If he says he is using arms but is not quite sure about them, then he makes an inquiry with the Lyon and finds out all about it. He very soon knows whether he is using arms with authority or not; and if he is not, then he can without great expense put the matter right, either by having an entirely new grant, which costs about fifty pounds, or else by matriculating his arms as the cadet, that is to say, the younger branch of some recognized family.

The Lyon Office has jurisdiction in theory, and to a large extent in practice, over people of Scottish descent throughout the world, and therefore many Scots in Canada, Australia, and the United States have their particulars registered in the Lyon Office.

The system is that the matriculator has a grant of the arms which is valid for himself for life and for his eldest son. But the younger sons must rematriculate, and their arms are then said to be differenced by some addition made by the Lord Lyon. There are recognized difference marks which enable anyone who understands the subject to pick out the different branches of Campbell or Graham and to decide where they belong in the main family tree.

So the Lyon Office is not only a center of heraldry in Scotland but also a court of law, and in addition a government department dealing with heraldic inquiries in Scotland. Correspondence can be sent to:

*The Lyon Clerk*
*Lyon Office*
*H. M. Register House*
*Edinburgh*

After this, correspondence may well be with the Lord Lyon, who is addressed by whatever his name may be, as Sir Thomas Innes of Learney, K.C.V.O. (this is the name of the present holder), The Lord Lyon, at His Court, H. M. Register House, Edinburgh.

For those who are interested in going into the matter further, there is a very useful book by the present Lyon called *Scots Heraldry,* which was first published in 1934 and has gone through several editions. This explains the whole position as regards Scottish heraldry and records and is very useful to the inquirer.


## THE SCOTS PEERAGE

Owing to the ramifications of Scottish family history and the enormous number of cases which are known in which the apparently humble inquirer is a branch of an ancient and noble family, great importance attaches to any records which are in writing concerning what are known as collaterals of peerage families.

In this connection, the *Scots Peerage* is a very great help. It is in eight volumes and has an index and is very good. It is on the lines of the *Complete Peerage,* to which references have been made in the chapter on England, but it has an immense advantage over the latter work, because it gives not only the names of the holders of the titles but a sketch of the family history and its ancestry before the title was obtained. It then goes on to give the true family descent, so that very often all sorts of younger sons whose names would otherwise not be found in any printed work are available to the inquirer in these excellent volumes.

Another useful book, although some of the statements must be taken with great caution, is William Anderson's *Antiquity of the Scottish Nation.* This book was published about 1840, and what it does is give an account of every Scotsman of note up to that time. Not only is his biography given but also as much as possible of his ancestry. In the case of peers or lairds (see below), the account is given of each holder of the title, so that within one compass it is possible to trace these details right through. Some of the statements in Anderson's book need to be taken with great caution, for there are a number of mistakes there. On the other hand, there is an enormous amount of material in the three volumes and much of it is very useful.

In Scotland a great deal of importance attaches to the records of the Church since the Reformation. The information before the Reformation has often been destroyed. In England the cartularies which remain concerning the great monasteries are sad relics of what could have been spared for us if in the Tudor period some care had been taken. This is even more true of Scotland, but since the Reformation every effort which one could reasonably expect has been made to provide a large amount of information. One of the best sources of information regarding the Scottish Church is a book under the title *Fasti Ecclesiae Scoticanae,* in seven volumes, which were produced between 1915 and 1928. These records of the Scottish Church begin with particulars of the ministers, and as the Presbyterian clergy have always been allowed to marry, there is a lot about their families there and it is extremely useful.

## UNIVERSITY REGISTERS

It has always been the proud claim of Scotland that while England had only two universities, namely, Oxford and Cambridge, in Scotland there were four, Glasgow, Edinburgh, St. Andrews, and Aberdeen. The position has now been very greatly altered, and it is at times difficult to know how many universities there are in England, as a university college is always being founded in a new city. However, the Scottish universities were never as big or as important in the lives of their country as Oxford and Cambridge in that of England. Nevertheless, they have extremely valuable records and, like all university records which have been kept, they do give us the names of the parents in most cases. These university registers are printed volumes, and the best way for an inquirer to find out anything from them is to write to the secretary or chancellor of the particular university and ask if the person in question is mentioned in the records. If this particular ancestor matriculated at one of the four Scottish universities, then his particulars will be obtainable and will be very helpful.

## KIRK SESSION RECORDS

These are useful because the Reformation in Scotland introduced a very exacting system dealing with the regulation of the lives of the people of the parish. Everyone knows that this was very unpleasant and entailed a great deal of clerical supervision which at times was quite tyrannous. Like many other things in the past, it was very unpleasant but the records of it are very useful now. These Kirk Session records are usually in the keeping of the parish minister and they give information of the date and reason for a person's having left the parish. Indeed, it was not usual for anyone to leave, except irregularly, without receiving what are known as letters of demission. These were really letters of permission and must have been a very unpleasant imposition. However, the inquirer will be able to see how useful this feature is when he wants to find out why his ancestor left a parish and whether he left permanently. It should be mentioned also that a list of record agents, or searchers, is given in the directory of Edinburgh. As to seeking the address of the parish minister, if you know the parish for which you are making the inquiry you will easily be able to get that from a good gazetteer.

## THE CLAN SYSTEM

Now it is time to give some attention to the clan system and to explain more or less what it means. If anyone wishes to go into it in the antiquarian sense, he can, of course, study such works as *Scots Heraldry*, which has been mentioned above. The fact that the book is about heraldry does not prevent the author quite rightly from dealing with the clan system. There is also a book by Frank Adams called *Clans, Regiments and Septs of the Highlands of Scotland*. This work was recently reissued after a very extensive revision by the present Lord Lyon, Sir Thomas Innes of Learney.

The clan sysem is a relic of the days when Scotland was a Celtic country. The clan was viewed as the family of the chief, and no doubt in the first place the clan was very closely united by blood with the head of it, but, as mentioned above, this blood connection was weakened as time went by, as many people sought protection of the chief who were not of his family or even of his previous clan. They were broken men, that is to say, those whose clans had broken up and who were themselves wanderers. They sought the protection of some powerful magnate and this led to their taking his name and coming into his clan. On the other hand, there have been sub-divisions in clans, and as a result we get many septs where we have a name which apparently has nothing whatever to do with the main clan; for instance, the Shaws are a sept of the clan Macpherson. When a clan Macpherson association was brought into being and extended after the last war, one of the people who were induced to join it was George Bernard Shaw. There is something rather curious in this ironic Irish dramatist being in some way connected with a clan. His connection with it is, in fact, a perfect illustration of how the clan system enables people to claim ancestry which could never be deduced by genealogical research. Shaw came of a family of English baronets who settled down in Ireland as part of the old ascendancy. Shaw himself belonged to a very poor branch of this family, but originally the family had come from Hampshire, although the first person who went to Ireland appears to have been a Scottish soldier of fortune. There is not, I think, very much real connection between this family of Shaw and the Macphersons, who were, of course, a Highland family. However, there are many such cases and the reader who takes the trouble to read Sir Thomas Innes' revision of Frank Adams' book will find long lists of the clans with their appropriate septs; and to trace yourself to a sept means that you then trace yourself to one of the clans.

There is a whole complicated system of clan law and clan custom, but a great deal of this, I think, has originated through the work of antiquaries, because the old clan system, whereby a clan had a tribal territory in which they lived, has, completely passed away. Not long ago the McNeill of Barra announced that he was going to sell the greater part of his ancestral land. He will retain only a small holding in Barra if this scheme goes through. There are already cases of Scottish chiefs who live in America or Australia and whose families no longer own any of their ancestral property. There are many efforts to revive clan ceremonial and clan gatherings, but there is something rather artificial about some of these. However, they do serve a very useful purpose in encouraging genealogical research and bringing people to a thorough knowledge of their ancestry and taking a pride in it.

There has been a great deal written on the origin of the kilt, and it has even been claimed by quite serious writers that the tartan originated through the efforts of an English contractor who was living in Scotland and who found that his workmen needed to have their clothes girt up in order to get on with their job more easily when working in the quarries. This story, of course, gives great offense to many Highland people, but in fact the kilt may be very much older and go back to a remote period. The tartan varies very greatly and it is quite impossible to describe the different patterns. The only thing that can be said is that it is very dangerous for anyone who is not familiar with the tartan to assume that he knows the right one and it will be wise for him to study them in the various books mentioned above.

There are clan badges and, there are also arms in the clans; however, these coats of arms are not the property of the clan but rather of the clan chief and descend according to the rules of Scottish heraldry.

## SCOTTISH SOCIETIES

As in most countries where genealogy flourishes, there are societies in Scotland which exist for the purpose of helping with the study of family history. Foremost among these is the Scots Ancestry Research Society. This society was established as a nonprofit-making organization by the Rt. Hon. Thomas Johnston when he was Secretary of State for Scotland, in 1945. The object was to assist persons of Scottish blood in tracing facts about their ancestors in Scotland. During the first thirteen years of its existence the Society has investigated more than 13,000 inquiries from people of Scottish descent both at home and overseas. Particulars as to the fees of the Society are as follows (I quote from the Society's leaflet):

"Anyone who desires help in tracing Scottish ancestry should fill up and return to the above address the registration form. . . . The fee for registration is 10/- or 2 dollars (£1 or 3 dollars if the latest known Scottish date is prior to 1855), and the fee for the actual research work and report, which is additional, does not normally exceed the sum of Ten Guineas (dollars 30.00). In actual fact, the average fee charged is less than the maximum, but it should be noted that the above charges cover the cost of investigating one ancestral line only, i.e., the paternal, unless otherwise instructed, and each additional line to be traced involves payment of separate Registration and Search Fees."

It is particularly important for inquirers who live out of Scotland to realize that, in all cases where the latest known Scottish date is prior to 1855, precise details of birthplace (i.e., town or village) *must* be given, as the old parochial registers of births, and so on, in Scotland are not indexed before that date.

The application form to which reference has been made above is as follows:

*Name of person whose ancestry you wish to trace*
*Date of birth*
*Place or parish in Scotland where born*
*If married, name of spouse*

*Date and place of marriage*
*Date of death*
*Place of death (if in Scotland)*
*Was the person the owner or tenant of any land or house
property in Scotland? If so, give address.*
*What was his profession or trade?*
*Was he or she resident in Scotland in or after 1841? If so,
where and when?*

The address of the Society is:

*Scots Ancestry Research Society*
*4a North St. David Street*
*Edinburgh 2, Scotland*

Closely connected in aims with the Scots Ancestry Research Society is the Scottish Genealogy Society. This exists to promote research into Scottish family history and to undertake the collection, exchange, and publication of information and materials relating to Scottish genealogy by such means as meetings, lectures, and others. By the expressed desire of the original members, the Society was to remain an academic and consultative body and was not to engage itself professionally in record searching. Arrangements can be made by which the Society can supply a list of those members who are professional searchers, but any commissions of this kind must be carried out independently of the Society. There are monthly meetings of the Society in the St. Andrews Society Rooms, 24 Hill Street (Castle Street end), Edinburgh.

The Society publishes each quarter a magazine, *The Scottish Genealogist,* edited by Miss Jean Dunlop, B.A., Ph.D., 30 India Street, Edinburgh.

## BOOKS AND DOCUMENTS

In the sections which follow, more information is given about Scottish records, and in some cases a certain amount of duplication arises. The writer does not think this a bad thing, however, as duplication may prevent the inquirer from forgetting some essential facts, while it will also serve to fix some details of importance firmly in his mind.

### "A Guide to the Public Records of Scotland"

*A Guide to the Public Records of Scotland Deposited in H. M. Register House, Edinburgh,* by M. Livingstone, I.S.O., late Deputy Keeper of the Records. 1905.

The author of this work makes the point that the records of Scotland have suffered from neglect and bad housing, but also from the removals of large portions of them by the English. He points out that from an early period a high official, the Lord Clerk Register, was appointed to deal with the Scottish records and that this official was an officer of high rank and an officer of state in Scotland.

After this, Livingstone points out that many documents were removed to England; first by Edward I, then by Cromwell, where some still remain, others having been destroyed or lost. A book on the subject of records in England is Joseph Bain's *Calendar of Scottish Documents Deposited in H. M. Public Record Office in London.* Livingstone adds: "In view of the many vicissitudes and losses . . . it is matter both of surprise and congratulation that so much material has survived. . . . There are at present deposited in the Register House about 60,000 manuscript volumes, and an equivalent in bulk of unbound warrants and other papers.

Livingstone's work is divided into four parts, and while all the records are immensely valuable, they will not all interest a genealogist.

CLASS I. CROWN, PARLIAMENT, REVENUE, AND ADMINISTRATION

These include many fascinating items, such as Oaths of Sovereigns at Coronation or Accession; the Privy Council; State Papers; and Crown Patrimony and Revenue Exchequer and Treasury. Some of these items could be of assistance to an inquirer on genealogy. Thus, there are numerous rolls of peers who were elected in the elections which took place after 1707 to ascertain what peers should go to sit at Westminster. There are also such things as Army and Navy Accounts, and Muster Rolls. A long-lost ancestor may be recovered through this source. There is an interesting account (page 67) of records and papers relating to particular estates forfeited for the rebellions of 1715 and 1745. Six pages are taken up with the particulars of the estates and the names of those forfeited.

CLASS II. JUDICIAL RECORDS

These records, as in England, are often of great importance, and without them many an inquiry would come to an end. They are listed as:

| | |
|---|---|
| *The Council (i.e., records of)* | *High Court of Admiralty* |
| *The Court of Session* | *Jury Court* |
| *Court of Exchequer* | *Court of Teinds* |

This last-named court dealt with the provision of stipends for the ministers of the Reformed Church of Scotland from the teinds, or tithes, derived from each parish.

## Court of the Lord Lyon

This has already been dealt with above. It will be sufficient to say here that the Court of the Lyon is part of the Court of Session of Scotland to this day.

## Commissary Courts

These were the old ecclesiastical courts, which were similar to those in England and whose jurisdiction survived the change of religion in Scotland, as in England, at the Reformation. It was not until 1830 that jurisdiction in cases relating to marriage, separation, divorce, and legitimacy were transferred to the Court of Session, and in cases of alimony to the Sheriff Court.

The Commissary Courts are very important from the point of view of a genealogical inquirer because they contain records of wills. Thus, the Commissariat of Edinburgh has among its records the record of testaments from 1567 to 1829, making 154 volumes. There are gaps in these volumes, but even so, they constitute a wonderful record of immense value. There are many other records relating to wills and disputes arising out of them, indices, and inventories.

Aberdeen Commissariat. Earliest records were destroyed by fire in 1721.

Argyll. Records of testaments from 1674 to 1819.

Brechin. Testaments from 1576 to 1823.

Caithness. Testaments from 1661 to 1679 and from 1790 to 1824.

Dumfries. Testaments from 1624 to 1827, with some gaps (see previous note on commissariats).

### Regality, Sheriffs' Courts and Baronial Courts

Regalities were conferred on the immediate vassals of the Crown in the form of special jurisdictions in all cases except for high treason. They were specially privileged jurisdictions.

Baronial courts were, as in England, the prerogative of the lesser lords and carried many feudal powers with them. All these privileges were abolished by the Hereditable Jurisdiction Act of 1748 after the 1745 Rebellion. The records of these courts are thus deposited in the Record Office and are of great value.

### Diligence Records: Registers of Hornings, Inhibitions, Interdictions, and Adjudications

In Scotland a diligence was a legal process making an order of the court effectual against the person or estate of a debtor. He was considered to be in rebellion against the Crown and therefore was put to the horn, that is, outlawed. Process was made against his estate by letters of inhibition, by which the debtor was restrained, or inhibited, from alienating his property to the prejudice of the creditor's claim. Interdiction forbade the debtor to alienate his property without the consent of persons named. There are Registers of Hornings, etc., which go back to the sixteenth century for many counties in Scotland.

CLASS III. CROWN GRANTS AND TITLES TO LANDS, DIGNITIES, AND OFFICES

### The Great Seal

The Register of the Great Seal is the record of Crown grants to which the Great Seal of the Crown is affixed. There are no records of the Great Seal before the reign of Robert I (1306–29). There are 12 rolls and 268 volumes of the Register. There are 47 folio volumes of the Paper Register, 4 volumes of the Register of Confirmations and Registrations, and 2 volumes of the Register of Crown Writs.

There are many other classes of records connected with the Great Seal, such as warrants which had to bear the Sign Manual. The earliest date for these documents is 1561.

## The Prince's Seal

This relates to grants and other deeds in the principality of Scotland, in other words, to the lands of the heir to the throne.

## The Privy Seal

The earliest date here is 1488.

## The Register of Tailzies

These are what are known in England as entails. They were first formally legalized by a statute of 1685. The Register consists of 220 large folio volumes, beginning with 1688 and ending with 1903.

## The Register of the Interruptions of Prescription

This deals with the interruption of the prescription of real rights, by which, for example, the question of actual ownership might be kept open.

## Register of Inventories of Heirs Entering cum Beneficio Inventarii

*Cum Beneficio Inventarii* meant that the heir, on entering upon his property, had a right to enter upon inventory to see what property he wished to give up to be liable for the debts of his ancestor.

## The Register of Sasines

The word "sasine" means the same as "seisin," or taking possession of land, or the giving of land to a new proprietor. These exchanges had to be made in the presence of witnesses. Very early in Scotland's legal process, it was felt desirable to have a Register of Sasines. A statute was passed in 1540 in which it was suggested that there should be a public Register of Sasines. This was also put forward in a statute of 1555, and the latter was ratified in 1587. There was a checkered period during which a Register of Sasines was kept for a while in certain parts, but in 1617 the present Register of Sasines was established, under the control of the Lord Clerk Register. In 1681 an act was passed establishing similar burgh registers.

## The Old General Register under the Act of 1617

The records are in 3779 volumes from 1617 to 1868. Then there are particular registers for parts of Scotland. Some of these begin earlier than 1617. The current General Register in County Divisions is in 20,255 volumes from 1868 onward.

## Notarial Protocols

These are valuable as containing a record of sasines in land and of other private transactions of which the originals are no longer extant or for which a contemporary register is unavailable. These books are mostly of the sixteenth and seventeenth centuries.

CLASS IV. ECCLESIASTICAL AND MISCELLANEOUS RECORDS AND DOCUMENTS

Of these documents, the work records that only a few volumes are in the possession of the General Register House, while many more documents are held by private collectors or in other public sources. Those which are in the General Register House are some volumes of the judicial records of the diocese of St. Andrews, an early register of the diocese of Glasgow, and other registers, with some accounts of a few of the abbeys, papal bulls, and a few other items from the pre-Reformation Church.

In this section the author also puts Universities, the Highlands, the Solway Salmon Fisheries Commission, County and Burgh Valuation Rolls, Reports on Local Registers, Special Collections of Papers, Letters, and Inventories of the Records. Some of these sections may contain information of value to the searcher; for example, in the Highlands section there are accounts of proceedings to relieve destitution in the Highlands. No one ever likes to think that his or her ancestors were among the destitute; nonetheless, some of them were, and these records may have something about their sufferings some 120 years back. The transactions of the aid given to emigrants from the Western Isles and the Highlands to the British colonies in and after 1851 may well have the names of many whose descendants have found affluence in America.

### "The Surnames of Scotland"

*The Surnames of Scotland: Their Origin, Meaning and History,* by George F. Black, Ph.D. This work, the result of many years of research, deals with the origin, meaning, and history of several thousand Scottish surnames.

The use of fixed surnames or descriptive names appears to have commenced in France about 1000 A.D., and such names were introduced into Scotland through the Normans a little over one hundred years later, long before the custom of using them became common.

Many Scottish surnames are:

*1. Patronymics—e.g., Dickson, Robson, Thomson, Watson, Wilson—which began in the fourteenth century.*

*2. Local and territorial names. The first persons who had fixed surnames were nobles and landowners, whose names came from their lands.*

*3. Official and trade names.*

*4. To-names, or tee-names—e.g., Alexander White was called "goup-the-lift" to distinguish him from other Alexander Whites.*

Dr. Black has some very important remarks concerning the use of the same Christian name by all the sons of a family and on the fact that many people took the surname of a great family, thus building up the clan system. "In clan societies one can enroll as a member if he bears the name under which the society is organized. Thus an individual bearing the name Macdonald may join the Clan Macdonald Society, but how many individuals named Macdonald are really Macdonalds? A present-day John Macdonald may boast of the ancient greatness of that clan, when as a matter of fact he may actually be descended from some 17th-century Donald Campbell, and therefore the scion of a clan which was the hereditary and deadly enemy of Clan Donald."

### "Scottish Family History"

*Scottish Family History: A Guide to Works of Reference on the History and Genealogy of Scottish Families,* by Margaret Stuart.

To this work is prefixed an essay, "How to Write the History of a Family," by Sir James Balfour Paul. 1930.

This work is valuable for several reasons. In the first place, it has a delightful introduction by Sir Balfour Paul, who was the author of the *Scots Peerage,* to which reference has been made, and also of an Ordinary of Arms. In this introduction, Paul describes the various ways in which a pedigree can be prepared: he describes tabulated pedigree charts, the various dangers which can attend the preparation of a pedigree, the value of anecdotes, portraits, and illustrations. In the second part of the introduction, Paul describes the public records and tells the student (as I have already explained in the case of England) that he must learn to read the handwriting of the old records or else employ someone to do it for him. Wright's *Court Hand Restored* (ninth edition, 1879) is a good work; so, too, is *Facsimiles of the National Manuscripts of Scotland* (three volumes). Paul, of course, refers to the work already covered some pages earlier, namely, Livingstone's *Guide to the Public Records of Scotland.* Therefore, in this part I shall merely refer to those records which appear not to have been dealt with in the previous section. (The second part of the book, by Margaret Stuart, gives 300 pages of histories of Scottish families in alphabetical order. As this list was published in 1930, other references have since accumulated.

### "Retours of Services of Heirs"

The Latin name of this is: *Inquisitionum ad Capellam Domini Regis Retornatorum Abbreviatio.* It is contained in three volumes. They contain "an authentic history of the transmission by inheritance of by far the greater part of the landed property in Scotland, as well as that of the descent of most of its leading families from about 1550 down to 1700." Succession to the property could not take place until passed by the sheriff of the county. This procedure bore certain resemblances to the English system of I.P.M. (see chapter on England), but the latter died out much earlier. The main importance to the searcher is that these documents must show the relationship of the heir to the ancestor from whom he inherits.

## THE UNPUBLISHED RECORDS

### Register of Deeds

This is a huge collection of no fewer than 621 volumes extending from 1554 to 1657, but only a portion of it has been indexed. It contains for preservation and execution all deeds which contain a clause of consent to registration. The information is there for the genealogist but naturally requires much sifting and searching.

### Parish Registers

There are records of over 900 parishes, but few go back to the Reformation period, some beginning in the seventeenth century and a greater number in the eighteenth century. There are also records of similar nature which are not in the General Register House, such as the burials in Greyfriars Churchyard, Edinburgh.

### Lyon Office Records

These are in the custody of the Lyon King of Arms (see above under description of that office). There are two principal records: the Register of Genealogies and the Register of All Arms and Bearings in Scotland. The former begins in 1727, with a gap between 1796 and 1827. The latter begins in 1672, the date when the Scots Parliament ordered the keeping of the Register and the matriculating of arms. The Register since that date has been kept with regularity, and the volumes in which it is recorded are very beautiful productions, including some fine colored illustrations of the arms. In Lyon Office there is also a copy of the Heraldic Register of Sir David Lindsay, a former Lyon, which was begun in 1542. The original is in the National Library. Other documents of great value to the searcher are those concerned with birth brieves, funeral entries, and others. They have been indexed and published by the Scottish Record Society.

### Ecclesiastical Records

The *Fasti Ecclesiae Scoticanae*, although a private work, must come under the above heading. It takes up seven volumes, and its value can be gauged by the simple statement that "it contains many thousand biographical notices of all the ministers of the Church of Scotland since the Reformation with their wives and families." Also useful in this sphere of inquiry is *Sons of the Manse,* by the Rev. A. W. Fergusson of Dundee.

## SOCIETY AND CLUB PUBLICATIONS

*The Society of Antiquaries of Scotland.* The proceedings of this society contain little of interest to genealogists, but some items do occur and there is also occasionally some heraldic material. As the first volume appeared in 1792 and others have been produced up to the present day, it is best to inquire of the secretary of the Society with reference to any particular item. The address is: The Secretary, The Society of Antiquaries of Scotland, National Museum, Queen Street, Edinburgh.

*Abbotsford Club.* Some family-history material, especially with reference to Cameron of Lochiel and Hume of Wedderburn.

*Ayrshire and Galloway Archaeological Association.* 1877–97. Some items on family history in those areas.

*Banffshire Field Club.* Began 1880.

*Bannatayne Club.* 1823–61. Of particular interest are the volumes dealing with the ancient criminal trials from 1488 to 1624. The inquirer's ancestor need not have been a criminal for the inquirer to find these works of use.

*Berwickshire Naturalists Club.* Began (as far as genealogical details are concerned) in 1887.

*Buchan Field Club.* Volumes began after 1887.

*Dumfriesshire and Galloway Natural History and Antiquarian Society.* Publication began in 1864, but there is little of genealogical interest. Irving of Hoddesdon figures in Vol. XXIV.

*The Gaelic Society of Inverness.* Transactions began in 1872. Many useful articles on Highland families, clans, and chiefs. The American inquirer need not worry over the "Gaelic" of the title. Too many folk of Gaelic descent cannot speak or read Gaelic for some parts of these transactions not to be written in English.

*The Grampian Club.* Family histories therein will be found in the Bibliography of Scottish Family Histories.

*Hawick Archaeological Society.* Volumes from 1863. Many genealogical histories.

*The Iona Club.* 1833–38. One volume published. Name: *Collectanea de Rebus Albanicis.* Contains some Highland clan genealogies.

*The Maitland Club.* 1828–59 publications.

*New Spalding Club.*

*Spalding Club.* 1839–70.

These three last-named club transactions contain much useful material for the family historian.

*Scottish Burgh Record Society.* 1868–1908. The names of burgesses and burgh officials are given in twenty-two volumes dealing mainly with Edinburgh, Glasgow, Aberdeen, and Peebles.

*Scottish History Society.* 1886. Much useful information, particularly with the rebels in such items as the 1745 Rebellion, or with Scottish exiles in Holland.

*Scottish Record Society.* 1887. Began as a part of the British Record Society. This society has indexed many registers of testaments, printed many parish registers, and calendared many charter chests of the nobles and others.

*Spottiswoode Society.* 1843. A little information on genealogy, especially of the great family of Spottiswoode.

*Stirling Archaeological Society.* 1868.


## CARTULARIES OF RELIGIOUS AND OTHER HOUSES

Cartularies are collections of charters, and the importance of these to the inquirer is that charters often go back to a date earlier than that of any other document known in the particular family and give information about names and lands. Most of those which have been published are the work of the various clubs mentioned above.


## UNIVERSITY RECORDS

These have been treated above under one of the earlier sections, but some additional details may be of service.

*Aberdeen.* The register of matriculations is available from 1601 to 1686, and of the Marischal College (forerunner of the University) from 1593 to 1860. Officers and graduates of the University from 1495 to 1860 (New Spalding Club).

*Edinburgh* (youngest of the Scottish universities) has a catalogue of the graduates in arts, divinity, and law, 1858.

*Glasgow.* Matriculations from 1728 to 1858. Roll of graduates, 1728–1897.

*St. Andrews* (oldest university in Scotland) has matriculation roll, 1747–1897.

## THE SCOTTISH LEGAL SYSTEM

The Scottish legal system differs considerably from that of England. Some of these differences are well known, for example, that in Scotland in a murder trial a verdict of not proven can be returned apart from the usual English verdicts of guilty or not guilty; also that in Scotland a coroner does not exist, a matter always claimed by the Scots as a proof of the superiority of their law. The Scottish law is based on the Roman, whereas English law, though treating Roman law with respect, does not base itself upon it. It is a native growth.

Scottish law can have important consequences for the student of family history, as differences of detail with the law of England or of the United States (based on the Common Law of England) can mean difficulties in interpretation. For example, in the matter of registration of land transfers, in Scotland the register for this has existed for a long time, in England for only a short while. Consequently, the student of family history should bear this in mind.

A useful book on the study of Scottish law, and which explains also the many terms puzzling to the non-Scot which recur in Scottish legal documents, is *Principles of the Law of Scotland,* by John Erskine of Carnock, Advocate. This book went through many editions, and the one to which I have referred is that of 1911. It can be obtained from Edinburgh booksellers secondhand. Terms such as "wadset," "warrandice," "teinds," and others, which have a nasty habit of recurring in genealogical documents, are here explained in full detail.

# IRELAND

## INTRODUCTION

Anyone who wishes to make researches into his family history in Ireland must first understand the political structure of the country; otherwise he will waste time and money by going to the wrong places to discover the records which he seeks.

Until December 6, 1921, all Ireland was united as a kingdom under the British Crown, and it was the second kingdom in the United Kingdom of Great Britain and Ireland; but after December 6, 1921, it was divided into two separate countries. There are thirty-two counties in the whole of Ireland, and of these, six counties now form Northern Ireland, which is shown in the official title of the United Kingdom of Great Britain and Northern Ireland.

These six counties are Antrim, Armagh, Down, Fermanagh, Londonderry, and Tyrone. Northern Ireland is usually referred to as Ulster—the ancient Irish, or Celtic, name of that part of Ireland. The capital of Northern Ireland is Belfast.

The remaining twenty-six counties of Ireland now form the Republic of Ireland, the capital of which is Dublin. The Republic is a state entirely independent of Great Britain (so much so that it remained neutral in the war of 1939–45) and can only be described, in a very broad sense, as a member of the British Commonwealth.

The twenty-six counties, each after the name of its province are: Leinster Province: Carlow, Dublin, Kildare, Leix (formerly known as Queen's County), Longford, Louth, Meath, Offaly (formerly known as King's County), Westmeath, Wexford, and Wicklow.

Munster Province: Clare, Cork, Kerry, Limerick, Tipperary, and Waterford. Connaught Province: Galway, Leitrim, Mayo, Roscommon, and Sligo. Ulster Province (a small part of this is included in the Republic of Ireland): Cavan, Donegal, and Monaghan.

Before the partition of Ireland in 1921, most Irish records would have been found in Dublin, since the city was then capital of all Ireland. Since the partition some records are to be found in Belfast and others in Dublin. It should be added that even before the partition some records existed in the North of Ireland which were not to be found in the South.

It is also essential to success in research into Irish records to understand clearly the main outlines of Irish history. From remote times Ireland has been inhabited by a branch of what, for want of a better word, is called the Celtic race. Ireland was known to the Romans, but it was never invaded by them; nor did it form part of their empire. In the fifth century the Irish were converted to Christianity by St. Patrick. They were divided into tribes under the rule of chiefs. In each of the four provinces—Ulster, Leinster, Connaught, and Munster—there was a king, and out of these four a High King (*Ard Rig* is the Irish term) was chosen, unless he asserted himself by right of conquest. One of the most important of these High Kings was Brian Boru, or Boroimhe, who in 1014 defeated the Danes at Clontarf. He was the ancestor of the great family of O'Brien. The High King was supposed to make the circuit of all Ireland and to receive the homage of the other kings. In fact, there was never a national monarchy in Ireland which developed into a central government over the whole country. This was a source of weakness which led eventually to the English conquest of Ireland.

In 1166, the King of Leinster, who had been driven out of Ireland, appealed to the King of England for help. The English (or, rather, the Anglo-Normans) invaded Ireland, and their connection with that country lasted until 1921. For some four hundred years the English rule over Ireland was nominal and did not extend much beyond Dublin and a few of the counties around Dublin. But under the reigns of the Tudor sovereigns of England (1485–1603) all Ireland was conquered. Many of the native landowners were deprived of their estates, and their lands were given to Englishmen. When James VI of Scotland became James I of England there were fresh Irish rebellions, and it was decided in 1609 to clear the whole of Northern Ireland of its Irish inhabitants and put settlers from Scotland and England in their place. This act was known as the Plantation of Ireland, and it is the reason for the separation of Northern Ireland from the Republic of Ireland.

The people of Northern Ireland are mainly of Scottish or English stock, and they are Protestant in religion; in the Republic of Ireland most of the people are of the Celtic race and are Roman Catholic in religion.

During the seventeenth and eighteenth centuries there were renewed Irish rebellions, and in each case more Irish landowners were dispossessed and their lands given to the Scots and English. Penal laws against Irish Catholics were enacted.

This brief historical sketch is necessary in order to help the searcher in Irish ancestry. There are several classes of Irish pedigree material connected with the race of the people concerned.

### Celtic Families

In many cases these families changed their names to an English equivalent in order to escape persecution, and for this reason their records are often difficult to trace. Many Irish families in this group have a tradition of descent from one of the ancient Irish kings. Certain changes of name occur in the dropping of the "O'," as in Kelly, where the real name was O'Kelly; in less obvious instances, like Keane, which was originally O'Cahane. There are other instances today which are much harder to trace at first sight. For example, Smith was once O'Gowan, meaning "Son of the Smith"; and in the days, two hundred or three hundred years ago, when a Celtic and Catholic name might be a danger to a family, it was changed to the English form, Smith. Another example of a name's being Anglicized is McLoughlin, which in its Irish form is Maelseachlainn. Again, "Mac" was sometimes dropped, so that MacLysaght became Lysaght. All of this makes it very important for the researcher to find out if there are any traditions in his family of a change of name.

### Anglo-Norman Families

Anglo-Norman families settled in Ireland in the Middle Ages between 1172 and 1485. These are not numerous (many of them have died out) but some of them are very important, such as Fitz-Gerald, FitzMaurice, or De Courcy and De Stacpool, and their names are widespread.

### English Families

English families settled in Ireland between 1485 and 1690. These were the ruling class, the "old ascendancy," as the Irish called them, and their records have been well kept. An instance of one of these families is that of the Duke of Wellington. His real name was not Wellesley but Colley, the surname of an English settler who went to Ireland about 1500 and whose descendant married the heiress of the Wellesleys (this is the same name as Wesley). It should be remembered, however, that many of the English settlers who went to Ireland became more Irish than the Irish themselves in the course of a few generations. In a recent list of the cabinet ministers in the Republic of Ireland there are such (originally) non-Irish names as Norton, Everett, Keyes, Sweetman, and Blowick. These are not Irish names in origin, and they may have been adopted by the ancestors of the present bearers, as noted above; but it is more probable that the ancestors were from England or Scotland. The Keyes family certainly went to Ireland after living for centuries in England. Many of Cromwell's soldiers were granted land in Ireland, but their children and grandchildren became completely Irish. In the Irish telephone directory there are many instances of Collins, an English name. Michael Collins, who helped to bring about the treaty with Great Britain in 1921, was one of the leading Sinn Feiners. The name of Joyce is more common now in Ireland than in England, but it was originally English and derived from Joyce, a medieval Christian name. Pyne figures among the list of English settlers under Cromwell and again under William of Orange. In Ireland now it is found fairly often as an Irish name. Therefore, the inquirer who is apparently of Irish stock may well find himself of ancient English descent.

### The Ulster Families

As already explained, these are of Scottish and English descent.

I shall deal with each of these groups in turn, but I shall begin with the last and work backward, because the majority of Irish inquiries in America will belong to the Celtic-family group and it is this group whose genealogy is now receiving most attention in the Republic of Ireland.


## NORTHERN IRELAND

### The Registrar-General

Before 1921, the Registrar-General in Dublin dealt with all Ireland in respect to the registration of births, marriages, and deaths. Since 1921 and the establishment of a government in Northern Ireland, a separate Registrar-General's office has been created in Belfast. The name and address of this department is:

> *The Registrar-General*
> *General Register Office*
> *Fermanagh House*
> *Ormean Avenue*
> *Belfast*

In this department are kept the records of birth, marriage, and death in Northern Ireland since 1921. The adoptions of children are also recorded there. The Registrar-General of Northern Ireland is also concerned with the taking of the census of population, and therefore the records of the censuses of 1931 and 1951 will be kept with him. Owing to the war, no census was taken in 1941. The department of the Registrar-General is under the Ministry of Finance.

Fees for the issue of certificates of births, deaths, and marriages are:

> *Search, covering period of five years*     1*s*. 6*d*.
> *Certified copy*                            3*s*. 6*d*.

Fees have been prescribed for general searches which are carried out by the applicant or his agent. In the case of births and deaths, the fee is one pound for a search during any number of successive hours not exceeding six without stating the object of the search; and in the case of marriages, a fee of one pound in respect to a search during any number of successive days not exceeding six.

The questions to be answered in completing the forms of application are:

BIRTH

> *Name in full and surname of child*
> *Date of birth*
> *Place of birth (if in a town, state street)*
> *Father's name, and rank or occupation*
> *Mother's name and maiden surname*

DEATH

> *Name in full and surname of deceased*
> *Date of death*
> *Place of death*
> *Age of deceased*
> *Rank or occupation of deceased, and condition as to marriage*

MARRIAGE

> *Names and surnames of the parties married (the name and*
> *surname to be written in full in each case)*
> *Date of marriage*
> *Place of marriage (name and address of church)*

## The Public Record Office

This was created by an act of Parliament in 1923. It is under the Ministry of Finance, the minister being ex officio Keeper of the Records. There is a permanent official who is styled the Deputy Keeper. Anyone who wishes to write to the Public Record Office should address his letter as follows:

> *The Deputy Keeper*
> *Public Record Office of Northern Ireland*
> *May Street*
> *Belfast*

The Public Record Office receives all records of court cases in Northern Ireland, and departmental records from the various departments of the Northern Ireland Government. Although the Office was not created until after 1921, many of the records go back to an earlier date. As examples, there are official copies of wills for Northern Ireland district probate registries dated back to 1838, and the original wills from 1900. Court records in the Office date from about 1890, and some grand jury records from about the late eighteenth century. The records of the government departments go back to the early nineteenth century, and private archives from Northern Ireland families of importance, and from estate and solicitors' offices, back to 1600. Photostat copies are held in the office of parish registers as far back as 250 years ago in some cases.

The account of the acquisitions of the P.R.O. during three years fills a small quarto volume of more than 300 pages, and it is impossible to give an account of every item. To sum up, however, the P.R.O. contains:

> *1. The usual documents to be found in a P.R.O.—law court proceedings, voting lists, and indoor and outdoor relief;*
> *2. The papers relating to families—letters, diaries, business transactions—found in County Record Offices in England; and,*
> *3. Wills—which in England would be in the keeping of Somerset House.*

*Charges at the Public Record Office, Belfast.*

Persons who can sign a declaration that they are bona fide literary searchers are allowed to search free of charge. Application for permission is made to the Deputy Keeper, and a form has to be completed which states: "My search in the Public Records is Exclusively for purposes of Historical, Genealogical, Antiquarian or Academic research. The subject of my research is——" Otherwise, fees are charged as follows:

TABLE OF FEES, PAYABLE IN EVERY CASE BY STAMPS

|  | £. s. d. |
|---|---|
| *For the inspection of any book, roll, file, bundle, or document,* per diem | 1. 6. |
| *For the inspection of a number of books, etc., not exceeding ten, in any one suit, action, or matter,* per diem | 4. 0. |
| *For attendance at the Supreme Court of Judicature of Northern Ireland or elsewhere to produce records for purpose of evidence,* per diem | 3. 3. 0. |
| COPIES OF RECORDS | |
| *Copies of records will be made at the request of any applicant at the following rate:* | |
| *For photographic copies of records:* | |
| Photostat negative, *13" x 8"* | 1. 0. |
| " "    *18" x 14"* | 1. 6. |
| " "    *22" x 15"* | 1. 9. |
| " positive  *13" x 8"* | 2. 0. |
| " "    *18" x 14"* | 2. 6. |
| " "    *22" x 15"* | 3. 0. |
| *For making copies of maps, plans, drawings, etc., by the hour* | 5. 0. |
| CERTIFIED COPIES | |
| *made under subsections (1) and (2) of section 6 of the Act* | |

| | |
|---|---|
| *For certifying photographic copies, per sheet* | *1. 0.* |
| *For certified typescript copies of records for which a certified photo-graphic copy could issue, for a copy not exceeding 3 folios of 72 words* | *9. 0.* |
| *For certified typescript copies of records for which in the opinion of the Deputy Keeper of the Records no photographic copy can issue, for a copy not exceeding 3 folios of 72 words for* | *3. 0.* |
| *longer copies per folio* | *1. 0.* |

Postal queries are always answered, but the following rules are applied: All genealogical queries should be addressed to the Ulster-Scot Historical Society (see below for full account). Legal searches are not undertaken and the applicant is advised to employ a Belfast solicitor. Requests by genuine academic persons are fully answered, particularly if they live outside the British Isles and a journey to Belfast is, therefore, not easy for them. In general, a short preliminary search is undertaken free of charge. The profession of searcher has not developed to any extent in Belfast; but there is a firm which conducts legal searches, namely:

*Messrs. Ellis*
*78 May Street*
*Belfast*

### The Ulster King of Arms Office

Until 1940 all inquiries relating to heraldic matters were dealt with by an official named Ulster King of Arms, whose office was in Dublin Castle. He was appointed by the British Crown and was responsible for registering pedigrees, making grants of coats of arms, and conducting genealogical searches. When the Ulster King of Arms, Sir Nevile Wilkinson, died in 1940, the Government of the Republic of Ireland stated that it did not want any new Ulster King of Arms in Dublin and appointed its own Chief Herald of Ireland, whose office is in Dublin Castle. The office of Ulster King of Arms was then united by the British Crown to that of Norroy King of Arms, at the College of Arms (or Heralds' College), London. The address of this functionary is:

*Norroy and Ulster King of Arms*
*The College of Arms*
*Queen Victoria Street*
*London E.C.4*

Any inquiry concerning coats of arms in Northern Ireland should be addressed to him. He has photostat copies of all arms material which is in Dublin. It is his province to grant arms in the six counties of Northern Ireland.

### Other Registers

Many families in Northern Ireland were, and are, Presbyterian. Their records are often kept in Belfast, and application should be made to:

*The Secretary*
*Church House*
*Belfast*

### The Ulster-Scot Historical Society

This was recently established as a nonprofit-making organization to assist persons of Ulster ancestry to trace facts about their ancestors in Ulster. Correspondence should be addressed to:

*The Secretary*
*Ulster-Scot Historical Society*
*Law Courts Building*
*Chichester Street*
*Belfast*

This society in its forms of application states: "If you wish a search to be made you should fill up this form as far as you are able and send it to the Society together with a registration fee of £1 (or $3) which is not returnable. When the completed form is received by the Society, the relevant records will be searched and a report sent to you. Since many Irish records have been destroyed, searching is more difficult here than in the rest of the United Kingdom. Searches involve a great deal of work and there can be no certainty of success but an average search and report should not exceed £3 ($9) and a more difficult search should not normally exceed £10 ($30). All remittances should be made payable to the Ulster-Scot Historical Society."

The form to which reference has been made sets out in a very clear manner the procedure for anyone who wishes to make researches.

### How to Make Researches in Northern Ireland

It is at first essential to have as many particulars as possible about the person whose ancestry you wish to trace. Assuming that your grandfather lived in Northern Ireland and was called James Weir, you must first of all tabulate the information which you already have concerning him. Thus:

*Surname.*
*Christian names* (be sure to include all of them, since many people may be named James Weir and so may be hard to identify; whereas James Brown Weir or James Keith Weir will be easier to trace).
*Residence* (the best and most exact address you have for your grandfather).
*Date and place of birth* (if you don't have this, you may have particulars of his baptism).
*Religion.*
*Profession or business occupation.*
*Date and place of marriage.*
*Name and parentage of wife.*
*Names of children* (with dates and places of birth—or baptisms—and marriages).

If you work on this basis you can adapt the style of the tabulation easily to suit the particulars of your father, your grandfather, your great-grandfather, and so on, for each generation. It will make your task much simpler if you work out what you know in this suggested tabulated form, and you will then be able to see at a glance what you still want to discover.

When you have obtained from the Registrar-General and the Public Record Office in Belfast, and the other sources listed above, all the information that is obtainable, what must you then do?

It is possible that you cannot trace your ancestry any earlier. This happens sometimes with Ulster families because the settlers were more concerned with their lands than with their pedigrees, and some generations may have passed before they became interested in making pedigrees. In the case of the famous general in the last war, Viscount Montgomery of Alamein, his descent is traced to Samuel Montgomery, a Belfast merchant who was born in 1723. Previous to that date the family has only traditional knowledge of its origin; but this tradition takes it back to Scotland, whence a branch of the Montgomeries emigrated to Northern Ireland in 1628. The parent stock of the family is that of the present Earl of Eglinton and Winton, who is head of the family.

It is possible, on the other hand, especially if your family's roots in Ireland are recent, that only a small part of your family history can be found in Northern Ireland, and you may therefore have to seek the remainder in Dublin.

It should be made very clear, however, that the inquirer should make the most careful and exhaustive inquiries in the Public Record Office in Belfast. Although (as will be seen below) many records perished in 1922, there are many cases of parish registers and other documents of which copies exist in Belfast. The very large number of family papers now being deposited in the Public Record Office, Belfast, will yield the answer to many genealogical inquiries.

## THE REPUBLIC OF IRELAND

Anyone who has to make inquiries into records in the Republic of Ireland must face the fact that in a civil war (after the connection with Britain had been broken) many of the records of Ireland were destroyed. This happened because the Irish Republicans had their own quarrels, and on April 13, 1921, the Public Record Office in Dublin was occupied by armed men, and on June 30, 1921, the portion of the Office in which the records were kept was destroyed. Vast quantities of records which are used by genealogists were thus lost. For example, out of the collection of wills, only eleven wills of the Prerogative Court and one diocesan will were saved.* Of the parish registers, 817 were burned. These registers were those of the (Protestant) Church of Ireland, which was disestablished in 1869.

This fact must strike a searcher into Irish genealogy as most distressing, but it has happened that the great loss sustained when the Public Record Office was destroyed has to a very large extent been offset by the labors of modern Irish genealogists.

It can now be stated definitely that the descendant of Irish emi-

---

* The meaning of the court titles referring to wills, and the position of the former Established Church of Ireland, will be explained later.

grant stock can rely on being able to trace his ancestors for three generations in the majority of cases.

Ireland has never had a large population. Until the nineteenth century the population of all Ireland was never more than two and a half million. By 1845 it had risen to eight million but it slipped back to six and a half million in 1851, owing to the horrors of the Potato Famine. Many people emigrated between then and now, and today only three million live in the Republic.

Ireland has always been an agricultural country and, because of the absence of minerals, it is likely to remain so. Consequently, the small population, remaining very much in the same area for long periods, makes it possible for information to be more easily found.

The best method of beginning a search in Ireland is to visit the village or locality where the family lived originally. The Irish have always had long memories for historical events, and the oldest inhabitants of the district where one's family has lived may be able to furnish much information about grandparents or great-grandparents.

In many instances affidavits are supplied and are accepted on the sworn testimony of people who can remember predecessors of the living inquirer. One case which I saw recently was that of Maelseach-lainn (McLoughlin, in Anglicized form), whose line of ancestry goes back to Niall of the Nine Hostages, an Irish king who lived about 400 A.D. Owing to penal laws and religious persecutions, this family lost much of its land, and the records of some of the more recent generations lacked exactness. Sworn affidavits were produced from very elderly people who had known the predecessors of the present generation. Such affidavits are accepted in a court of law.

The records of the Republic can be consulted at the following centers:

### The Registrar-General's Office

This office dates from January 1, 1864, when the registration of births, deaths, and marriages became compulsory in Ireland. Therefore, the first step for those seeking information before 1921 is to inquire at the Registrar-General's Office.

This office also contains other valuable documents, including (this is very important) records of all Protestant marriages from 1845.

It should be noted here that in the Twenty-ninth Report of the Registrar-General there is given a treatise on Irish surnames, a subject of great importance to the inquirer, since changes of name are more frequent than in England and are often the clue to the genealogy. The full address of the department is:

*The Registrar-General's Office*
*Customs House*
*Dublin*

### FORMS OF APPLICATION AND SCALE OF CHARGES

### *Birth Certificate*

Application for a search. A form will be sent from the Registrar-General's Office in response to an inquiry, and on this form the following questions must be answered:

*Surname of person whose birth record is desired*
*Christian name(s) in full*
*Date of birth, or approximate age*
*Place of birth (if in a town, name of street to be given)*
*Father's name*
*Father's occupation*
*Mother's Christian name(s)*
*Mother's maiden surname*

With the completed form the applicant must send the sum of four shillings; if a full birth certificate is required, he must send eight shillings and sixpence. These sums are made up as follows:

Search made by the staff in the Registrar-General's Office over a
       period of five consecutive years                3*s.* 6*d.*
Certificate                                5*s.* 0*d.*
                                      8*s.* 6*d.*

Each additional full certificate costs 5*s.* 0*d.*

Should the search be for a short certificate      2*s.* 6*d.*
Certificate                                1*s.* 6*d.*
                                      4*s.* 0*d.*

Each additional short certificate              1*s.* 6*d.*

NOTE: The short form of birth certificate gives *only* the name, sex, date of birth, and district of registration. The full certificate gives particulars of parentage, which is what most inquirers will want.

The form, with the questions listed above completed as far as possible, must accompany the application; so, in the first place, the inquirer should write to the Registrar-General's Office for a form.

*Marriage Certificate*

The questions on the application form which are to be answered are as follows:

*Name and surname of the parties married (to be written in full in each case)*

*Date of marriage (or if date is not known, period of five consecutive years within which marriage took place)*

The form, when completed as far as possible, must be returned with the sum of eight shillings and sixpence. This sum is made up by search by the Registrar-General's staff:

| | |
|---|---|
| For each period of five consecutive years or portion | 3*s*. 6*d*. |
| Each certified copy required | 5*s*. 0*d*. |
| | 8*s*. 6*d*. |

*Death Certificate*

The questions on the application form which are to be answered are as follows:

*Surname of deceased*
*Christian name(s) in full*
*Date of death (or if the date is not known, period of five consecutive years within which the death occurred)*

The charge for the above information is eight shillings and sixpence, made up as in the case of the marriage certificate.

### The Public Record Office

All correspondence to this office should be addressed as follows:

*The Deputy Keeper*
*Public Record Office of Ireland*

*The  Four  Courts*
*Dublin*

The Irish equivalent of the title of the office is *Oifig Iris Puibli.*
The Public Record Office was established in 1867, the reason
being that the public records in Ireland were scattered and preserved very badly in unsuitable buildings. It seemed the most sensi-
ble thing to establish one central record office, though subsequent
events may have led to second thoughts on the matter.

Despite the destruction of this office (to which reference has been
made above), there has now been built up a large collection of
documents of great value to the genealogist.

CENSUS RETURNS

To bridge the gap between the beginnings of registration in the
Registrar-General's Office in 1864 and the parish registers, the census returns are of great value. A census was first held in Britain in
1801 and thereafter at ten-year intervals (except in 1941, owing to
the world war). In Ireland, census keeping began in 1813. There
were returns for the censuses of 1813, 1821, 1831, 1841, and 1851
in the Public Record Office of Ireland in 1922. By means of these
returns many people were able to prove their rights to old-age pensions in 1908, when the Old-Age Pension Act was passed in the
United Kingdom Parliament (southern Ireland was then part of the
United Kingdom). As public registration of births became compulsory only in 1864, and as parish registers before that date were
often defective, it would have been difficult for anyone to establish,
from official sources, that he or she was over seventy years of age
without the aid of the census returns. In 1911 alone, over 85,000
searches were made in the Public Record Office of Ireland on behalf
of claimants to pensions.

Only remnants of the census returns before 1922 remain. For
1851 there are twenty-three volumes for county Antrim; for 1821,
fourteen volumes of copies for county Cavan; and for 1831, six
volumes for county Derry. By a curious contrast with the procedure
in England, the census returns for 1861, 1871, 1881, and 1891
were not kept.

Even the fragments of the census returns for the counties of Antrim, Cavan, and Derry are invaluable for anyone whose family lived
in one of these three counties. Suppose that Michael Duffy's grand-

father was married in 1865, but he does not know his date of birth. If he knows that the grandfather was living in Antrim at the time of his marriage, it is likely that he will trace him through the census returns of 1851, which will give the grandfather's birth date and the names of *his* parents.

## PAROCHIAL RECORDS—PROTESTANT

When we refer to parish records of baptism, marriage, and burial we mean primarily the records of the Protestant Church of Ireland. At the Reformation in western Europe in the sixteenth century, the buildings and endowments of the Church of Ireland remained in the hands of the Protestant reformers. In England, the Church of England was reformed and came under the rule of the Crown instead of the Pope. Ireland was under the political control of England, and therefore the Reformation settlement applied to the Irish Church. But three quarters of the inhabitants of Ireland remained Roman Catholics, and therefore the Church of Ireland, although it was the Established Church and had the backing of England, was the Church of a decided minority of the Irish people. This fact had a considerable influence over the keeping of parish records; so, too, did the fact that in 1869 the British Government disestablished the Church of Ireland. For in 1875 and 1876, acts of Parliament, known as the Parochial Records Acts, were passed, and under these acts the records of baptisms and of burials before 1871, and of marriages before March 31, 1845, of the formerly Established Church of Ireland were constituted public records.

This meant that the parish registers of the Protestant churches were to be placed in the Public Record Office in Dublin. Had they all been placed there, they would in all probability have been destroyed in 1922. But fortunately an amending clause in the acts allowed the clergyman in charge of a parish to retain his records in the parish custody—provided that he could prove that an adequate place of storage was available. There were, in all, 1643 parishes in Ireland. In 1922, 1006 of these had deposited their pre-1871 records with the P.R.O., where the great bulk was destroyed. Fortunately, more than 600 parishes had retained their parish records in their own possession, and these therefore still exist, with the local clergy or in the P.R.O.

The clergy of the Protestant Church of Ireland were not ordered to keep registers of baptism, marriage, and burial before 1634. Very few of the registers go back to that date. During the seventeenth and eighteenth centuries the parish registers were kept very badly indeed. Neglect was a greater enemy of them than the destruction wrought in 1922. One instance is that of the curate of St. Fin Barre's, the cathedral church of Cork, who had a quarrel with his bishop and then in a fit of rage threw the earliest volume of the registers in the fire. This was in the eighteenth century, and the register thus destroyed is said to have gone back to the sixteenth century, possibly the oldest in Ireland.

To counterbalance this sorry tale, some of the registers in Cork are quite old. The oldest is that of Christchurch, in the city of Cork. It begins in 1643 and has a gap between 1665 and 1708. A transcript of the register was made, a copy of which is in the British Museum.

Other seventeenth-century registers in county Cork are Youghal, which begins in 1665 and has a short gap in the eighteenth century, and Kinsale, which begins about 1696.

The names of Catholics do appear in old Irish Protestant registers. The marriage of two Catholics when conducted by a Catholic priest was legal, but when a Catholic married a Protestant it was necessary, in the eyes of the law, for the service to be taken by a Protestant clergyman. A mixed marriage is therefore likely to be found in the appropriate Protestant register.

Then again, many Catholic entries are found in Church of Ireland burial registers. In Cork, at St. Anne Shandon, the registers, which begin in 1778, contain about 40,000 burial entries, of which about two thirds are Catholics.

The Baptist church in Cork has a good deal of information about the family of Riggs. Edward Riggs left a manuscript history of the foundation of the church, which has been preserved and from which we learn that he was married three times, though no other source mentions more than one marriage.

The registers of the Quakers, or Society of Friends, have been well kept and are now preserved at the headquarters of the Society,

*The Society of Friends*
*5 Eustace Street*
*Dublin*

As an example of the information which can be obtained from the Quaker records, it can be mentioned that in the pedigree of the Pim family a very extensive amount of information was produced from the Card Index of the Society of Friends. The old Irish Quaker families were very numerous in the early days, and names such as Neale, Bewley, Goodbody, and Hogg recur again and again. Whenever a Pim, to return to the family mentioned, married a girl of a Quaker family, an exact reference could be given to that family's number in the collection of pedigrees in the registers of the Society of Friends in Ireland.

Those who want to consult a parish register of the Protestant Church must remember the following facts:

*1. Those recorded are Protestants. This may appear of no help to Catholics; but they must remember that in Ireland during the seventeenth and eighteenth centuries many Catholics became converts in order to save their lands. The name of a Catholic ancestor may therefore appear in a Protestant register. These conversions were not, of course, permanent in the majority of cases (see Convert Rolls below).*

*2. A complete list of parish registers is to be found in the Public Record Office, and an inquiry as to the existence of a particular register should be sent there.*

*3. The name and address of the clergyman in a parish can be obtained from:*

> *The Editor, Crockford's Clerical Directory*
> *Oxford University Press*
> *Amen Corner*
> *London E.C.4.*

*or from:*

> *The Editor, Thom's Directory of Ireland*
> *Alex. Thom & Co., Ltd.*
> *Crow Street*
> *Dublin*

*When writing for information it is advisable to send postage to cover the cost of the reply. United States stamps are often sent to Great Britain and Ireland, but they will not be accepted by the post offices of these countries for outgoing mail. The best medium is the International Postage Coupon, with its world-wide currency.*

*4. The following list gives particulars of parochial registers which were (in 1952) actually in existence in the P.R.O., Dublin:*

| DIOCESE | PARISH | DIOCESE | PARISH |
|---|---|---|---|
| Dublin | Baggotrath | Lismore | Curragh Camp |
| Cloyne | Ballyclough | " | Newbridge Garrison |
| " | Castletownroche | " | Dungarvon |
| " | Macroom | " | Templemichael |
| Armagh | Clogherny | Ferns | Killinick |
| Glendalough | Inch | Cork | St. Mary Shandon |
| Meath | Nobber | | |

The above are original registers. *Copies* of registers exist for the following:

| DIOCESE | PARISH | DIOCESE | PARISH |
|---|---|---|---|
| Cloyne | Aghabullog | Kilmore | Ashfield |
| " | Carrigtwohill and Mogeesha | Cork | Ballymartle |
| " | Castletownroche and Bridgetown | " | Fanlobbus or Dunmanway |
| " | Killeagh | Dublin | Cloghran |
| " | Magourney | " | Crumlin |
| " | Midleton | " | St. Paul |
| Clonfert (formerly Elphin) | Ahascragh | Ferns | Clonmore |
| | | Ossory | Clonmore |
| Limerick | Ardcanny and Chapel Russell | Cashel and Emly | Doon |
| " | Fedamore | " | Toem |
| Elphin | Drumcliff | Ross | Glengarif |
| Ardagh | Templemichael | Kildare | Killeigh |
| | | Armagh | St. Peter (Drogheda) |
| | | Meath | Drumcree |
| | | " | Killochorogan |

The following extracts from registers are available:

| DIOCESE | PARISH | DIOCESE | PARISH |
|---|---|---|---|
| Cashel | Ballingarry | Cloyne | Churchtown |
| Ferns | Carne and Kilpatrick | Ossory | Durrow |
| Meath | Castlerichard | Dublin | St. Andrews and St. Kevin's |

NOTE: The object of the above list is to enable the inquirer who knows that his family lived in one of the above parishes to write to the P.R.O., Dublin, for information.

PAROCHIAL RECORDS—CATHOLIC

The records of the Roman Catholic churches were not regarded as official, since the Roman Catholic Church was not established and therefore had no official status. Moreover, owing to the operation of the penal laws against Catholics, very few of the Catholic registers date back further than the beginning of the nineteenth century. The emancipation of the Catholics in the British Isles was passed by the British Government in 1829, but before then any keeping of records by the Catholics was frowned upon.

In Dublin some of the Roman Catholic churches have records going back nearly two hundred years (and this is true of some of the larger towns). Elsewhere, as far as the villages and small towns are concerned, very few registers date before 1800. The early portions are very badly kept. One case is known of a woman, the housekeeper of a Catholic priest, who used regularly to tear a page from the early registers of the church to use as curling paper for her hair.

Anyone who wishes to secure information concerning an entry in one of these Catholic registers should write to the priest of the parish. *Thom's Directory of Ireland,* to which reference has been made above, contains a complete list of all Roman Catholic priests in Ireland, together with their addresses.

PAROCHIAL RECORDS—MISCELLANEOUS

There are a few other records of a parochial nature which are to be found in the P.R.O. These include an account of the civil administration of St. Thomas' parish, Dublin; a small number of vestry books (which are important because they contain the names of persons living in the parishes in question); and a Methodist register by the Rev. M. Lanktree of county Down, which covers the period 1815–49.

It should be added that, apart from the parochial records mentioned as being in the P.R.O., there are some extremely useful records in Cork. The Unitarian Church there—previously known as Prince's Street Presbyterian Church—has registers which go back to 1717, and of even greater value, minutes of the church meetings, which begin in 1700. These vestry minutes give much genealogical assistance; they include the names of new members of the congregation, the place they came from, and their relationship (if any) to other members.

**How to Proceed Thus Far**

The inquirer who is searching in the Dublin records will probably begin with the Registrar-General's Office, remembering that compulsory registration of births, marriages, and deaths began in Ireland in 1864 and that records of all Protestant marriages are held there from 1845.

If, therefore, the inquirer seeks information about his grandfather Thomas Sweeny, who was born in 1870, he should write to the Registrar-General's Office. If Thomas Sweeny was born before 1864 and was a Catholic, information must obviously be sought in the Public Record Office.

There, the first source of inquiry is the census returns, such as have been preserved, as mentioned above. If Thomas Sweeny's place of residence is known, he may be sought in one of the existing census returns. Failing that, existing parochial registers (both Protestant and Catholic) should be consulted.

Now, owing to the destruction of so much in 1922, some of the obvious sources of the genealogical inquirer have been lost. They have to be made up from other sources, and so, continuing still with the P.R.O., we come to wills.

WILLS

No documents are more valuable to a genealogical searcher than wills, because they often contain the names of several persons in a family of whom we would otherwise hear nothing. From the earliest times after Ireland became Christian, wills were made and were very much the concern of the Church. Wills were proved in the Church courts for many centuries; in the diocesan courts when a man had property in only one ecclesiastical jurisdiction, that is, in one diocese. If his property was in more than one diocese, the will was proved in the Prerogative Court of the Archbishop of Armagh. From 1858, wills were no longer proved in the Church courts but in a special Probate Court. There were, and are, principal and district probate registers for this purpose.

The Public Record Office has the largest collection of wills in Ireland, over 300,000 of them.

The whole series of wills from 1904 is complete, and almost complete from 1858 for the district registries. What of the wills proved in the Church courts before 1858?

As mentioned already, only eleven of the original Prerogative Court wills and one of the diocesan wills were saved from the destruction of 1922; but there are some will books which contain copies of wills and which were saved. These are:

Prerogative will books for the years 1664–84, 1706–8, 1726–29, and portions of those for 1777, 1813, and 1834; diocesan will books (for Connor) for the years 1818–20 and 1853–58, and (for Down) 1850–58. Many of the earlier wills (before 1858) were never deposited with the P.R.O. before 1922, and over 10,000 of these wills or other testamentary papers have been given to the P.R.O. and have been card-indexed.

In addition, in Ireland many abstracts of wills were made in past centuries for genealogical purposes, and of these a considerable collection is held in the P.R.O. The collection goes back as far as 1536, but it is not, by any means, complete.

All the above collections of wills, or abstracts of wills, are in the P.R.O.; but before leaving the subject of wills, other repositories of wills should be mentioned. In the Genealogical Office in Dublin Castle (see below for a full description) there are abstracts of all the Prerogative Court wills before 1800. These are set out in the form of chart pedigrees, which are very useful to the inquirer. Transcripts of these abstracts were made by Sir Bernard Burke, and they are now in the Public Record Office in Belfast (for address see under Northern Ireland section above).

Also at the Genealogical Office in Dublin are a large number of abstracts of the diocesan wills of Dublin, Cork, and Waterford. In the Registry of Deeds in Dublin (for full details, see below) there are a number of memorials, as they were called, of eighteenth-century wills, which deal with real estate. A collection of abstracts of Irish wills was brought together by Mr. W. H. Welply of Dublin and presented to:

> *The Society of Genealogists*
> *37 Harrington Gardens*
> *South Kensington*
> *London S.W.7*

Some Irish wills were proved in England, and the originals are preserved in Somerset House, London. The address is:

> *The Probate Registry*
> *Somerset House*
> *The Strand*
> *London W.C.2*

It should be added that the authorities of Somerset House, London, have presented to the P.R.O., Dublin, some registers of Irish wills and administration, namely, Irish will registers, 1829–39 (these volumes summarize the dispositions made by wills proved in Ireland); Irish will indexes, 1829–79; Irish administration registers, 1929–39; and Irish administration indexes, 1829–79. By "administration" is meant the power of administering the will.

It should also be mentioned (though more detail will be given presently) that there is an Irish Genealogical Research Society, the secretary and archivist of which is the Rev. M. Wallace Clare. He has printed a list of Irish wills which gives the names of the testators. For the address of this society, see below.

As an example of the wealth of family information in wills, an instance is given of one copied in 1920 and now destroyed.

"Will of Dominick Morrogh of Ballyhenig in the Diocese of Cork and Ross, 1681. Copied from the original in the Public Record Office of Ireland, Four Courts, Dublin, which were later destroyed in the Civil War of 1922.

"In the name of God Amen, I Dominick Morrogh of Ballyhenig in the County of Cork, Gentleman, being at the present time of perfect mind and memory, do make and ordain this my last Will and Testament in manner and form following. First I do leave and bequeath my Soul to Almighty God my Creator and Redeemer and my body to be buried in a Coffin in Cahirlag Church where my mother and sister are buried. Item—I do leave and bequeath to my son James Morrogh as his stock the sum of fifty pounds sterling, likewise I do leave, appoint and ordain my said son James Morrogh sole Executor of this my last Will and Testament. Item—I do leave and bequeath to my son John Morrogh the sum of twenty pounds sterling. Item—I do leave and bequeath to my daughter Catherine Morrogh the sum of twenty pounds sterling and leave her besides to the care of her mother. Item—I do leave and bequeath to my son Patrick Morrogh the sum of ten pounds sterling for his care taken about my occasions and I do likewise leave him the said Patrick a haine of Gould. I do leave and bequeath to my cousin James Morrogh a ring of Gould, or to make him one and to his son Andrew another ring and to his daughter Anne Morrogh the sum of five pounds sterling, to my nephew Dominick White another ring or rather to make him one, to my cousin Patrick Sarsfield FitzJames a ring or rather to make him one. Item—I do leave and bequeath to my son and heir Thomas Morrogh all my right, title and interest to Ballyhenig he the said Thomas paying and discharging all my debts and legacies immediately after my decease to him and to his heirs male forever."

## INTESTATE ADMINISTRATIONS

When a person died without making a will, the courts had still to deal with the disposal of the property of the deceased. The matter came before the court, which then proceeded to grant letters of administration to the next of kin. If, therefore, the searcher cannot find the record of his ancestor's will, it is worth looking into the records of intestate administration. A transcript of the Prerogative Court series before 1800 is preserved at the Genealogical Office, Dublin Castle. A copy of most of the collection from the diocese of Ossory is in the Genealogical Office.

The indices to the intestacies in the different dioceses are in the P.R.O., Dublin.

## THE REGISTRY OF DEEDS

Now, if the seeker after Thomas Sweeny has drawn a blank with parochial records, he has certainly got a wide field in which to search in the Irish wills; but if they should not supply the necessary information, there are many other sources open to him. Owing to the peculiar features of Irish history, there are records which would not exist in other countries. The fact that Irish land frequently changed hands (owing to religious and political changes) made it necessary for records to be kept, and these have in many cases been preserved. To discover one of the most valuable of these series of records, the searcher must go to the Registry of Deeds. The full address is:

> *The Secretary*
> *The Registry of Deeds*
> *The Four Courts*
> *Dublin*

In this registry can be found abstracts of all transactions relating to landed property throughout Ireland from 1708. There is no record in England of landed transactions which goes back for 250 years. There are in Dublin memorials, or abstracts, of deeds, wills, marriage settlements, leases, and other documents relating to landed

property. These documents deal not only with the wealthy land-
lords but with numerous lowly families, and from them pedigrees
of three or four generations can be gathered. In one case of a pedigree of Morrogh, the family had owned land in Cork, and through
the Registry of Deeds they were traced for several generations. The
contents of the Registry are not too well indexed, and much work
may be put into the examination of them; but it is eventually well
repaid, because if an ancestor had dealings in real estate in the
period after 1708, the particulars will be in the Registry.

COURT RECORDS

Most families at some time have been involved in court cases,
and much useful information to a genealogist can be deduced from
this source. The Public Record Office contains the following, which
were saved in 1922 because they were kept in the fireproof strong
room. These are:

> *The bill books of the Chancery and Exchequer courts*
> *The cause books of the Chancery Division*
> *Judgment book of the common-law courts*
> *Bankruptcy petition registers*

CONVERT ROLLS

These cover the period from 1703 to 1772 and give the names
and places of residence of all Catholics who gave up Catholicism
and became Protestants. These Catholics acted in this manner in
order to be able to enter one of the professions (from which they as
Catholics were barred) or to save their property. Of course, they
were not good Protestants, as their conversions came about from
material reasons. An interesting story is told of a Mr. Geoghegan
of Castletown, Westmeath, the descendant of the MacGeoghegans,
a famous family. Mr. Geoghegan was afraid that one of his kinsfolk
would become a Protestant and therefore secure his property. He
therefore turned Protestant on Sunday, sold his estates on Monday,
and was reconciled to the Catholic Church on Tuesday. He preferred, he said, to trust his soul to God for one day rather than
his property to his friends for one day. On the Sunday evening he
went into a favorite haunt, the Globe Coffee Rooms on Essex Street,
and with his hand on his sword, shouted, "I have read my recanta-

tion today [that is, his recantation from Catholicism], and any man who says I did right is a rascal!"

Whatever the value of these conversions from a religious point of view, there can be no doubt of their use to the genealogist. For the period of nearly seventy years when the greatest effort of the law was directed to crushing out Catholicism, these Convert Rolls exist to give the names of thousands of so-called converts. If Thomas Sweeny was one of them, his name will be found in the Roll.

These Convert Rolls exist in manuscript volumes and were the work of a famous scholar, John Lodge. It should be added that all his manuscripts are in the P.R.O. They include, besides the Convert Rolls, Crown Presentations, Enrollments, Exclusive Grants, Irish Chiefs, General Pardons, Peerage, Baronetage, and Parliamentary Registrations.

### SCALE OF CHARGES AT THE PUBLIC RECORD OFFICE

Where an inquirer is able to call at the Public Record Office in Dublin, no fees are charged for the inspection of records in cases where the Deputy Keeper is satisfied that the purpose of the inquiry is purely literary or historical. In other cases, an inspection fee of two shillings and sixpence is charged.

Indexes and calendars in the public search room may always be consulted free of charge.

Now, in cases where an inquirer cannot go to Dublin, but has to write to the Public Record Office, the position is more difficult. The Public Record Office does not undertake research on behalf of clients, and inquiries of a nature involving research cannot, therefore, be dealt with through the mail. In such cases, where a personal visit is not possible, an agent should be employed. For names and addresses of genealogical agents or searchers, the Public Record Office should be consulted; or application made to the Irish Genealogical Research Society (for full particulars and address, see below); or by application to the author of the present book.

*Photostats.* Negative photostat copies of records are supplied at two shillings per sheet measuring up to twelve by eighteen inches, and four shillings per sheet of larger size up to eighteen by twenty-four inches. A further charge of three shillings and sixpence for a first sheet and one shilling and sixpence for each additional sheet is made for sealing and certification under the Public Records Act of 1867. For purposes of translating the above charges into American currency, it should be remembered that at the time of writing one dollar equals approximately seven shillings.

NOTE: The inquirer who has obtained his basic information about his immediate ancestors from the Registrar-General's Office, and has gone on to the Public Records Office, is not likely to be satisfied with the results. There are still other sources of genealogical inquiry which ought to be consulted. The next most important is the Genealogical Office.

### The Genealogical Office, Dublin Castle

It should be explained that this occupies the same place as the former Ulster Office, and all the records which were in Ulster Office are held there. In the case of the Genealogical Office, the politics of Ireland have to be taken into account. The old Ulster Office dated from 1552, when King Edward VI of England instituted a Herald who was to have jurisdiction over the whole of Ireland. This jurisdiction lasted from 1552 to 1940, when the last Ulster King of Arms to work in Dublin Castle died. He was Major Sir Nevile Rodwell Wilkinson, and on his death Mr. Eamon de Valera, the Premier of the Republic of Ireland at that time, stated that he did not want the appointment of another Ulster King of Arms by the British Crown, but would wish to appoint a Herald of his own. Accordingly, the British Crown added the office of Ulster to that of the Norroy (for the meaning and derivation of "Norroy," see chapter on England) King of Arms of the College of Arms in London.

The Norroy and Ulster King of Arms has jurisdiction in matters of arms in the six counties of Northern Ireland (see under Northern Ireland, Ulster King of Arms Office).

On the other hand, the Republic of Ireland appointed a Chief Herald of Ireland, who has sole jurisdiction in matters of arms in the twenty-six counties of the Republic. The College of Arms in London gives official recognition to grants of arms and confirmations of the use of arms issued by the Chief Herald within the Republic.

Thus, since 1943 (the actual date of the appointment of the Chief Herald of Ireland; there was a Deputy Ulster from 1940 to 1943), the Chief Herald has been in the office in Dublin Castle which was formerly occupied by the Ulster King of Arms. The office is now known as the Genealogical Office, but the important fact to realize is that all the old records of the Office are there. Genealogical searchers would be very unwise to neglect the records in Dublin Castle, as they are extremely valuable. There may well be particulars there relating to the hypothetical Duffy or Sweeny whom we have postulated. Researches must be conducted through the staff of the Genealogical Office; but they are always courteous and willing to assist. The fees of the office are moderate (for full scale, see below).

Before going on to explain the workings of the Genealogical Office and how it can assist the inquirer, a description of the records should be given, after which it will be seen that an enormous amount of useful genealogical material is available.

## ORIGINAL CELTIC PEDIGREES

The chief source of information about these is a volume called *Linea Antiqua,* written by Roger O'Ferrall in 1709. The papers are closely written in a very small hand and are illustrated by drawings of coats of arms. This volume gives most of the reliable information on the pedigrees of the ancient Irish families whose surnames begin with "O'" and "Mac." Fortunately, the book was transcribed in a larger hand during the time (1820–53) that Sir William Betham was Ulster King of Arms. Thus, the *Linea Antiqua* was expanded into three volumes, with the addition of many notes in Sir William Betham's hand and an index of surnames.

These Celtic pedigrees are of the greatest value to many people of Irish stock in different parts of the world. The subject is so important that a full account of the value and authenticity of ancient Irish pedigrees is given at the end of this chapter.

## SIR WILLIAM BETHAM'S MANUSCRIPTS

These are his own recordings of pedigrees and are in twenty-four volumes, in two series. The most important part of Betham's work was in connection with the Irish wills (see under "Wills," above). In 1808 Betham began to compile chart pedigrees out of the particulars in the wills proved in the Irish Prerogative Courts. In the result, over thirty volumes were compiled of all wills. The pedigrees are in two series, those before 1700 and those from 1700 to 1800. There is an index of marriage alliances, and many pages of these volumes have notes added by some of the Ulster Office staff. The value of this last-mentioned collection can be understood in light of the destruction of almost all the original wills in the Public Record Office at Dublin.

As already explained in the Northern Ireland section, a transcription of the Betham will pedigrees was made by Sir Bernard Burke and is now in the Public Record Office at Belfast.

In addition to the above, Betham made abstracts of all the Irish Prerogative intestate administrations up to 1800.

## FUNERAL ENTRIES

It was the custom in former times for the Irish Heralds to arrange for the funeral of many families, and in the funeral certificates, or entries, there is an enormous amount of data. They give not only the names of the dead person but also details of his marriages and children, and often grandchildren and great-grandchildren. There are eighteen volumes of funeral entries for the period 1575–1729. One of the original volumes, for the years 1634–1729, is in the British Museum and has been printed in *The Memorials of the Dead* (see below under "Printed Sources"). All these pedigrees, although extending through only a few generations, are of very great value. They are always attested by a near relative of the deceased.

## GRANTS OF ARMS

Registers of these fill many volumes. They are in two series, from 1552 to 1698 (where in some cases only the name of the grantee is given) and from 1698 to the present day (where full particulars of pedigree are included with the description of the arms).

## VISITATIONS

It was the custom for the Heralds in olden days to go around the country inspecting arms and to decide who had the right to them. There are only three volumes of visitations left in Ireland. These are the visitations of Dublin in 1568 and 1607 and the visitation of county Wexford in 1618.

## REGISTERED PEDIGREES

Many volumes exist here. It was, and is, the function of the Heralds not only to grant coats of arms but also to record or register pedigrees. In many cases pedigrees are recorded without coats of arms.

## CITY OF DUBLIN FREEMEN ROLL

This covers the period from 1670 to 1770 and is very helpful in tracing the parentage of many Dublin tradesmen during the century mentioned.

## MISCELLANEOUS

It is not possible to mention all the sources available in the Genealogical Office, but items can be mentioned, such as the nine volumes of obituary notices taken from local newspapers for the period 1778–1810, which came into the Genealogical Office in a manuscript collection. There are also many hundreds of documents stored in the Genealogical Office, and a moderate fee will secure a great deal of useful information about any surname, however common it may appear to be.

## FEES

The scale of fees at the Genealogical Office, as in force from April 22, 1955, is as follows (inquirers should remember that £1 is equivalent to $2.80):

|  | £ | s. | d. |
|---|---|---|---|
| *Hand-painted colored illustration and written description of armorial bearings* | 2. | 0. | 0. |
| *Black-and-white sketch (with engraver's lines) and written description of armorial bearings* | 2. | 0. | 0. |
| *Colored or black-and-white sketch of crest only* | 1. | 0. | 0. |
| *Design for armorial bookplate* | 4. 4. 0. to | 7. 7. | 0. |
| *Grant of arms, including stamp duty, emblazon, and registration* | 60. | 0. | 0. |
| *Grant of supporters, including stamp duty, emblazon, and registration* | 100. | 0. | 0. |
| *Grant of badge, including emblazon and registration* | 15. | 0. | 0. |
| *Confirmation of arms, including emblazon and registration* | 25. | 0. | 0. |
| *Copy of patent of arms, including emblazon, on vellum* | 15. | 0. | 0. |

| | |
|---|---|
| *Certificate of arms, including emblazon, on vellum* | *15. 0. 0.* |
| *Certificate of Chief Herald and Genealogical Officer* | *5. 0. 0.* |
| *Search limited to six hours in Genealogical Office or* | |
| *outside sources (expenses, if any, extra)* | *3. 0. 0.* |
| *Registration of a pedigree, per generation* | *1. 0. 0.* |
| *Copy of registered pedigree, per generation (on vellum,* | |
| *with emblazon—£4 extra)* | *10. 0.* |
| *Extract from will books or other manuscripts* ⎫ | *0. 5. 0.* |
| *Copy of funeral entry (arms colored, £2 extra)* ⎬ | *per folio of* |
| *Copy of royal or government warrant or license* ⎭ | *70 words* |
| *Change of name and arms by government license, including* | |
| *stamp duty, emblazon, registration, and* | |
| *gazetting* | *120. 0. 0.* |
| *Change of name by government license, including stamp* | |
| *duty, registration, and gazetting* | *60. 0. 0.* |
| *Designing and registering flag for civilian use* | *5. 0. 0.* |
| *Registration of flag already in civilian use* | *3. 0. 0.* |

Fees payable in advance. Checks, money orders, postal orders, etc., should be crossed and made payable to the Accountant, Department of Education.

It should be emphasized that the public are not allowed to make their own researches into the records at the Genealogical Office, but have to put their inquiries into the officials' hands. Inquiries are therefore constantly dealt with through official correspondence.

The full address of the Office is:

> *The Chief Herald of Ireland*
> *Genealogical Office (Office of Arms)*
> *Dublin Castle*
> *Ireland*

In Irish:

> *Oifig Gheinealais*
> *An Caislean*
> *Baile Atha Cliath*

### Libraries

No one who is trying to trace his ancestry should neglect to search in the Irish libraries. There is a great deal of genealogical material in the principal libraries in Dublin:

## THE NATIONAL LIBRARY OF IRELAND

There is, unfortunately, no guide or catalogue to this library, but the work of indexing the very great quantity of genealogical material has begun, and it is hoped that a useful index will be compiled in the next ten years. In the meantime it should be noted that the Library possesses about 14,000 volumes of manuscripts, many of which are family papers. There are about 16,000 manuscripts of Irish interest on microfilm, mostly from libraries and archives in England, France, Spain, and other countries. There are large collections of Irish newspapers of the seventeenth and eighteenth centuries. All the indexes of the Registry of Deeds (mentioned above in connection with the Public Record Office) and a great number of parish registers have been microfilmed, but the latter are not available to the general public.

Among the documents in the National Library is *Forfeited Estates of 1688,* under the heading: "A List of Claims as they are entered with the Trustees at Chichester House, Dublin, on or before 10 August, 1700." Also: *The Book of Postings and Sales of Forfeited and Other Estates and Interests in Ireland.*

There was a rebellion in Ireland in 1688, which was put down, and many Irishmen had their estates confiscated or were forced to sell them. In *The Book of Postings* the names of the old owners are given, together with those of the persons who purchased the estates and the prices paid for them.

In the case of one family—Maelseachlainn, or McLoughlin—whose property was confiscated, the head of the family got away to the extreme West of Ireland, where he built himself a small house on an island in a lake, to guard against surprise!

The address of the Library is:

> *The Director, National Library of Ireland*
> *Kildare Street*
> *Dublin*

## TRINITY COLLEGE, DUBLIN

This has the greatest library in Ireland. Under the law of copyright in Great Britain, copies of all books published in Britain have to be sent to the library of the British Museum and to certain other libraries. Among these was the library of Trinity College, Dublin;

and this still remains the case despite the separation of southern Ireland from the United Kingdom.

As regards printed books, an account is given below as to how far they can assist the genealogical searcher. It should be obvious, of course, that to use the library of Trinity College, Dublin, it is necessary to go there in person, since books cannot be lent out.

There are, besides printed books, several manuscripts in the library of Trinity College which do give information on the early history of Irish families. There is also a collection of fifteenth-century wills of the diocese of Dublin.

There is another source of the utmost value to the inquirer. Trinity College is the premier university of Ireland and for some centuries was the only university in the country. Consequently, most families of any note among the Protestants sent their sons to Trinity College (T.C.D.), and in the records of entry particulars of parentage are given. This is of great use to the inquirer, and it is worth while making an inquiry for details of anyone under the particular surname; for in this way an unknown or unthought-of ancestor may be brought to light. The Admission Registers of T.C.D. have been prepared and published in book form under the title of *Alumni Dublinenses*. In this book will be found the names of all persons entered as students of T.C.D., with their dates and their university attainments; also, the names of their fathers, their fathers' professions or occupations, and the counties of the students' births. A great deal of other genealogical information has been added by the compilers of the *Alumni Dublinenses*, G. D. Burtchell and T. U. Sadleir, both of whom were at different times working in the old Ulster Office.

*Alumni Dublinenses* can be seen in many large libraries, but if it is not accessible to the inquirer, he should send his query (as to the presence of his ancestors as students of T.C.D.) to:

> *The Assistant Registrar*
> *Trinity College*
> *Dublin*

THE ROYAL IRISH ACADEMY

This cultural institution possesses many valuable manuscripts. Among these is one called *The Books of Survey and Distribution*, compiled in 1677 by Thomas Taylor at the order of the government.

In these books there is a complete account of all the lands in Ireland in 1677, with the names of the old owners in 1640, and those of the new owners after the confiscations under Oliver Cromwell. There was a very bloody rebellion in Ireland in 1640, when the English were nearly swept out of the country. Some years later, Oliver Cromwell landed in Ireland with an army, which suppressed the rebellion as bloodily as it had been conducted. There was a great confiscation of land, and the old Irish proprietors were driven out in favor of many of Cromwell's soldiers. The Curse of Cromwell became the worst imprecation that an Irishman could use. Curiously enough, the descendants of Cromwellian soldiers who settled in Ireland became more Irish than the Irish, and it was principally from their ranks that the leaders came during the 1916–21 movement against England. A name like Haugh, for instance, borne by a typical Irish family, betrays an origin which is certainly not Celtic, unless, of course, the name was assumed by an ancestor who had to change his name.

Inquiries should be addressed to:

> The Secretary, The Royal Irish Academy
> 19 Dawson Street
> Dublin

### THE ARMAGH LIBRARY

This includes much useful information and manuscripts, including one which gives a list of "Innocent Papists," that is, Catholics who took no part in the 1640 rebellion and who, by establishing their innocence, were allowed to keep their lands. This manuscript gives the names of all claimants and of those through whom they claimed, with exact relationships, dates of death, and names of lands.

### MASONIC SOURCES

Ireland being largely a Catholic country, it would not be reasonable to expect a large number of Freemasons in Ireland. Nonetheless, an inquirer may well find some help from Masonic records. It is popularly supposed that a Catholic cannot become a Freemason, but this is incorrect. The bar is not on the part of Freemasons, but from the Catholic side, on the ground that Freemasonry is a secret society.

The story is told in Ireland that, in the troubled period of 1916–21, a band of Sinn Feiners arrived at the Masonic Hall, 17 Molesworth Street, Dublin. They announced with courtesy that they had come to burn the hall. The master who met them remarked that he thought it strange that they should wish to burn a building which housed the Masonic memorials of Daniel O'Connell, the great Irish patriot. On being shown the Masonic certificates of O'Connell, the Sinn Feiners withdrew and the hall was saved.

However this may be, it is undoubtedly true that in many cases genealogical facts can be brought to light from the Masonic records. In the family of Sirr (located in Dublin, and in county Monaghan, and derived from a Huguenot family, Sers) some of the eighteenth-century members were prominent as Freemasons in Ireland, and I have traced three generations of them in this way.

Incidentally, a pamphlet on the Sirr family (*The Sirr Family and Freemasonry,* by H. Sirr, 1906) just mentioned is available in the library of Trinity College, Dublin; which merely goes to show how carefully the searchers should inquire of the great Irish libraries. There are members of the Sirr family in America and Canada.

Inquiries for Masonic records should be addressed to:

> *Grand Secretary's Office*
> *Freemason's Hall*
> *17 Molesworth Street*
> *Dublin*

### THE BRITISH MUSEUM LIBRARY

There may seem to be something particularly Irish about the suggestion that Irish inquirers seek information in London; but the fact remains that some useful information can be obtained at the British Museum Library which cannot be found anywhere else about Irish genealogy, namely:

*1. In the Library there are two copies of* The Book of Postings and Sales of Forfeited Estates, *with manuscript notes (see mention under "National Library of Ireland" above).*

*2. The Egerton MSS., which are of special value in connection with the settlement of Ireland in the period of Oliver Cromwell and after.*

*3. The Lansdowne MSS., collected by the first Marquess of Lansdowne.*

*4. The Clarendon MSS., collected by Sir James Ware and bought in 1686 by the second Earl of Clarendon, who was the Lord Lieutenant of Ireland.*

*5. The Cottonian MSS., collected by the famous antiquary Sir Robert Cotton.*

*6. The Sloane MSS. These include the collection of one of the Irish (Protestant) bishops, Dr. Pococke, Bishop of Meath.*

An American visitor to London who does not find it convenient to go on to Ireland may therefore be able to get some useful information in London. He must, of course, previously have some inkling that his family is mentioned in the particular manuscripts; but this is not difficult, as no one would seek to search in manuscripts in the British Museum unless he had some idea that they covered his ancestors and had seen a reference to them.

Manuscripts, like books, can be seen at the British Museum by those who hold a ticket. The American visitor must therefore write well in advance, requesting a ticket, to:

> *The Director, The Library*
> *The British Museum*
> *Bloomsbury*
> *London W.C.1.*

If required for genealogical research by an overseas visitor, the request is almost invariably granted.

LAMBETH PALACE LIBRARY

This has the collection of papers of Sir George Carew, President of the Munster Province in the seventeenth century. There are bound to be references to numerous Irish families. Lambeth Palace is the home of the Archbishop of Canterbury, and therefore permission to consult the Library must be sought. Application should be made to:

> *The Librarian, The Library*
> *Lambeth Palace*
> *London*

## THE BODLEIAN LIBRARY

A collection known as the *Carte Papers,* which contain many Irish state papers and entry books belonging to the Earl of Ormonde, is deposited at this library. Application should be made to:

> *The Librarian*
> *Bodleian Library*
> *Oxford*

## IRISH STATE PAPER OFFICE

The records in this case are, as the name implies, concerned with affairs of state, but as large numbers of Irish families were in trouble with the authorities in the past, they contain much that is useful to an inquirer. The Office is in Record Tower, Dublin Castle.

### Printed Sources

Printed books are useful in Irish genealogy, as in other countries, although often the inquirer can be misled by an account in a book of some family of the same surname as his own. With this proviso in mind, an inquirer can still use the printed sources in Irish genealogy. There are many families in the United States, Canada, Australia, and other countries who have been put on the track of their ancestors by finding a record in a book of printed pedigrees.

*O'Hart's Irish Pedigrees,* or (to give it its full title) *The Origin and Stem of the Irish Nation,* was published in 1875 by John O'Hart and passed through several editions. Few books dealing with genealogy can have been more ambitious than this. It begins with Adam and goes through various genealogies of Irish families. The most extraordinary genealogies are given, generally, however, only as strings of names. The book ought never to be taken as reliable unless a statement can be checked from some other source. As to the Milesian fables, or legends, see full account below.

*Burke's Landed Gentry of Ireland.* There have been four editions of this book—1899, 1904, 1912, and 1958. Before 1899 the Irish landed-gentry families were included with the similar families in *Burke's Landed Gentry* (established in 1836 by John Burke and carried on by Sir Bernard Burke, who was Ulster King of

Arms). The editions of 1899, 1904, and 1912 can be obtained only at secondhand, but the 1958 edition can be obtained from the publishers:

> *Burke's Peerage, Ltd.*
> *Mercury House*
> *109–119 Waterloo Road*
> *London S.E.1.*

The price is £7.7.0.

The number of families dealt with in these volumes varies from edition to edition as much as from 800 to 1500. In earlier editions, the families were mainly of the "Old Ascendancy" pattern, being of English or Scottish descent, but in the current (1958) edition, many families of the submerged Celtic type have appeared, often with representatives who are settled across the Atlantic. A case in point is that of the Tooles, whose present head lives in Canada; he owns the family property in county Wexford. The family name is really O'Toole, meaning "Son of Tuathal," who was King of Leinster in 950 A.D.

*D'Alton's King James's Irish Army List, 1689.* This deals with those Irish officers who settled in France and Spain after the battle of the Boyne and gives an account of the officers' families. Families like the O'Kellys, the O'Mahonys, the McMahons, and the Sarsfields rose to eminence in the service of various European powers, and some of the modern representatives of such families have returned to settle in Ireland.

*The Calendar of State Papers* relating to Ireland contains references to all sorts of people and has information as to the places of origin in Britain of many of the settlers in Ireland.

*Newspapers.* A very valuable printed source is found in a newspaper which began publication in 1763 and continued until 1924. This was the *Public Monitor,* or *Freeman's Journal.* The issues which have been preserved contain thousands of references to Irish men and women from the eighteenth century. The paper was issued weekly, and in each issue there was a column headed "A View of St. Stephen's Green." The idea behind this column was that two friends took a walk each day in St. Stephen's Green, Dublin, and talked about the people whom they met. Some of the remarks are not very pleasant, and therefore the inquirer should not have too thick a skin about his ancestors. One anecdote which is related concerned a famous duelist, John Geoghegan. He is described as a man who "has been early in life much off his guard, by which he fell into some errors, but the propriety of his conduct now amply atones for any former levity."

The *Freeman's Journal* is kept in its files at the National Library of Ireland (see above). It continues to be romantic, for the project of the indexing of the contents of this newspaper is now being undertaken—by convicts.

In 1954, with the co-operation of the Department of Justice and of Major Barrows, Governor of Portlaoighise Prison, the indexing of the *Freeman's Journal* was begun. The task was entrusted to long-term prisoners of good education. "Everything of Irish interest, including all the advertisements, has been catalogued for the National Bibliography under the names of persons, subjects, place-names and date. The typing of the cards has also been done by the prisoners. The indexing of five years of the newspaper has now been completed and some 15,000 cards have been typed. The quality of the work has been excellent. It is checked in the National Library as it proceeds, and a very high standard of bibliographical accuracy has been maintained. The data available in this index has already proved its value in answering a number of inquiries. It is estimated that the index of the whole journal (which ran for 161 years) will eventually contain about three million cards, and the work will take about 20 years to complete." (From a report of the Council of Trustees of the National Library of Ireland, 1954–55.)

*Walker's Hibernian Magazine* (1771–1812). An index to Irish marriages mentioned in the magazine was compiled by Henry Farrar and printed in England (Phillimore & Co., London) in 1897.

### Historical Manuscripts

In 1889 a Royal Commission was appointed by the British Crown to inquire into manuscripts and papers which belonged to private families and which might be useful for historical purposes. The report was published in 1914.

A *Guide to the Reports of Collections of Manuscripts* issued by the Royal Commission for Historical Manuscripts is very useful in trying to trace Irish records.

## Societies

There are a number of Irish record societies which can be extremely helpful to inquirers, not only because of papers and publications which they may hold but on account of the pooled resources of knowledge from the members.

THE IRISH GENEALOGICAL RESEARCH SOCIETY

This society has always had its center in England. It was established on September 15, 1936, and had its headquarters at 6 South Square, Gray's Inn. It remained there until just after the beginning of the world war in 1939. It was thought advisable to remove the Society's headquarters from London to greater safety in the country, and, in fact, when London was severely bombed by the Germans, the former headquarters was destroyed.

The objects of the Society are: (*a*) to promote and encourage the study of Irish genealogy; (*b*) to collect manuscripts and books of genealogical value and, above all, existing copies of records of particular interest to the family historian which were destroyed in the Public Record Office, Dublin, in 1922; and (*c*) to card-index the contents of all manuscripts acquired by the Society, so that names of persons mentioned in the manuscripts may easily be looked up.

The library of the Society consists of:

*A large collection of printed works, including numerous reference books, family histories, parish and admission registers, eighteenth-century directories, diocesan and county histories, indices to Irish wills, a copy of the Chichester House Claims, MS. rulings, and an interleaved copy of* Burke's General Armory (*see under "Heraldry" note*), *with many Hussey-Walsh MSS., in eleven volumes; these embody innumerable copies of Chancery Bills (i.e., proceedings re property in the Chancery Court) and abstracts and copies of Irish wills made by Valentine Hussey-Walsh of Nul Hussey and Cranagh, county Roscommon, before the destruction of public records in 1922. Other MSS. are:*

*The Farnham MSS., in twenty-nine volumes. These were collected by Henry Maxwell, seventh Lord Farnham, and contain numerous pedigrees, coats of arms, copies of family records submitted to Sir John Bernard Burke (editor of* Burke's Peerage *and* Burke's Landed Gentry *until 1892), Irish bookplates, and a large collection of autograph letters of noted Irish genealogists and historians of the nineteenth century.*

*The Butler MSS. include a vast number of Chancery and Exchequer bills, pedigrees, and will extracts.*

*The De la Ponce MSS. (a copy) are a collection dealing with the genealogies and military services of the officers from Ireland who served in the Irish brigades in the service of France. These records are particularly useful to descendants of Irish families which left Ireland in the troubled period after 1689 and took service with European powers in their armies.*

Also with the Society are:

*Sketches of arms registered at the old Ulster Office (see above) and made in 1816 by Patrick Kennedy, heraldic painter of Dublin.*

*Sir William Betham's (at one time Ulster King of Arms) personal index to the large collection of MS. pedigrees acquired during his lifetime.*

*Transcripts of deeds relating to the Taylor family of Dublin and their leases (1336–1731).*

*Numerous typescripts of leases, census returns, and will abstracts from Catholic and Church of Ireland parish registers.*

*The Card Index of Births, Marriages, and Deaths, from 1769 to 1818, covers the announcements of these events in some of the older Irish newspapers, such as* The Hibernian Chronicle *and* The Cork Mercantile Chronicle; *and there is also a similar index of the announcements in* Faulkner's Dublin Journal *for 1759 and 1760.*

The address of the Society is:

> *The Rev. Wallace Clare, F.R.S.A., F.I.G.R.S.*
> *Secretary and Archivist*
> *Oak Hill, Belstead Road*
> *Ipswich, Suffolk*
> *England*

It is unfortunate for inquirers who want to consult the Society's records as listed above to have to visit Ipswich, which does not have a good train connection with London, and perhaps most of them will prefer to write to the Secretary. But fortunately the Society has permission from the Committee of the Irish Club, 82 Eaton Square, London S.W.1, to house some of its books in the Club. Books can be borrowed from the library through the mail.

*The advantages of membership.* Apart from the means of consultation set out above, members can:

> *1. Attend meetings of the Society, held throughout the year at the Irish Club;*
>
> *2. Receive the* Irish Genealogist, *the official organ of the Society, free of charge; and*
>
> *3. Insert queries in the* Irish Genealogist. *An example is given below (see note at end of section).*

Membership is open to persons of Irish descent or sympathies residing in any part of the world. There is an entrance fee of one guinea and an annual subscription fee of twenty-five shillings. Members under the age of twenty-one and law and medical students are admitted without entrance fee and at an annual subscription of one guinea. Application forms for membership may be obtained from the secretary.

NOTE: An example of the type of query which appears in the *Irish Genealogist* is given below:

> O'Toole, John, of Ballyfad, Co. Wexford, eldest son of Laurence and Eliza (née Masterson) O'Toole, was described as "late Irish Brigade" when commissioned Lieutenant-Colonel of the 2nd. Regiment, Irish Brigade, in the British service on 3rd. March, 1796. His name has also been quoted as James. Which was his correct name and are any details known of his career in the French Irish Brigade from which he emerged a Count and Chevalier of the Order of St. Louis? Also can it be confirmed that his only son, John, was the same John O'Toole who entered the French service in 1786 as sous-lieutenant of the Regiment of Berwick, and who died in 1791?

Replies to these queries are sent in to the Secretary of the Society. Many monumental inscriptions are also given in the *Irish Genealogist*.

THE MILITARY HISTORY SOCIETY OF IRELAND

This society was founded in January 1949 to further the study of Irish military history, which was defined as the history of warfare in Ireland and of Irishmen in war.

This definition is a very comprehensive one, as it needs to be; for the troubled history of Ireland has involved Irishmen in military affairs not only in Ireland but in all parts of Europe and indeed, of the world. After the various rebellions in the seventeenth and eighteenth centuries many Irishmen left Ireland to take service with foreign powers, and consequently the history of some of the greatest Irish families—like the Mahonys, the O'Kellys, O'Donevens, and O'Tooles—cannot properly be investigated without reference to the archives of France, Spain, Austria, and other countries. In addition, there have been, over the past two hundred years, large numbers of Irishmen in the armed forces of the British Crown.

It is to gather and to disseminate information on this important subject that the Military History Society exists.

The annual subscription is one guinea. In return for this, as well as participating in all the Society's activities, members receive *The Irish Sword* (the journal of the Society), which is published twice a year. In the contents of this journal many references to Irish families occur. Queries and answers are printed in *The Irish Sword*. A typical query is as follows:

> *M. MacDermott—The French nautical journal* Neptunia (*No. 38, 1955*) *in a series of extracts from the memoirs of the nineteenth century French Admiral Baudin mentions that, during Napoleon's absence in Egypt, Barras took Jerome Bonaparte away from school and placed him at St. Germain with a M. MacDermott. Who was this MacDermott?*

The price of the journal to nonmembers is fifteen shillings. The Hon. Editor is:

> *G. A. Hayes-McCoy, M.A., Ph.D., D.Litt., M.R.I.A.*
> *4 Richview Villas*
> *Clonshea, Dublin*

Correspondence about the Society should be addressed to the Correspondence Secretary:

> *The Military History Society of Ireland*
> *1 Northgate Street*
> *Athlone, co. Westmeath*
> *Ireland*

## THE MILESIAN PEDIGREES, OR CELTIC GENEALOGIES

Nothing is more common among Irish people who are interested in genealogy than the claim to descend from a period far anteceding the longest pedigrees among the European nobility. Once, in Dublin, I was talking with an Irishman who admittedly possessed a long ancestry. He assured me that he could show a documented pedigree back to 150 A.D., and he added that if he had his rights he should be King of Ireland!

The claim to go back to 150 A.D. is not quite as fantastic as it may sound. In *O'Hart's Irish Pedigrees* there are plenty of instances where the pedigree is taken back to Milesius, about 1500 B.C. For this reason alone Hart's book is nearly valueless as regards ancient Irish ancestry.

On the other hand, these Milesian tales have been current in Ireland for a long time, and it is not much help to an inquirer merely to dismiss them as farfetched fables. When did they become fables, and how far can any authenticity be attached to any part of them?

The position now taken by scholars is that the traditional Irish genealogies are accepted as being substantially accurate from about the middle of the sixth century A.D. The mission of St. Patrick in Ireland began in 432 A.D., and by the end of that century (the fifth century) Western learning—that is, Latin learning—had been introduced into Ireland. There was a pre-Christian alphabet called Ogam, which was used for inscriptions on gravestones, but not for recording events. When Ireland became Christian, the Irish language began to be written down by means of Latin letters.

There was a very strong oral tradition in the Ireland of the fifth and sixth centuries, and this came to be written down under the influence of the monks, who were then the only literate class. A body of men had always existed among the Irish whose business it was to memorize valuable knowledge, and there was a good reason why genealogies should be remembered. The ancient Irish, like other Celtic peoples, did not follow the rule of primogeniture, or inheritance by the eldest son. The succession to the kingly position (that is, as king of one of the provinces of Ulster, Munster, Connaught, and Leinster) did not necessarily go from father to son. Anyone in the royal family could inherit the kingship, provided he could show descent in the male line from a common great-grandfather who had held the kingship. Gradually it became the practice to elect during the lifetime of the king a successor, who was known as the Tanist.

These rules of succession made the knowledge of descent a necessity, and so it came about that at any time from the end of the fifth century it would be fairly safe to say that the ancestry of the leading men would be known for five generations. About the eighth century, the Irish genealogies were compiled and formed into a corpus of alleged historical knowledge. The ancestry of all the great families is made to converge upon a small number of ancestors who are located in time about a century before the coming of Christianity. These ancestors are then traced back through strings of ancestral names to Mil, or Milesius. This Milesius was supposed to have come with his son, Heber, from Spain about 1500 B.C. There may be some faint racial memory here of a migration of ancestors from Spain to Ireland. The genealogical corpus just mentioned is not content with a pedigree from Milesius; Milesius himself is said to be descended from Japhet, son of Noah, and so on, of course, back to Adam. This part of the genealogies corresponds to what was found in ancient Wales and in Anglo-Saxon England. Alike in Ireland, Wales, and England, the Christian monks would take the oral traditions which they found and would then tack onto them the genealogies which are found in the Book of Genesis.

It need hardly be said that the genealogies of the Milesian style are now abandoned by all Irish scholars. But the position as now taken by learned men is one which gives Irish pedigrees pride of place in western Europe. The corpus is regarded as reliable as far back as 600 A.D., and certain pedigrees may be genuine back to the fifth century, that is, to about 400 A.D.; consequently, pedigrees which begin with Niall of the Nine Hostages are usually acceptable. Niall was so called because of his warlike exploits in taking hostages from the surrounding nations. The O'Neills descend from him. He died about 400 A.D., and thus the O'Neills have a pedigree of a millenium and a half, 1500 years. There are few traditions in Europe which can equal this, that is, if there are any outside Wales.

From the twelfth to the fifteenth centuries there were great compilations of genealogical research in Ireland, such as the *Book of Leinster,* the *Book of the Dun Cow,* and the *Great Book of Lecan.* The corpus itself is now being published under the title *Corpus Genealogiarium Hibernicarium;* but this compilation will need great scholarly care and attention in its handling.

For the average inquirer, some facts must be borne in mind. Irish surnames were well established by the eleventh century, before the Anglo-Norman invasions. O'Clery is the first-known case, in 916. These native surnames follow a general form. "Ua" or "O'" denotes "grandson" or "descendant" of the original prince, or kingly ancestor, who founded the family. The surname alone—for example, O'Neill—was the prerogative of the chief, and this usage still persists among the Irish, so that the head of a great Celtic family will be referred to as the O'Callaghan, the O'Donovan, or the O'Conor Don. "Mac," meaning "son of," is much less used in

Ireland than in Scotland, though some names of this form are ancient, such as MacDermot of Moylurg.

Only native Irish families can be found in these native genealogies. They deal with the Goidil (a name which is more familiar to us in the form "Gaels"). The Goidil were regarded as the old ruling classes of Ireland. In fact, they must have represented the last wave of conquerors a long time before the Anglo-Normans. FitzGerald and Burke are not found in the Irish genealogies because, although nowadays they would be looked upon as typically Irish, they were not originally so.

Moreover, only families of great importance are recorded in the original genealogies, so that many real Irish names, like Moylan (O'Maolain), are omitted, and not merely names that are not of native Irish origin.

The subject of the various ancient Celtic clans, and the surnames derived from their founders, has engaged the attention of many Irish scholars. Early in the nineteenth century it became the practice for the representatives of the last holders of the Irish chieftainries to revive the appropriate designations. It is thought that there are some seventy of these chieftainries, and the Genealogical Office in Dublin Castle is now engaged in working out the descent of the chieftainries from the last person who was chieftain. The following cases have been investigated and cleared up (the name of the present holder is given in the right-hand column):

| | |
|---|---|
| *MacDermot, Prince of Coolavin* | *Charles John MacDermot* |
| *MacDermott Roe* | *at present dormant* |
| *McGillycuddy of the Reeks* | *Major J. P. McGillycuddy* |
| *McMorrough Kavanagh* | *Col. Sir Dermot McMorrough Kavanagh* |
| | |
| *O'Brien of Thomond* | *Rt. Hon. Lord Inchiquin* |
| *O'Callaghan* | *Don Juan O'Callaghan* |
| *O'Conor Don* | *The Rev. Charles Denis O'Conor* |
| | |
| *O'Donel of Tirconnell* | *John O'Donel* |
| *O'Donoghue of the Glens* | *Geoffrey O'Donoghue* |
| *O'Donovan* | *Brig. Morgan John Winthrop O'Donovan* |
| | |
| *O'Morchoe* | *Capt. Arthur Donel MacMurrough O'Morchoe* |

| | |
|---|---|
| *O'Neill of Clandeboy* | *H. E. Dom Hugh O'Neill* |
| *O'Sionnaigh (The Fox)* | *Capt. Niall Arthur Herbert Fox* |
| *O'Toole of Fer Tire* | *Charles Joseph Anteoine Thomy O'Toole, Comte O'Toole de Leinster* |

Also the following titles:

| | |
|---|---|
| *O'Grady of Kilballyowen* | *Major Gerald Vigors de Courcey O'Grady* |
| *O'Kelly of Gallagh and Tycooly* | *Capt. Walter Lionel O'Kelly, Count of the Holy Roman Empire* |

It does not follow that only the above are genuine, but merely that they have been examined and the present chieftain definitely ascertained. The wife of a chieftain is usually addressed as Madame.

It should be noted that some of the above live on the Continent, not in Ireland, and that others, like the O'Kellys, bear foreign titles. This again emphasizes the many lines of Irish family history which are to be traced in the archives of France, Spain, Italy, and Austria.

## IRISH SURNAMES

The subject of Irish surnames has been mentioned above, but it will help the inquirer to have some idea of what type of name he bears. Not all Irish surnames are of Irish origin, and some which are now considered to be purely Irish are of foreign origin. The "Macs" and the "O's" were well established a century before the Norman invasion of 1172. This invasion brought in a new set of surnames, which belonged to the Norman families, and prominent among these are FitzGerald and FitzMaurice (the "Fitz" means "son of"). Burke, another Norman name, is derived from De Burgo. Among the names brought in by the Normans may be mentioned Barry, Costello, Cusack, Cogan, Dalton, Dillon, Nagle, Nugent, Power, Purcell, Roche, Sarsfield, and Walsh.

In the seventeenth century, as mentioned above in the brief sketch of Irish history, there was a tremendous change, and many native Irish families were rooted out and replaced by settlers from England and Scotland. From this source have come many of the greatest names in Irish literature: Ussher, Goldsmith, Shaw, and Yeats. Most Irish settlers in the end became more Irish than the natives, and names like Tone, Collins, Emmet, Mitchell, and Pearse are found among the leaders of the movements for Irish independence.

To sum up, three quarters of the leading families in Ireland today still bear names which show that they were derived from England or Scotland. West of the Shannon River, in Clare and Connaught, Celtic and Norman names are more common. The reason for this is that in the various forfeitures of the seventeenth century the land west of the Shannon was regarded as not being such an attractive proposition for the settlers and could therefore be left to the natives.

But apart from the old landowning families and ruling classes, the bulk of the names to be found in directories are of Celtic Irish origin, except in the case of Belfast and its neighborhood. An inquirer will be interested to learn that many native names are still found in the areas where they originated. This is a great help in record tracing.

Thus in Clare, MacMahon, MacNamara, and O'Brien are the most frequent names. In Limerick and Tipperary, Regan is the commonest name, as is O'Reilly in Cavan.

The old Norman names, like the old Norman families, have long since been assimilated by the Irish, and thus the names listed above under this heading are classed as Irish.

The "Macs" often denote the formation of a sept, or small clan, from a larger one, for example, MacConsidine and MacLysaght, from the O'Briens of Thomond.

There are a number of native Irish names which are without "O'" or "Mac," such as Kavanagh, Kinsella, Deasy, Bane, and Minnagh.

During the centuries of English domination many native names became Anglicized or distorted; MacGiolla Brighde is the Irish original of Macgilbride (but another version is Mucklebreed), while both Grehan and Grimes have been formed from O'Greachain. Lennon has been made into Leonard, Markahan into Markham, as well as cases like MacGowan into Smith.

For full information on Irish surnames, the reader should consult the work by Dr. Edward MacLysaght entitled *Irish Families* (Dublin, 1958).

## NOTE ON COATS OF ARMS

For the convenience of those who are making inquiries in the Genealogical Office, Dublin Castle, regarding matters of heraldry, the following notes will be useful, though it must be understood that heraldry is a vast subject which can be explained here only in the briefest outline.

In all ages of recorded history, nations and individuals are found to be using emblems, mostly in war. An example can readily enough be seen in the designs shown on the shields of Greek warriors in illustrations to Homer's *Iliad* and *Odyssey*. These examples are often quoted as being heraldic, but true heraldic designs can best be defined as being symbols used in war which became hereditary in the families of the users.

In the sense of this definition, heraldry is found (with certainty) in only two regions of the world, in western Europe and in Japan. In the latter country the *mon*, or family symbol, is the exact equivalent of the crest in European heraldry.

In western Europe heraldry developed in the twelfth century, when armorial bearings began to be used on shields and surcoats (linen garments worn over the armor) all over western Europe, from Norway to Italy and from Poland to England. It is thought that as the armor of the knights became more enveloping, and particularly as their faces were covered by the helmet, the need for means of identification between one mailclad man and another made the use of symbols imperative.

Whatever the cause, the use of armorial bearings quickly developed. They were used (a) on the shield, (b) on the surcoat—hence the term "coat of arms," (c) on the pennons, banners, and standards, (d) on the trappings of war horses, and later (e) on the helmet, when an object known as the crest was placed there. The crest is part of the coat of arms, but there can be coats of arms (that is, shields) without a crest to surmount them.

Very soon in the Middle Ages heraldic designs were used apart from war. They were carved in stone and on wood, on domestic articles such as dishes, and they were also adapted by ladies for use on their dresses. This peaceful use of heraldry paved the way for the continued use of the heraldic designs when armor ceased to be worn in war. The possession of a coat of arms began to be considered as one of the signs of a gentleman. Thus, centuries after heraldry had ceased to be used in war, it survived to be employed in various ways. Coats of arms are now borne not only by individuals and by families but also by corporate bodies, such as governments, banks, trusts, and insurance companies.

From Europe heraldry has spread all over the world, to North, Central, and South America, to Australia, New Zealand, and South and East Africa. The former Indian princes adopted the idea of coats of arms from the British, and in countries in eastern Europe, such as Russia, coats of arms were adopted from the example of western Europe.

In Celtic countries—Ireland, Wales, and the highlands of Scotland—heraldic designs were not used until they were adopted from imitation of the Normans or Lowlanders. In the case of a very ancient family, such as Maelseachlainn, there is no coat of arms properly speaking, but they have a royal standard, that of Tara (the old crowning place of the kings of Ireland), which is far older than coats of arms.

There are thousands of Irish coats of arms, and those who want to see if there is a coat of arms for their name should look in *Burke's General Armory* under their surname, where they will find descriptions of over 80,000 coats of arms.

Those who want to learn more of heraldry, and the meaning of the terms, should consult the *Encyclopedia Americana,* under "Heraldry" (by L. G. Pine), and *Teach Yourself Heraldry and Genealogy* (by L. G. Pine).

# WALES

## INTRODUCTION

The course of development in genealogical studies in Wales is very much the same as in England after 1542. Nowhere is an understanding of the history of a country more needed than in Welsh genealogy, for 1542 is a dividing line before which Welsh genealogy has features which are distinctive and which mark it off from England. In 1542, Wales and England were united administratively. Curiously enough, this was done at the wishes of a king of England who was partly of Welsh descent, Henry VIII. In 1284, Edward I of England had conquered Wales and annexed it to his dominions; he had divided Wales into counties and had made English laws prevail there, but only to a limited extent. The Welsh customs of inheritance and, in fact, the old Welsh tribal laws had still gone on. Under Henry VIII things were very different. Wales and England were thenceforth linked together, and so still remain, though there is now a movement to obtain for Wales what is known in British politics as Dominion status.

From 1542, therefore, records concerning Wales are in the same categories as those of England. Births, marriages, and deaths for Wales will be found at Somerset House for the period from 1837 to the present day. Before that time, parish records can be consulted as in England. For the names and particulars of Welsh ecclesiastical parishes, the reader is advised to consult an old copy of *Crockford's Clerical Directory* as for England. In fact, the inquirer can be referred to the chapter on England for the main outlines of records back to 1542. Particulars of the disposition of many Welsh records in England and in Wales is given in the sections below.

But the differences between Welsh and English genealogy manifest themselves very greatly as soon as the inquirer has any hope of getting back before 1542. For one thing, anyone who has made any sort of acquaintance with Welsh family history must know that some of the most distinguished families in Wales have very common names. Williams, Jones, Price, Hughes, Green, Howell, Powell, and others are names which command a very long pedigree in Wales. Why is this? Because surnames were adopted quite late by the Welsh. Then, when they did so, they took names on the English model which were really translations of their Welsh Christian names. If a man's father's name was John or William, he inclined to take the name of Jones or Williams, that is, son of John or William. This was because the Welsh had used a system of nomenclature which ran somewhat like this: Ievan ap ("ap" means "son of") Caradoc ap Griffith ap Meurig ap Gwillim ap Morgan. In this way a Welshman had a ready means of rehearsing his pedigree through six generations in a single sentence.

Now, most inquirers will not be content with a string of Joneses or Williamses going back a few hundred years. They will know that in medieval days the Welsh princes were numerous and held small tracts of land which made them sound very important and rendered necessary the keeping of pedigrees, to insure their possession of land legally as representing a certain ancestor. What are the chances of going back before 1542 in Wales and of dealing with specifically Welsh records?

A very valuable exposition of Welsh pedigrees is in the last definitive edition (1952) of *Burke's Landed Gentry*. There, in an article by Major Francis Jones, one of the leading Welsh scholars of our time, is a careful account of Welsh genealogy. I give now a summary, without going too far into detail, of his thesis, but those who become deeply interested in this subject are advised to read the whole article, which runs to about 8000 words.

In the first place, a great deal of merriment has been expressed by English and other scholars at the length of a Welsh pedigree. The example which I gave in the chapter on England, of a son of Noah born in the Ark, is to be found again and again in old Welsh pedigrees. Descent from knights of King Arthur's Table is not at all uncommon, and ascriptions of descent from people who lived before the Christian Era is at least as common as it is in Ireland. These claims cannot be substantiated, but it has been observed that a tradition of Arthurian descent which was talked about in the ninth century is at least of respectable age and does show that a family was known in the ninth century. Another reason for disbelief and dislike of Welsh pedigrees has been the barrier of language. Few scholars in England who have been interested in genealogy have been concerned to learn Welsh, and so the matter has gone by default.

The basis of old Welsh genealogy lies in the tenure of the land before the English conquest in 1284. In those days the Welsh held their lands by reason of their blood relationship through their family groups. It is noticeable that in Welsh genealogy there is no servility. There are kings and nobles, but the mass of the Welsh are freemen, who are known as *bonheddig* (this means a man of pedigree). Below these was a small class of serfs, but all the freemen were classed in one sense as equal; in other words, they all took pride in their pedigrees and, indeed, had good reason to do so. The possession of land and many rights and privileges, such as taxation and dues, depended on blood relationship. Consequently, a man had to know who he was and to be able to give his parentage, and several generations of predecessors, or there would be persons near by who would dispute his rights. Land in old Wales was divided by the method known as gavelkind, which means equal division among a man's sons or relatives. This custom prevailed in certain parts of England at one time, such as the county of Kent. The general English principle was, however, of inheritance by the eldest son, primogeniture. This system, despite the conquest under Edward I, did not prevail in Wales until 1542, so that for any really old family it is necessary to trace the ancestry under the Welsh rules.

To the medieval Welshman, it was a matter of necessity that he know his pedigree. It meant possession of land, right to certain dues and privileges, or exemptions from certain burdens. Major Jones points out an interesting example in England where the villeins (that is, the unfree people) often tried to prove their freedom by showing descent from a free ancestor. In both this instance and the old Welsh pedigrees, the motive is the same, a strictly utilitarian method of keeping a pedigree to prove some advantage to oneself.

Now, with reference to the oldest pedigrees, where many mythical personages are found, or where a line is traced back to Biblical times, it should be noticed that this was not peculiar to the Welsh. In several countries of western Europe, as the people became Christian the monks and priests tried to connect the genealogies of their princes with the old scriptural genealogies of the Old Testament. They were not always successful, and in some of the Welsh pedigrees a pagan survivor has got through the net of Christianity without being baptized into a Biblical form. The same thing occurs in the pedigree of Her Majesty Queen Elizabeth II, where the god Wotan (Woden, or Odin) has been gently grafted onto the Biblical pedigrees regardless of the fact that he was a pagan deity. Therefore, a very long Welsh pedigree falls into four sections: (1) The Biblical section. This goes to Noah or Adam. (2) The Classical section. This contains the names of Greek and Roman gods or has the names of Roman rulers or governors in Britain during the times of the Roman occupation. There is one case which used to occur in accounts of the British peerage. Lord St. Davids used formerly to claim an ancestor who derived from Maximus, Roman governor of Britain during the third century. Also in this pedigree was included Vortigern, who was the king of Kent who invited the Saxons into England. These two sections are not to be taken seriously when considering old Welsh pedigrees, because for obvious reasons they cannot possibly be substantiated. The next section (3) is the Dynastic. This contains many genuine names and rudimentary pedigrees even back to the sixth century. These parts of the pedigrees represent genuine old traditions, and from the ninth century up to 1284 they can be accepted as reliable. (4) The *Bonheddig* section. This gives us from 900–1200 A.D. a series of pedigrees of princes, lords, and lesser families. These pedigrees are good, and many of the lines shown may be descended from the old dynastic houses referred to in section 3. The great Welsh aristocratic families come from this group in section 4.

The study of the pedigrees in sections 3 and 4 above requires archaeological and philological research, and to understand them thoroughly a sound knowledge of Welsh history and economic conditions as well as the language of Wales is essential.

The conquest of Wales by Edward I in 1284 did away with the great dynastic houses and imposed a superstructure of Anglo-Norman lords. But the *bonheddig* referred to above did not cease to hold their lands, and many of them remained in possession into the twentieth century. There was an effort made to connect these families of the lesser gentry with the great dynastic houses. To do this, an elaborate scheme was worked out whereby the houses of the *bonheddig* were all supposed to be derived from the dynastic lines by a common descent, just as a Highland clan in Scotland was supposed to descend from a common ancestor. Just as the Mackintoshes, for instance, in Scotland are supposed to be all the descendants of Shaw, son of the Thane, and the Macgregors of Gregor, so in medieval Wales there arose a genealogical scheme whereby the Welsh noble families descended from the Five Royal Tribes of Wales or the Fifteen Noble Tribes of Wales.

I am mentioning these arrangements because it will be impossible for anyone to go far in Welsh genealogy without coming across mentions of the Noble Tribes. For example, there is a well-known book on Welsh genealogy called *The Noble Tribes of Wales,* by Philip Yorke of Erthig, written in the eighteenth century. There is no harm in these schemes of Welsh genealogy, provided that they are known for what they are, namely, schemes or schematic arrangements which do not have validity behind them.

In some cases it is possible to trace out a connection between an alleged ancestor and the family group descending from him. Thus, Major Jones gives some interesting examples. Ednyfed Fychan, who died in 1246, was tenth in descent from Marchudd, who lived in the ninth century. Gruffydd Unbais, who was living in 1292, was eighth in descent from Elystan Glodrydd, who lived in the tenth century.

It is clear from these cases that descent for notable Welsh families goes back much further than in England or in Scotland for families of a similar social status. The inquirer can therefore be encouraged by the possibilities which open before him.

These medieval pedigrees were not in the form which would now be considered suitable for an entry in a book of family history. They were very simple and consisted simply of names of ancestors in each generation; no dates, few details of any sort, whether personal or biographical. The reason for this is found in the nature of Welsh law already mentioned; the pedigree was required for legal purposes, to show the descent from a given person. Dates and details were not needed. The pedigrees were recited, and it is natural that many of them should have been preserved by the bards, who in their songs and lays included pedigrees of the patrons for whom they worked.

Great changes were produced in Wales by the Tudor dynasty. Not only was Wales brought into a closer union with England but the habits of the English Heralds and genealogists prevailed. The College of Arms made itself felt in Wales, and Welshmen were appointed as Deputy Heralds. Pedigrees began to be constructed in which ancestors were magnified and given princely titles which they had never possessed in real life. This is not to say that these Tudor Welsh pedigrees are not reliable. They do carry a large amount of reliable information, and they give the pedigrees of the *bonheddig*. In England, at the visitations (see chapter on England) the general rule was that pedigrees should give only the descents of the eldest son in each generation. This was because of the rule of primogeniture. In Wales, on the other hand, despite the fact that primogeniture had taken the place of the old gavelkind, the Welshman was still interested in his widespread pedigree and wanted to include all his cousins, so that a full pedigree was given. Needless to say, this is extraordinarily interesting and useful to an inquirer.

The position about Welsh surnames already mentioned is further brought out by examples taken from Scotland and Ireland. The interest here is that these are all Celtic peoples, whose outlook on pedigree is quite different from that prevailing among the English.

In Scotland there is an example quoted from no less an authority than the Lord Lyon: Alistair MacIan MacSheumas MacIan Beg. This means: Alistair, the son of Ian, son of Sheumas, son of Ian Beg. Here we have four generations; it would be useful if a similar system could have prevailed among the more legalistic English. The Irish case is quoted by Major Jones from an inscription which appeared in 1722 carved on the family vault of the O'Neills of Shane Castle: Shane MacBrien MacPhelim MacBryan MacShane MacBryan O'Neill. This is: Shane, son of Brien, son of Phelim, son of Bryan, son of Shane, son of Bryan O'Neill. "Mac" and "O'" are the signs of "son of" among the Highland Scots and the Irish, respectively; "ap" meant the same thing among the Welsh. Among the Normans, "Fitz" was used in the same way, but this very soon was dropped or became a part of the family surname.

For the Tudor period there are many cases where the old and the new systems of nomenclature appeared side by side. Thus: John Gough or Gowgh alias John ap Howell ap Griffith of Anglesey, clerk. The alias, as was exactly the case in England, was not a term of abuse or of suggested criminality as it would now be. Among minor families the old usage was retained much later, and some say that it has hardly now become extinct among the peoples of pastoral districts in Wales.

It appears that there are great collections of Welsh manuscripts, concerning which something will be said below. Before going on to that, it should be noted that Wales has been invaded by more than one race. Saxon and Norman alike did so and left traces of their invasions in various families which have survived for centuries. The Irish also settled in Wales in older days. Among the names which are not Welsh but which are found in Wales may be noted: Hanmer, Mortimer, Mansell, Holland, Conway, Salesbury, Bulkeley, and Turberville.

## MANUSCRIPT COLLECTIONS

The most important of the manuscript collections is that in the National Library of Wales at Aberystwyth.

I paraphrase from a pamphlet put out by the National Library under the heading "A Brief Summary of Its History and Its Activities."

The National Library of Wales: Founded by royal charter, granted in 1907, the National Library came into existence on January 1, 1909. It is maintained by an annual grant-in-aid from Her Majesty's Treasury. It is one of the six libraries in the British Isles which is entitled to certain privileges under the Copyright Act, not the least of which is that it shall receive the copies of all books printed in Britain. In 1955, when figures were available to me, the number of books in the Library was 1,500,000; there were also 30,000 volumes of manuscripts, and about 3,500,000 deeds and other documents, together with a very large collection of maps, prints, drawings, and portraits. It is a general reference library; it specializes also in printed, manuscript, and graphic material relating to Wales and the other Celtic countries.

Admission is by reader's ticket, an application form for which may be obtained from the Librarian. The address of the Library is simply:

*The National Library of Wales*
*Aberystwyth, Wales*

For the older manuscripts, the Reports published by the Historical Manuscripts Commission are essential. These will be found in
the Public Record Office in London. They are supplemented by
the National Library's own publications of catalogues of manuscripts and documents listed at the end of the Annual Report. For
example, in the Annual Report for 1957–58, which is before me as
I write, there are numerous works listed, which fill two pages. There
are catalogues of deeds and documents, of many papers recovered
from private collections, and, what will prove of immense interest to
American inquirers, *A Bibliography of Welsh Americana,* by Henry
Blackwell of New York, edited and with an introduction by William
Williams, 1942.

To turn to the side of the Library which will appeal to most of
our inquirers, there is a booklet called *The Department of Manuscripts and Records in the National Library of Wales,* by E. D. Jones,
which was printed in 1947. It appeared originally in the *National
Library of Wales Journal.*

To begin with, the Library had the immense advantage of being
helped from the earliest days by the efforts of Sir John Williams; he
spent large sums on acquiring manuscripts of Welsh history and
literature. He bought, among other things, the reversion to the
Hengwrt-Peniarth Collection in 1905 from William Robert Maurice
Wynne of Peniarth. By this means alone, the National Library
was endowed with the finest collection of Welsh manuscripts ever
gathered under one roof. This Hengwrt-Peniarth Collection was
mainly the creation of Robert Vaughan (1592–1666), who was an
antiquary. It can therefore be understood that the documents in this
collection are of value to the genealogical inquirer.

In the present account I shall give some details of the most valua-
ble contents (from the genealogical point of view) of the National
Library. Some of the post-1660 subsidiary papers of the Court of
Great Sessions were transferred from the Public Record Office in
London to the National Library. As can be seen in the account of
Welsh records in the Public Record Office below, by no means all
the Welsh records have been returned to Wales.

The library of Edward Humphrey Owen was purchased in 1910.
Its chief interest lay in its printed books on history, genealogy, and

heraldry; it also contained several historical and genealogical manuscripts relating to Anglesey and Caernarvonshire.

In 1914 the Kinmel Library was purchased; it had been collected by Hugh Robert Hughes and reflected his interest in genealogy and heraldry. It includes the manuscripts of John Williams of Beaumaris and of Angharad Llwyd of Caerwys, afterward of Ty'n y Rhyl. Another item of great genealogical interest was the collection from the library of the Myttons of Halston. This was a family famous on the Welsh borders and having extensive possessions in the area.

In 1915 the first of the larger deposits of deeds and documents, which numbered over 35,000, came in from the offices of Messrs. Williams and Williams, solicitors, of Haverfordwest.

1918. The collection of Edward Griffith of Dolgelley was presented.

1919. The Panton Collection, which included the papers of the Wynn family of Gwydir, came into the Library's possession.

1920. The papers of Sir Henry Watkin Williams Wynn were presented. Also the deposit of the manorial records of the lordship of Ruthin. Also the Castell Gorfod Library, which included the genealogical collections of Joseph Joseph of Brecon, and an elaborate transcript in twenty-one folio volumes of Walbrook paper of the *Book of Golden Grove* genealogies (see below for information concerning this).

1921. There were deposited in the Library over 2000 deeds relating to the estates of the Pulestons of Emral and Worthenbury.

1922. The Clark manuscripts were acquired. They give invaluable aid to students of Glamorgan history and genealogy.

1926. Viscount Combermere presented sixteenth- and seventeenth-century correspondence of the family of Salusbury of Llewenni and deeds relating to the northern counties of Wales.

1938. Mrs. Spence-Colby, who had deposited manuscripts relating to the deeds of the Ffynone Estate, gave an interesting collection of early deeds relating to the Kidwelly district.

The gifts to the Library and other acquisitions may perhaps best be summarized, the above account serving as an illustration of the mode of accumulation of the manuscripts and other records of the Library.

Manorial records are of great value, and of these, a large quantity is in the Library. So, too, are large collections of private papers and other works of a genealogical interest. It is certain that few

Welsh families can be indifferent to the value of the Library when they are searching for their ancestors.

Among those who have given valuable papers to the Library is the Honourable Society of Cymmrodorion. This society is of great value to Welshmen, as it exists under a royal charter for the encouragement of literature, science, and art as connected with Wales. In the transactions of the Society there is a great deal of information about Welsh genealogy. Each year there is published a volume of the transactions of the Society, and a history of the Society from 1751 to 1951 was published some years ago.

The address of the Society, with that of its Secretary, is:

*Sir John Cecil Williams, M.A., LL.D.*
*Hon. Secretary, The Honourable Society of Cymmrodorion*
*20 Bedford Square*
*London W.C.1*

The subscription is one guinea per year.

Apart from those in the English Public Record Office (see under this heading), some valuable genealogical manuscripts are stored in Bangor University College Library and the Cardiff Public Library. The Bodleian Library, Oxford, and the British Museum Library both have some early Welsh genealogical records. In the British Museum are the Harleian Manuscripts, which contain some Welsh papers.

In the British Museum (see chapter on England for a full description) there are many Welsh materials. These include many manuscripts. They have been catalogued, as far as the older collections have been dealt with, in a *Catalogue of Welsh MSS.*, by Edward Owen. There are many additional manuscripts, and for reference to them, the searcher must see the officially indexed (calendared) lists of manuscripts.

Owing to the facts detailed in the introduction to this article, Welsh genealogy has been treated as either something incomprehensible or else as a vast realm of fairy tale. Few genealogists know Welsh, and therefore in collections of manuscripts and books in England there is a tendency to neglect the Welsh side.

With the Society of Genealogists there is a considerable Welsh section containing many books, but the inquirer, unless he or she already knows the difficulties, will not be likely to gain elementary help from them. They will, however, be very helpful when he comes to the later stages of his inquiries. Most of the printed calendars referred to in various sections above are given in the Society's Welsh section. There are important works such as Sir Joseph Bradney's *History of Monmouthshire* and the *List of the Parish Registers of the Diocese of Llandaff.* There is also a list of Welsh wills proved 1601–78 at the Carmarthen Probate Registry; index to the wills of the Peculiar of Hawarden; and sixty-five volumes of pedigrees made by the Rev. Thomas Williams.

In the Society's library is a copy of a *Report on MSS. in the Welsh Language,* a volume issued by the Historical Manuscripts Commission.

## WELSH WILLS— THEIR PLACES OF DEPOSIT

The Probate Courts of the four Welsh bishoprics are now to be found as follows:

> *Bangor: the Probate Registry*
> *Llandaff: at Llandaff—this includes the wills of the diocese of Hereford*
> *St. Asaph: at Bangor*
> *St. David's: at Carmarthen*

## THE PUBLIC RECORD OFFICE

A valuable guide to the documents concerning Wales which are to be found in the Public Record Office is by M. S. Giuseppi, who was an Assistant Keeper of the Records. An edition of this work was brought out in 1923 by H. M. Stationery Office. On pages 317–24 particulars are given of the records of the Principality of Wales. After the union of England and Wales in 1542, to which reference has been made above, Courts for the Great Sessions were established by a statute of the thirty-fourth and thirty-fifth years of King Henry VIII (1543 and 1544). Assizes were indeed held in Wales from the latter part of the reign of King Edward I (1272–1307). Some of the Assize Rolls are held in the records of the King's Bench and others in the records of the Court of the Exchequer. (For particulars of these, see the chapter on England.)

Now, however, by the statutes of 1543 and 1544 mentioned above, Wales was divided into twelve counties. Eight of these were of ancient times. They were Anglesey, Caernarvon, Carmarthen, Cardigan, Flint, Glamorgan, Merioneth, and Pembroke. The other four, namely, Brecknock, Radnor, Denbigh, and Montgomery, were recent creations in the time of Henry VIII. Sessions were to be held in each of these counties twice every year, and it is mainly with records of a legal nature concerning Wales that the Public Record Office in London is concerned. These records can be divided into three sections.

### Equity Records

It has already been explained in the chapter on England, and also briefly above, that the English legal system went on for centuries with two separate legal jurisdictions, namely, Common Law and Equity. These include, in the Public Record Office, records for the following circuits: Chester, North Wales, Brecon, and Carmarthen. They consist of decrees, exhibits (these are often the counterparts of deeds and leases, extending over three hundred years, from Elizabeth I to George III), and pleadings.

### Common-Law Records

These include Calendar Rolls from Henry VIII to Charles II. They give the names of persons who were to be tried at the Sessions, and they also include abstracts of coroners' inquests, for Radnor, Glamorgan, Cardigan, and Pembroke.

*Fines and Recoveries.* These are from Henry VIII to William IV, and there are over 4000 files.

*Jail Files.* Jail files from Henry VIII to William IV, of which there are over 1000 bundles.

*Plea Rolls.* For all the twelve counties of the Principality. None of these are earlier than the Tudor period (Henry VII, 1485), but they contain a mass of information of cases which were brought before the Crown. The Ruthin records extend from 1343 to 1808 and include much information, such as lists of freeholders and other inhabitants in the lordship of Ruthin. (It should be noted that the Court Rolls of this lordship are placed with the general series of Court Rolls in the Public Record Office.)

### General

Under this heading there is a considerable amount of information relating to attorneys, such as their articles of clerkship, admissions and oath rolls, together with registers of articles and certificates. This information is mainly from the period of George II to William IV, but if your ancestor was a solicitor or attorney during this period, you will be likely to find much information in this section.

There are also a few ancient deeds which have come out of the records of Chester but which relate to places in Wales.

Then, under the heading of Miscellanea, there are 249 bundles and volumes covering the period from Edward III to William IV. There is a great deal of detail here, and obviously this section of the Public Record Office will be the last resort of the inquirer.

NOTE: It should be noted that many collections of what are really private papers have been presented to the Public Record Office. Of these, there is one set of pedigrees which will be of particular interest to Welsh inquirers; namely, the *Golden Grove Book,* which consists of three volumes with an index. This fine collection includes a great deal of heraldic and genealogical information.

# THE ISLE OF MAN and
# THE CHANNEL ISLANDS

## THE ISLE OF MAN

This island, which lies in the middle of the Irish Sea between England and Ireland, is not bound by the acts of the United Kingdom Parliament unless specially mentioned in them. It has its own legislature—called the Tynwald, or Assembly—which consists of the Legislative Council and the House of Keys. The word "Keys" is possibly derived from the Scandinavian word *keise,* meaning "chosen." The Norsemen ruled in Man for centuries.

### Registration of Births, Marriages, and Deaths

This is governed by the Civil Registration and Dissenters' Marriages Acts, 1924–33, and the Marriage Act of 1951. The compulsory registration of births and deaths came into operation in 1878, and that of marriages in 1849, the last under the Marriage Act of 1849.

### Custody of the Registers

The completed registers and other records of births, deaths, and marriages are deposited in the custody of the Registrar-General, Government Office, Douglas, Isle of Man. As mentioned above, they date from 1849 in case of marriages and from 1878 in case of births and deaths.

Records of dissenters' marriages are preserved from 1849 and ecclesiastical marriages from 1884. (The last sentence is taken from the official account published by the British Government and is a trifle obscure. By "dissenter" is meant a person who dissents from or does not conform to the Established Church of England; by "ecclesiastical" is meant here, I think, marriages in places of worship belonging to the Church of England.) Records of baptisms (Church of England) and burials from 1884 to 1910 are also preserved (with the Registrar-General).

*Compulsory registration of baptisms and burials* in the parishes of the Isle of Man came into operation in 1849 under the Parish Registers Act, 1849.

*Searches and certificates.* Searches can be made and certified copies of any entries in the registers can be obtained on application addressed to the Registrar-General, Government Office, Isle of Man. The fees are very low, being not more than two shillings and sixpence in the highest case.

*Wills* are recorded and preserved in the Probate Registry (of Deeds), Finch Road, Douglas, Isle of Man, under the Judicature (Ecclesiastical) Transfer Act, 1884.

*Title deeds* to real estate, wills, administrations, and so on, are recorded and preserved in the Registry of Deeds, Finch Road, Douglas, Isle of Man, together with certain entries of baptism, marriage, and burial which occurred in the Isle of Man prior to the year 1849.

### Ecclesiastical Parishes

Full particulars of these can be found in *Crockford's Clerical Directory,* to which reference has been made in the chapter on England.

### Arms

Manx arms come under the jurisdiction of the College of Arms, London, for a full account of which, see the chapter on England. There have never been protests against the authority of the College, so that I can only assume that the native Manx knew not coat armor, and that the Manx families whose pedigrees are extant are— like the Quayles of Crogga or the Macphersons of Countesswells— really invaders from Great Britain who imported their arms from their respective countries of England or Scotland. Otherwise, if really of Manx descent, as the family of Christian may be, they must have adopted arms from the example of the English. Inquiries concerning Manx arms should therefore be addressed to the College of Arms. Fletcher Christian, leader of the mutineers in *Mutiny on the Bounty,* was a member of the family referred to.

## THE CHANNEL ISLANDS

These are a group of small islands off the northwest coast of France. The main islands are Jersey, Guernsey, Alderney, and Sark, and they are the only portions of the duchy of Normandy (once held by William the Conqueror) which now belong to the British Crown. Jersey has the States of Jersey; and Guernsey, with its dependencies (that is, the other islands), has states likewise. There is a Lieutenant Governor appointed by the British Crown in both Jersey and Guernsey. Acts of the British Parliament do not apply to the States without their consent.

### Jersey

*Births, marriages, and deaths* have been officially recorded in Jersey since 1842 under the *Loi sur l'état civil.* This was passed by the States of Jersey following the British Parliament's acts of 1836–37 which set up the procedure in England and Wales for registration of births, marriages, and deaths (see chapter on England). The law passed by the States of Jersey was given force by the King in Council (Order in Council). The law of 1842 has been subsequently amended on several occasions, but is still the governing statute.

*Custody of the registers.* Completed registers of births and deaths are kept by the registrar of the parish concerned. In the case of registers of marriages, one register is kept by the registrar or rector of the parish or the vicar of the ecclesiastical district concerned, and the other by the Superintendent Registrar. Registers date from August 1842. Information may be obtained by application to the Superintendent Registrar, States' Building, St. Helier, Jersey.

Registration of baptisms and funerals is carried out by the rector of the parish or by the vicar of the ecclesiastical parish in which the baptism or funeral takes place. Further inquiries on this subject should be addressed to the Acting Dean, St. Saviour, Jersey. Parish registers date from about 1542, in some cases.

*Searches and certificates* can be obtained on application to the rector, vicar, or registrar of the parish concerned, or to the Superintendent Registrar, whose address is given above. For list of parishes and particulars of incumbents, see *Crockford's Clerical Directory* (see chapter on England).

*Fees* are seven shillings and sixpence for a general search and two shillings for a simple search (that is, for one item only). Fee for an extract is three shillings.

*Wills* of realty are registered in the Royal Court of the island, whereas wills of personalty are registered in the Probate Division. All wills are copied into books specially kept for that purpose, and the originals are preserved in the strong room of the Judicial Greffe. They are open to inspection by members of the public.

*The Public Registry of Contracts* contains records of contracts relating to real property. There is no Chief Registry of Central Archives. These records may be inspected on application to the Judicial Greffier, States' Building, St. Helier, Jersey.

*States' Assembly* (that is, the island Parliament). Inquiries concerning the proceedings and decisions of this body may be obtained on application to the States' Greffe, Jersey.

It should be observed that the official language of the islands is French, hence the reason for the 1842 law being written in French.

### Guernsey

The States of Guernsey are concerned not only with the island of Guernsey but also with its dependencies, Alderney, Sark, Herm, Jethou, and Brecqhou.

*Registration of births and deaths.* This is governed by an Order-in-Council of March 9, 1935.

*Registration of marriages* is governed by an Order-in-Council of May 6, 1919.

*Registrar-General's Office, Greffe, Guernsey,* has completed registers of births and deaths since 1840, but before this date registrations of births and burials were maintained at the parish churches. Also maintained in this office are registers of marriages from 1919 onward, together with registers of all marriages in places other than churches of the Church of England since 1840.

Marriages according to the rites and ceremonies of the Church of England, Roman Catholics, Methodists, and others are in the custody of the church or chapel concerned. Records of baptisms, marriages, and burials before 1840 are in the custody of churches.

### Alderney

Some of the registers of Alderney were lost during the German occupation in 1940–45, but the following still exist: births, from August 3, 1850, to date; deaths, August 2, 1850, to date; marriages, July 1, 1891, to date. A duplicate of the registers of births and deaths in Alderney from 1925 and of marriages there from May 15, 1919, is in the custody of the Registrar-General of Guernsey. Fees for searches are very light.

*Wills* of realty are registered at the Registrar-General's Office. Copies of wills of personalty are kept by the Registrar to the Ecclesiastical Court, 9 Lefebvre Street, St. Peter Port, Guernsey.

All documents under seal, including deeds of conveyance, bonds, and deeds of division of property, have to be registered at the office of the Registrar-General, and copies are kept there. All historical records and archives are kept there, and these are at present in process of being catalogued.

Ecclesiastically, the Channel Islands come under the rule of the Bishop of Winchester; before the Reformation they were under the Bishop of Rouen.

*Coats of Arms.* As being part of the old duchy of Normandy, the Channel Islands have always claimed to be outside the jurisdiction of the College of Arms and to be able to use arms which may not be agreeable to the English College. An example can be given from *Burke's Landed Gentry* of 1952, in a footnote to the arms of Le Breton. "It is contended that Jersey, as a remnant of the Duchy of Normandy, was not affected by the various proclamations concerning the bearing of arms issued for the Kingdom of England, and it is pointed out that the islands of the Duchy were never subjected to an Heraldic Visitation by the English Officers of Arms."

There are many interesting facets to the study of the older genealogies in the Channel Islands, and anyone who knows that his ancestors came from there would do well to study the history of the islands. Many works have been written about them, and among these may be cited Falle's *History of Jersey* (1837) and Duncan's or Tupper's *History of Guernsey*. The standard work on Sark is perhaps *L'Ile de Serk,* by Louis Selosse, and there is also the Rev.

J. L. V. Cachemaille's *History of the Island of Sark*. The Guille-Alles Library in Guernsey contains much valuable information, as does the Priaulx Library, also in Guernsey, in St. Peter Port.

### Sark

In addition to the notes already given above, inquirers may like to know of a recent work, *The Story of Sark,* by A. R. de Carteret, published in 1956. This book is very interesting and useful, for it not only gives a good account of the island but relates the names of the original settlers. The economy of Sark is still feudal, and the management of the island is under the rule of La Dame de Serk, Mrs. S. M. Hathaway, O.B.E.

The De Carterets were the original settlers of the island, in the reign of Elizabeth I (1558–1603). Prominent among the early settlers were the names: Alexandre, Balleine, Chevalier, Cristin, Dupre, Gaudin, Guille, Hamon, Hotton, Le Brocq, Le Cerf, Le Couteur, Le Gros, Le Masurier, Nicolle, Noel, Poindestre, Vaudin, and Vibert. These names are given in case anyone may have an idea that his ancestors came from Sark, and from this list he may be spared a lot of trouble, but it should be emphasized that this list is not exhaustive.

# NORWAY

## INTRODUCTION

In the account which follows I am very much obliged to the Archivist of the Riksarkivet, Oslo, who supplied me with a copy of *How to Trace Your Ancestors in Norway*. This pamphlet was published in 1959 by the Royal Norwegian Ministry of Foreign Affairs, Office of Cultural Relations. It contains much useful advice, such as I have given in other sections of this book, about the general principles of tracing your ancestry. There is also a general likeness to the state of record keeping in Sweden.

## PARISH REGISTERS

According to the Central Bureau of Statistics, registration of births, marriages, and deaths began in 1687, as far as the law was concerned, but as in other countries, often the registration books do not begin until after 1700. The registers are kept by the clergy and contain information not only about baptism, marriage, and burial but also about confirmation and, since the beginning of the nineteenth century, movements into and out of the parish. Some of the older registers are very hard to understand, since until after 1800 they were not written in a standard form. Parish registers older than eighty-five years are kept in central files (*statsarkivs*) within the bishopric in question. Later registers are retained by the parish clergyman, to whom application should be made for particulars.

It is stated that "extracts from the parish registers since 1870 are held by Statistisk Sentralbyra (Central Bureau of Statistics), Oslo," and "for the period 1866–69 extracts are deposited at the Riksarkivet." To this may be added the following information from the Central Bureau: "All records of births, marriages, and deaths are kept in the churches, but all church books being 85 years old are sent to the state archives. In addition, the Central Bureau of Statistics keeps all the individual lists of births, marriages, and deaths sent from the parishes for statistical purpose."

In applying to the Central Bureau of Statistics, it is sufficient to write to:

> *The Chief, Demographic Section*
> *Statistisk Sentralbyra*
> *Dronningens Gate 16*
> *Oslo, Norway*

There also exist registers of religious communities other than the Church of Norway.

## CIVIL REGISTRATION

Civil registration of births was established by law on April 10, 1915. With regard to this, the Central Bureau of Statistics informed me that, for births, registration is civil, because all births must be registered in a special book, not in the church register, and this special book includes all births occurring in the parish. Marriages and deaths are registered in the parish register, also marriages by civil contract, and, of course, all baptisms. Thus, a great deal of what in England or America would be considered as civil registration is carried out by the parish clergy. The Central Bureau has the task of supervising the registers, and copies of parish registers are deposited with the Bureau. This is naturally very valuable should the documents in a parish be destroyed, for example, by fire.

## CENSUS RETURNS

A census was held in Norway in 1769 and 1801, thus being instituted even earlier than in the United States. Censuses were held every tenth year from 1815 to 1875, and from 1890 every tenth year. For 1900 and earlier, the census papers are available at the Riksarkivet for inspection. It will be advisable to explain that the Riksarkivet is the National Archives of Norway. The address is simply:

*The Archivist*
*Riksarkivet*
*Bankplass 3*
*Oslo*

All the census returns are in the National Archives, except for those of 1875 and 1901, these being kept in the *statsarkivs*. Many of these returns are unfortunately of more value to the statistician than to the genealogist. After 1865 the census returns give a person's place of birth.

Norway is distinguished by possessing older census records, the most important being the population rolls of 1664–66. It is not clear, however, whether these give details of names and families.

## WILLS

In Norway there are no rules saying how and where wills must be kept. The testator may keep the will, or, if he wishes, the will can be kept in the court of probate. After the death of the testator, the will is kept by the Probate Court. The oldest probate registers go back to about 1660. These records are now preserved in the *statsarkivs* (see below).

## PUBLIC RECORDS

There is a distinction here, as in so many other countries, between the national and the regional archives.

### The National Archives

The Riksarkivet, Bankplass 3, Oslo. This is the National Archives. No official register exists of its contents. It contains documents and records from government departments; for example, there are real estate books under the name of *matrikler*, which give the names of owners of farms for the years 1665–1723, which may be of great interest to the researcher. The books dealing with these years are in the Riksarkivet. Many account books dealing with counties and bailiwicks are in the same archives.

### Regional State Archives

*Statsarkivet.* These keep documents from the local government administration. Their addresses are:

*Statsarkivet i Oslo, Kirkegaten 14–18, for Östfold, Akershus, Oslo, Buskerud, Vestfold, and Telemark counties.*

*Statsarkivet i Hamar, Strandgaten 71, for Hedmark and Oppland counties.*

*Statsarkivet i Kristiansand, Vesterveien 4, for Aust-Agder and Vest-Agder counties.*

*Statsarkivet i Bergen, Arstadveien 32, for Rogaland, Hordaland, Bergen, and Sogn og Fjordane counties.*

*The principal records relating to Rogaland are lodged at the branch Statsarkivkontoret i Stavanger, Peder Klows Gate 27.*

*Statsarkivet i Trondheim, Högskoleveien 12, for Möre og Romsdal, Sör-Tröndelag, Nord-Tröndelag, Nordland, Troms, and Finnmark counties.*

*The principal records relating to Troms and Finnmark are kept at the branch Statsarkivkontoret i Tromsö, Petersborg Gate 21–29.*

ADDRESSES FROM PAGE 5: *How to Trace Your Ancestors.*


## HERALDRY

With regard to heraldry, all available publications on coats of arms, and incidentally on genealogical studies, are kept in the library of the Universitetsbiblioteket i Oslo, Drammensveien 42B, Oslo. Inquiries should be addressed to the Secretary. To him I am obliged for the following information. "The state of affairs with regard to Norwegian heraldry is as follows. Since 1814 there have been no titled families in Norway, and since 1821 it has not been necessary for family heraldry to be registered or regulated in any way, private individuals having free choice in the matter of coats of arms. Proposals regarding official heraldry are dealt with at ministerial level, with professional assistance from the Riksarkivet." Collections of particular coats of arms exist in the Public Record Office, or Riksarkivet, and in addition, small collections occur in local files. Heraldry has not apparently been used as extensively as in England or America. Mention is made of the *bumerker,* which are used as signets, etc., but which are not coats of arms. They are useful, through the initials used in them, toward solving some problems of research.

## GENEALOGICAL SOCIETY

The name of this is: Norsk Slektshistorisk Forening. The name and address of the Secretary are: Mr. Anthon Busch, Øvre Slottsgate 17, Oslo.

## NEWSPAPERS

As everywhere, these contain much useful information. The majority are kept on file at the Universitetsbiblioteket (see above).

## ADDITIONAL INFORMATION

For those to whom the above may be more useful if they have information as to their beginnings in the United States, there is a body called the Supreme Lodge of the Sons of Norway (1312 West Lake Street, Minneapolis 8, Minnesota). This body can give you much information which would be of value. There is also the Norwegian-American Historical Association, which publishes many volumes of interest to researchers. I understand that the publications of the Association can be consulted not only at the Library of Congress but also in the libraries of the following: the University of Minnesota, Minneapolis, Minnesota; St. Olaf College, Northfield, Minnesota; the University of Wisconsin, Madison, Wisconsin; and Luther College, Decorah, Iowa.

## LIBRARIES

Apart from the University Library at Oslo, the following may be helpful: *Universitetsbiblioteket, Bergen*

*Videnskapsselskapets Bibliotek (i.e., the Library of the Scientific Society), Trondheim*

*Deichmanske Bibliotek, Oslo*

# SWEDEN

## INTRODUCTION

In the account of Swedish genealogy, my sources have been the booklet *Finding Your Forefathers,* issued by the Press and Information Service of the Royal Ministry for Foreign Affairs; the booklet *Archives in Sweden,* by Ingvar Andersson of the Swedish Institute; the Swedish Embassy in London; and the various learned societies which are mentioned in their proper places. The author particularly wishes to acknowledge the curtesy of Mr. Andersson and the Svenska Institutet, for permission to quote extensively from the booklet *Archives in Sweden.* All inquirers would do well to obtain this booklet. In research into Swedish as into English genealogy (see chapter on England), it is of the greatest importance to know the name of the immigrant ancestor and to have the American side properly connected and ready.

## THE PUBLIC RECORD SYSTEM

This is under the control of the Ministry for Ecclesiastical Affairs and Education. It comprises the National Archives, seven provincial and county archives, and two municipal archives. The National Archives (Riksarkivet) corresponds to the Archives Nationales in Paris or the Public Record Office in London. Thus it holds the written documents of the government, the higher courts, and the central administration from the earliest times until modern days, and is the agency through which this material is placed at the disposal of the various administrative organs and of research workers. The National Archives is, moreover, the supreme authority for the public record system; under it are the regional offices—the seven provincial and county archives—and it exercises supervision over the formation, listing, and preservation of the records of the country's civil administration. The relationship between the National Archives and the central administration is paralleled by that between the provincial archives and the local administration: each of these preserves the older documents of the local administration and the legal authorities in its own area and keeps watch over the more recent documents which have not yet been delivered to it. The military archive system has its own authority, the Archives of the Army and Navy.

Because research is likely to begin with the local records, the account of this part of the Swedish archives precedes the account of the National Archives. For purposes of clarity, the following designations will be used throughout even though they do not exactly correspond with the Swedish terms: regional archives, for *landsarkiv;* district archives, for *länsarkiv;* and city archives, for *stadsarkiv.* A listing of the various archives is appended.

In the event that the home parish of the emigrant or the next of kin is known, it is possible to turn to the pastor's office in that parish if the record desired dates from the past one hundred years. (A listing of the clergy of the Church of Sweden as well as of Swedish officials in general, with their addresses, may be found in a catalogue entitled *Sveriges Statskalender,* which is available at some Swedish consulates. Information on the clergy of the Church of Sweden is listed under the heading "Ecklesiastikstaten"). Genealogical information not available in the parish archives must be sought in regional, district, and city archives (*lands-, läns-,* or *stadsarkiv*).

Subordinate to the Riksarkivet are seven *landsarkiv* (regional archives) situated in central towns in different provinces. They have in their charge the most important records for the genealogist: the parish registers (baptisms, marriages, deaths, and burials), the parish catechization lists, the inventories, the schedules of population, and the court records, each for its district. There are also two *stadsarkiv* (city archives), in Stockholm and Malmö. Addresses are given at end of the chapter.

## CIVIL REGISTRATION

This has for many years been entrusted to the clergy of the Established Church. General directives for the keeping of church records were first issued in the Church Act of 1686. Church records from an earlier period are therefore found only in a small number of cases. It is obvious that by no means all existing church records go back to the end of the seventeenth century, for in spite of fairly good supervision many such records have been destroyed or lost in the course of time.

From the above paragraph it can be seen that civil registration in Sweden, like the ecclesiastical registration in England, does not always begin at the date when it was ordered to be made.

In addition to the records of birth, marriage, and death, there are in the church records the notations of transfers into and out of the parish, and the communion records. The character of these documents is fairly obvious from their names. The household examination rolls (*husförhörslängder*) may require further explanation. These records, which from about 1895 have been called parish registers, are of considerable importance for genealogical research. At first their purpose was to record the knowledge of the Christian faith possessed by the parishioners; these entries were kept with varying completeness. From about 1750 these examination rolls give a more complete account of the population in the parish. They contain entries for each separate household with all of its members.

Following a reform in 1946, the keeping of church registers was changed in certain respects. In addition to the "church book," a parish ledger was introduced containing a separate personal record (*personakt*) for each one registered in the parish. Each record contains an extract of all the pertinent data appearing in the church register. When a person moves, this document is sent to the pastor's office in the parish to which the move is made; thus a record follows the citizen throughout life. If he dies or leaves the country, the document is sent to the Central Bureau of Statistics (Statistiska Centralbyrån). In the archives of this office (see below) the personal documents are kept in two categories: the registry of deaths and the registry of emigration. For the latter category, there is a supplementary register arranged according to dates of birth. It may be added that, as a result of a procedure now followed in the administration of each *län* (district), there are records of addresses alphabetically arranged for all persons presently registered in the *län*.

The general rule is that local records are passed to the regional archives or the district archives when they are one hundred years old; more recent records are left in the care of the appropriate local agency. However, this time limit is obviously rather flexible. Information regarding further limits for the delivery to the archives of specific local records can naturally be obtained from the archive authorities. Some forty Swedish parishes (most of them in Dalarna) have received permission to retain all their church records.

In the regional and district archives there are, in addition to the older church archives, many other records which are of importance for genealogical research. Here special mention may be made of the records of the lower courts with their especially valuable inventories of the estates of deceased persons (*bouppteckningar*). A considerable portion of these inventories is registered in alphabetical order in the regional archives. Here also are the records of court cases and decisions (*domböcker*) and the so-called "minor protocols" (*småprotokollen*), consisting of transfers of ownership of real property and records of marriage settlements, mortgages, and guardianships.

The regional and district archives also receive the records of the administration of the *län* and *härad*, which are of special interest for genealogy because they contain census rolls (*mantalslängder*), which are lists of the population made at the annual census, although they are often incomplete for earlier periods. They also contain the real property books (*jordeböcker*), which are lists of landed property together with tax and fiscal data and also some information about their owners. These records begin at the time when the *län* administration was organized (about 1630) and thus go further back than the church archives.

It is clear from the above that many of the records of Sweden have their counterpart in England. For example, the inventories of the estates of the dead correspond closely to the Inquisitiones post Mortem mentioned in the chapter on England.

# THE NATIONAL ARCHIVES

For a long period the National Archives was the central record office of Sweden before there were deliveries to the National Archives of material from central administration boards (*ämbetsverk*) outside the Royal Chancery. The latter was the Chancery of the Council of State, which began in the thirteenth century and was reorganized in 1634. The records of the Royal Chancery form a major part of the contents of the National Archives, which is divided into five sections. No comprehensive handbook on the Archives exists, but work on one is proceeding.

The various collections of the National Archives naturally contain a great deal of material which can be used by genealogists. The National Archives (Riksarkivet) is the central authority for the entire archival system in Sweden. It functions in part as a repository for archives of various types, primarily those of the Royal Chancellery (the Supreme Executive branch), and of certain central administrative agencies. Its collections also include many other archives, both from official and private sources, of unparalleled importance for the history of the realm. Here as well are to be found both genealogical collections and documents concerning particular persons. Especially when it is a question of persons employed by the state or whose affairs have come to the notice of the King in Council, valuable information can often be secured here. Records of qualifications, applications, and petitions of different kinds are of special interest, as are records of the settlement of Crown stipends (*likvidationerna*) found in the Cameral Archives.

*First section* contains some of the central series in the Royal Chancery, such as the National Registry. The latter contains copies of the documents on different subjects emanating from the king and the government. There are other documents which may well be of interest to the genealogical researcher. All documents coming in from authorities and from members of the general public are there. Following the division of the Chancery into departments, these documents were called departmental papers (*departements-akter*). Documents from private persons were formerly arranged to some extent according to subject, in series entitled "Biographica," etc. Documents from the archives of the Supreme Court are also included in these series.

*Second section.* Many constitutional documents, such as the Constitution of 1809, are here; also the national archives which deal with foreign affairs. The Ministry of Foreign Affairs (Utrikesdepartementet) keeps its documents for the last five decades on its own premises and in the care of its own archivists. Foreign research workers may gain access to this material by special permission.

The collections dealing with former Swedish possessions in Europe, under such titles as "Livonica," "Pomeranica," "Bremensia," and others, contain documents addressed to the government from the Swedish authorities in those areas, as well as other documents concerning these provinces from different sources.

*Third section.* This contains the archives of the Swedish kings and the royal family, with the exception of the archives of Gustavus III and the Bernadotte dynasty. It also contains the archives of the different estates of the Riksdag, with the exception of the archives of the nobles, which are kept at the House of the Nobility (Riddarhuset). Until 1865 the Swedish Riksdag consisted of four estates: the nobility, the clergy, the burghers, and the peasants.

There are also in the third section the collections of a number of private papers, including many dealing with the families and estates of the Swedish nobility during its political and cultural heyday; these have been presented to or deposited in the National Archives. In this connection, reference may be made to the archives of Count Magnus Gabriel de la Gardie (1622–86, Chancellor during the reign of Charles XI), and to the Skokloster and Rydboholm collections, which, among other things, contain documents dealing with the Brahe, Wrangel, and Königsmark families as well as a number of early manuscripts of great value.

*Fourth section.* This includes the older portions of the archives of a number of central administrative boards (see above). These boards are government offices which are separate from the Royal Chancery; for example, the Statskantoret (Treasury) and the Kammarrätten (Audit Court). The fourth section also contains the archives of the Svea Hovrätt (High Court), which was the supreme judiciary after the Crown in former times. This court was set up in 1614, and its archives also contain copies of the "judgment books" of the lower courts, which were submitted for inspection; these often fill the gaps which are found in the archives of the lower courts. Among the important biographical material in the High Court archives may be mentioned the inventories of the possessions of deceased members of the nobility for the years 1737–1916. There are, however, a number of *ämbetsverk* with exceptionally valuable archives which have not been transferred to the National Archives but are retained by the boards themselves.

*Fifth section.* This includes the Kammararkivet (Exchequer Archives). A copy of the census rolls and the real property books is also to be found in the Cameral Archives (Kammararkivet), which now form part of the National Archives in Stockholm. Some real property books, however, are in the archives of the Cameral College (Kammarkollegiet). The Cameral Archives also contain many other types of accounts which were originally submitted for auditing and which now are of the greatest value for research. From the point of view of genealogical research, the available material in the Cameral Archives cannot compare with that of the church registers, because family connections and migrations can only be cleared up with difficulty, if at all, with the help of the former. Thus, the use of the collections in the Cameral Archives is to be regarded as to some extent auxiliary to genealogical research. Nevertheless, the material has value for such research because it fills up gaps in the data in local archives and because it goes further back in time. From the period before the establishment of the *län* administrations (that is, before 1630) the Cameral Archives contain bailiff accounts (*fogderäkenskaper*), the so-called "provincial acts" (*landskapshandlingarna*), which extend from about 1540 to 1630 and which contain real property records, tithe rolls, etc. Under certain favorable conditions these may serve to complete the inquiry into a family history. When, for instance, information is sought on the ownership of a particular farm, research can be carried out advantageously at the Cameral Archives.

## THE REGIONAL ARCHIVES

It is to the regional archives that records are transferred, after one hundred years have passed, from the county administrative boards (*länsstyrelsen*), and other records come from the *häradsrätter* and *rådstuvurätter* (lower courts for the countryside and the towns) and from the ecclesiastical organization (*kyrkoarkiven*). These latter are, beyond comparison, the records in the regional archives that are most used by research workers, especially those engaged in genealogical research, which is becoming steadily more popular.

There are five provincial archives, and two corresponding institutions, known as county archives, for smaller districts. The provincial archives for southern Sweden—Skåne, Halland, and Blekinge—are situated at the university city of Lund, where they were established in 1903. The provincial archives at Uppsala, the other historic university city in Sweden, were established in the same year and are housed in the old castle. The Uppsala archives cover the administrative districts of Stockholm, Uppsala, Södermanland, Örebro, Västmanland, and Kopparberg and thus have a very large area to serve. The provincial archives at Vadstena (1899), which also have their home in a sixteenth-century castle, covered the counties of Östergötland, Kalmar, Jönköping, and Kronoberg, while the provincial archives at Göteborg (1911) exist for the administrative districts of Göteborg and Bohus, Skaraborg, Älvsborg, and Värmland. The latest provincial archives to be established are those at Härnösand (1937), which serve the greater part of northern Sweden. The two county archives at Östersund and Visby cover districts of special historical traditions (the counties of Jämtland and Gotland, respectively).

## THE ARMED FORCES
## AND DIPLOMATIC CORPS

For officers and to some extent for enlisted personnel, the military rolls and other documents in the War Archives (Krigsarkivet) constitute important sources. Valuable information about diplomats, and about Swedes in general, who reside outside the country can sometimes be secured from the archives of the Foreign Office (Kungliga Utrikesdepartementets Arkiv). For members of the nobility, the genealogical collections of the House of Nobility (Riddarhuset) should be consulted. At the Central Bureau of Statistics (Statistiska Centralbyråns Arkiv) there are extracts (*nominativa utdrag*) from registers of birth, marriage, and death for each year from 1860 to 1947 and extracts from household examinations rolls (*husförhörslängder*) and parish registers for each ten-year period from 1860 onward. In addition, there are so-called summary reports on population. In these there are, among other things, lists containing the full name of persons entering and leaving the kingdom. In these lists, in addition to the year of birth, the country to which or from which the migration took place is also stated. (See above regarding the personal records extracted from "church books," which are kept in these archives.)

## PRIVATE ARCHIVES

There are large quantities of these in Sweden, provided it is understood that by "private" is meant records which are not part of the state system or under the control of the state. Among these are the municipal archives. These are the archives of what are known as the popular movements, for example, the Labor, or Socialist, movement, nonconformist movements, temperance societies, women's organizations, co-operative movements, the Farmers' Confederation, and the organizations of salaried workers. The first of these has its own central records office, known as the Arbetarrörelsens Arkiv (archives of the Labor movement), in Stockholm, together with twenty-five branch offices in the provinces. In records such as these the value to the inquirer will be incidental, that is, giving information regarding someone who was holding office or was prominent in the movement, but there will not be specifically genealogical information.

Many of the larger Swedish industrial undertakings have considerable records.

Reference should also be made to the family and country-estate archives which are preserved in their original homes in various parts of the country. Some of these, however, have been temporarily sent to the central archives for arrangement and listing. Among these are the records at Ericsberg in Södermanland (the Bonde, Stenbock, Oxenstierna, and Tessin families), Esplunda in Närke (the Mörner family), and Kavlås in Västergötland (the Von Essen family). Among others may be mentioned Stafsund in Uppland (containing, among other items, the Fersen collection), Trolle-Ljungby (the Trolle-Wachtmeister and Von Brinkman families) and Kulla-Gunnarstorp (the Scheffer family) in Skåne, and Löfstad (Von Fersen and Piper) in Östergötland. A feature of the country as a whole is the number of archives which are preserved in all parts of Sweden in the *herrgårdar* (smaller manor houses) and which often contain documents which give insight into cultural developments and politics, biography, and economic history which would otherwise be difficult to obtain. Unfortunately, these manorial and family archives have not yet been thoroughly listed, although the desirability of doing so has long been realized.

Among archives with primarily local associations, there are, in addition to the manorial archives mentioned above, the records from farmsteads. In some places, particularly in Dalarna with its wealth of traditions, these farm archives have been listed and have been found to be well deserving of this work. Such records may have a value far beyond their utility for purposes of biography and local history. There have been Swedish farmers in the Riksdag for centuries, and the records from a farm may therefore prove to have political importance by reason of the memoirs, diary entries, and letters they may contain. The "letters from America" preserved in many Swedish homes are often of considerable importance for the study of Swedish emigration during the latter part of the nineteenth century.

The Swedish Historical Association has, with the support of the National Archives, proposed the setting up of a government committee to inquire into the problems connected with private archives. A great catalogue of the private archives in the public collections and in the hands of families or institutions has been made by Dr. Otto Walde, Uppsala. It is housed in the Uppsala University Library.

## SOCIETIES FOR GENEALOGICAL RESEARCH

*Genealogiska Föreningen, Riksförening för Släktforskning.* PRESIDENT: Lieutenant Colonel Börje Furtenbach, Gyllenstiernsgatan 17, Stockholm Ö. SECRETARY: Captain Lennart Zielfelt, Box 780, Skarblacka. FOUNDED: 1933. PUBLICATION: *Släkt och Hävd,* which appears three times each year.

*Föreningen för Släktforskning,* Olof Hermelins Väg 7, Stocksund. The purpose of this society is to begin and maintain the collaboration between persons and parties interested in the questions of genealogy, especially by publishing a periodical, *Genealogisk Tidskrift,* in which the results of genealogical researches can be published and questions belonging to this matter can be discussed. In addition, information is given to nonmembers by correspondence on how to undertake genealogical research, and which publications, libraries, archives, and record offices should be consulted. The Society also works out genealogical tables for anyone who wishes it to do so. Membership fee is 12.50 Swedish crowns yearly. CHAIRMAN: Jean Silfving, Börjessonsvägen 44, Stockholm-Bromma. SECRETARY: Mrs. Elsa Dalström-Söderberg, Olof Hermelins Väg 7, Stocksund.

*L'Institut d'Héraldique Communale Suédois.* SECRETARY: Mr. Uno Lindgren, Lindåsa Alvsjö.

*Personhistoriska Samfundet* (Society of Biography and Genealogy). SECRETARY: Docenten Bertil Broome, Krigsarkivet, Stockholm 80. Extensive details are available about this society and are given below.

In 1876, *Svenska Autografsällskapet* (*Swedish Society for Collection of Autographs*) was constituted as a society for special contact between some owners of large estates and learned circles in Stockholm. The purpose was to protect and save old and new manuscripts from destruction.

In February 1879 there appeared the first number of *Svenska Autografsällskapets Tidskrift* (*Review of the Swedish Society for Collection of Autographs*). In the rules for the Society in 1883, the sphere of interest was enlarged to include biography, genealogy, and heraldry. In 1898 the name of the review was changed to *Personhistorisk Tidskrift* (*Review of Biography and Genealogy*), and in 1905 the name of the Society was changed to *Personhistoriska Samfundet* (*Society of Biography and Genealogy*). *Personhistorisk Tidskrift* had appeared yearly since 1898 in volumes of about two hundred pages, containing biographical and genealogical essays and notices, and a section with critical reviews of biographical and genealogical literature.

The foundation and growth of *Svenska Autografsällskapet* was due to the increased interest in Swedish genealogy during the latter part of the nineteenth century. The founder of modern Swedish genealogical research, Gabriel Anrep, published in 1858–64 *Svenska Adelns Ättar-Taflor* (*Genealogies of the Swedish Nobility*), Vols. I–IV, which was mainly a print of defective genealogies belonging to the House of Nobility. Swedish genealogical research had, however, made great progress by the publication of this work.

Anrep then worked on the genealogy of common families and published in 1871–75 *Svenska Slägtboken* (*Swedish Family Book*), Vols. I–III, containing many well-known families and a few families of foreign nobility (not introduced in the Swedish House of Nobility). Anrep's contribution to the genealogy of Swedish common families was continued, in 1885–87, by Victor Örnberg in his four-volume *Svensk Slägt-Kalender* (*Swedish Family Calendar*). He produced a further work, in 1889–1908, under the title of *Svenska Ättartal* (*Swedish Genealogies*), in ten volumes. These fourteen volumes of Örnberg, all full of family information, were in 1939 supplied with a common index, containing also names of persons married into the families and many persons mentioned in the footnotes.

The work on the genealogy of common families was continued by Gustaf Elgenstierna with *Svenska Släktkalendern* (1913–50), in fourteen volumes. It contains in all about 1460 families; it is planned as a present list but has genealogical introductions.

Another book of the same type as those mentioned above is K. A. Leijonhufvud's *Ny Svensk Släktbok* (*New Swedish Family Book*) (1906), which contains about 160 families.

A great deal of genealogical data is available in the registers of special professions or of students, and especially significant for the genealogy of the common families are, of course, the series of collections of diocesan annals.

A short general description of Swedish genealogy and of the most useful handbooks and calendars is given in a chapter of S. E. Bring's *Bibliografisk Handbok till Sveriges Historia* (*Bibliographical Handbook to Sweden's History*) (1934). Another good bibliography is S. Agren's *Svensk Biografisk Uppslagslitteratur* (*Swedish Biographical Works*) (1929). A good help in searching after a special family are the indexes to J. A. Almquist's *Svensk Genealogisk Litteratur* (*Swedish Genealogical Literature*) (1905), and J. Wretman's *Släktvetenskapen Medhänsyn till Svensk Forskning* (*Family Science with Regard to Swedish Research*) (1924).

In 1925–36 were published nine large volumes, *Den Introducerade Svenska Adelns Ättartavlor* (*The Genealogies of the Introduced Swedish Nobility*), edited by Gustaf Elgenstierna. This great work was derived from the old genealogies of the House of the Nobility, but they have been considerably revised. The work is arranged in tables and gives most important data of everyone—birth, death, marriage, schools, career, orders, and so on—and it is a reference book of invaluable practical worth. As the title suggests, this work contains only noble families introduced in the House of the Nobility (this formal introduction was not enacted before the year 1625). Several important noble families which died out before the seventeenth century are therefore not treated. Some help is given in B. Schlegel's and C. A. Klingspor's *Den med Sköldebref Förlänade Men Ej å Riddarhuset Introducerade Svenska Adelns Ättartaflor* (*The Genealogies of the Swedish Nobility Who Have Been Invested with Letters Patent of Nobility But Are Not Introduced in the House of the Nobility*) (1875), but the work is now in many ways antiquated.

A modern critical work about the higher medieval noble families is in course of publication. The first part was published in 1957 entitled *Aldre Svenska Frälsesläkter. Ättartavlor* (*Older Swedish Noble Families. Genealogies*), edited by Dr. Folke Wernstedt.

Still living, unintroduced noble families (for example, those with foreign nobility) are to be found in two series of present registers, sometimes with complete genealogies. They are T. von Gerber's *Sveriges Ointroducerade Adels Kalender* (*Sweden's Unintroduced Nobility's Calendar*) Vols. I–IX (1912–35), and *Kalender över Ointroducerade Adels Förening* (*Calender of the Unintroduced Nobility's Society*) Vols. I–X (1935–58).

For the introduced nobility, there appears yearly a register called *Sveriges Ridderskaps och Adels Kalender* (*Calendar of the Swedish Nobility*), the eighty-second annual volume of which is now published, 1959.

*Personhistoriska Institutet.* Sweden was the first country in Europe to publish a large national biographical dictionary, the *Biographiskt Lexikon.* It appeared in a chief series of twenty-three volumes in 1835–57, and an additional series of ten volumes in 1857–1907. The dictionary has, however, great shortcomings, especially in articles concerning persons in the Middle Ages and the sixteenth and seventeenth centuries. A modern scientific series, *Svenskt Biografiskt Lexikon* (*Swedish Biographical Dictionary*), was started in 1917 by Professor Bertil Boëthius, chief of the Swedish Public Record Office, 1944–50, and fifteen volumes have been published (from *A* to *Fe*). Since 1937 the editor has been Professor Bengt Hildebrand, who is also chairman of *Personhistoriska Samfundet.* In recent years, as a support for the publication of the dictionary and for biographical research in general, there has grown up a biographical institution called Personhistoriska Institutet. This institute has the same locality in the Riksarkivet (the Public Record Office) and the same staff as the dictionary. It has a growing library and some important indexes—a continually increasing card index (about 158,000 cards) alphabetically ordered under names of persons and families. This index gives references to the literature and to some extent to other records.

Another modern biographical Swedish dictionary, *Svenska Män och Kvinnor* (*Swedish Men and Women*), was published in 1942–55 in eight volumes by a private publishing house and is now completed. It deals mainly with persons now living and with those who have died recently and is in many ways a very useful reference book.

## HERALDRY AND NOBILITY

There is in Sweden an official known as the *Riksheraldiker,* whose present task it is to draw up or examine drafts of coats of arms for new towns and also to examine coats of arms which are to be fixed on public buildings, flag standards, and coins. The *Riksheraldiker* also makes drafts for private individuals of seals, stamps, etc. In earlier days he was called upon to make drafts of coats of arms for those who were made noblemen, barons, or counts.

A record of acknowledged Swedish nobility is kept at Riddarhuset (the House of the Nobility) according to the rules laid down by the king and nobility in 1866. The Swedish nobility is nowadays, from a legal point of view, a private association. A certain amount of research is done by officials of Riddarhuset in Stockholm. Riddarhuset is governed by a board, *Riddarhusdirektionen* (the Directorate of the House of the Nobility), consisting of a president and six members, appointed during each ordinary meeting of the nobility. This body has to look after any rights of the nobility and to execute any decisions. It also has to administer properties and funds. If anybody is raised to the status of a nobleman by the king, it is the duty of *Riddarhusdirektionen* to ascertain that the conditions have been fulfilled entitling this person to be "introduced into Riddarhuset," which is the formal procedure of acknowledgment. In this connection it may be of interest to know that Sven Hedin is the last Swede who has been made a nobleman. This was in 1902. There is an association of "nonintroduced nobility," known as Ointroducerade Adels Förening, whose task it is to carry out genealogical research and draw up genealogical tables in respect to nonintroduced noble families in Sweden. The secretary is Captain J. Treschow, Kommendorsgatan 20B, Stockholm.

GENERAL NOTE: It should be pointed out that German script was used in Swedish documents until the beginning of the nineteenth century; therefore, the reading of old documents may require special training.

## SUMMARY

By way of summary, it may be said that the opportunities for genealogical research in Sweden are relatively good. Both the church archives and the property archives go far back and are fairly well preserved. Nevertheless, the prospects of achieving satisfactory results in any particular case must be judged with caution, as many obstacles and difficulties may arise during the course of the work. In addition, it should be borne in mind that this kind of research is often time-consuming, and therefore the costs should not be underestimated.

## ADDRESSES OF ARCHIVES

*The National Archives (Riksarkivet), Arkivgatan 3, Stockholm 2.*

*The Cameral Archives (Kammararkivet), Birger Jarls Torg 13, Stockholm 2.*

*Regional Archives (Landsarkivet) at Uppsala, for the districts (län) of Stockholm, Uppsala, Södermanland, Örebro, Västmanland, and Kopparberg. Address: Slottet, Uppsala.*

*Regional Archives (Landsarkivet) at Vadstena, for the districts (län) of Östergötland, Jönköping, Kronoberg, and Kalmar. Address: Slottet, Vadstena.*

*Regional Archives (Landsarkivet) at Lund, for the districts (län) of Blekinge, Kristianstad, Malmöhus, and Halland. Address: Dalbyvägen 4, Lund.*

*Regional Archives (Landsarkivet) at Göteborg, for the districts (län) of Göteborg and Bohus, Älvsborg, Skaraborg, and Värmland. Address: Geijersgatan 1, Göteborg.*

*Regional Archives (Landsarkivet) at Härnösand, for the districts (län) of Gävleborg, Västernorrland, Västerbotten, and Norrbotten. Address: Nybrogatan 17, Härnösand.*

*District Archives (Länsarkivet) at Visby, for the district (län) of Gotland. Address: Visborgsgatan 1, Visby.*

*District Archives (Länsarkivet) at Östersund, for the district (län) of Jämtland. Address: Museiplan, Östersund.*

*City Archives (Stadsarkivet) of Stockholm. Address: Rådhuset, Stockholm 8.*

*City Archives (Stadsarkivet) of Malmö. Address: Kyrkogatan 6, Malmö.*

*City Archives (Stadsarkivet) of Borås. Address: Stadshuset, Borås.*

*City Archives (Stadsarkivet) of Västerås. Address: Rådhuset, Västerås.*

*The Archives of the Foreign Office (Kungliga Utrikesdepartementetsarkiv). Address: Gustav Adolfs Torg, Stockholm 16.*

*The War Archives (Kungliga Krigsarkivet). Address: Banérgatan 64, Stockholm Ö.*

*The Archives of the Central Bureau of Statistics (Statistiska Centralbyråns Arkiv). Address: Linnégatan 87, Stockholm Ö.*

*The Archives of the House of the Nobility (Riddarhusets Arkiv). Address: Riddarhuset, Stockholm 2.*

# DENMARK

## REGISTRATION OF BIRTHS, MARRIAGES, AND DEATHS

This was originally kept in the various ecclesiastical parishes, and many parish registers exist from about 1600. In 1645 the obligation for the clergy to keep parish registers became statutory. From 1813–14 it was ordered that the registers be kept in two copies, one by the parish clergyman and the other by the teacher in the parish. The keeping of the registers was also made more systematic from 1814.

Up to 1891 the parish registers were collected in the provincial archives (*landsarkiver*), of which there are four, namely Aabenraa (South Jutland), Viborg (North Jutland), Odense (Fünen), and Copenhagen (Zealand, Lolland-Falster, Bornholm, as well as the former Danish colonies) (see below). Since 1891, one copy of the parish registers is delivered, thirty years after being finished, to the regional archives. A catalogue exists of all the parish registers in the archives. This is a publication, *Vejledende Arkivregistraturer* (*Designation of the Archives*), edited by the Rigsarkivet, (the Public Record Office). The fifth volume gives a complete designation of the church registers (*kirkeboger*) of Denmark. There is also a catalogue of all the registers in the archives, in *Danmarks Kirkeboger*, by S. Nygard (1933).

## THE PUBLIC RECORD OFFICE
## (THE RIGSARKIVET)

The Danish State Archives Department was set up by a law of March 3, 1889, which ordered that there be established a Public Record Office, consisting of a principal office at Copenhagen and three provincial offices, or *landsarkiver,* which since 1907 have been established in Copenhagen for Zealand and Lolland-Falster, in Odense for Fünen, and in Viborg for North Jutland. In addition to these, there is now a provincial office at Aabenraa for the South Jutland province, which was set up by a law of February 28, 1931, and opened in 1933. The head office, which has always been called the Record Office, came to embrace the old private archives, and in 1883 it took over, with all other records produced by the central administration, the archives of the kingdom (that is, the civilian ministry archives, formed in 1861 by the combining of the archives of the Chancellery and the House of Representatives). The provincial archives, on the other hand, act as depositories for the local government archives, including also those of the provincial county towns, while Copenhagen has its own special city records. The Copenhagen University archives were formerly deposited in the University Library but are now in the Public Record Office.

The War Office keeps the Army Archives, but those previous to 1868 are to be found in the Public Record Office.

Hours of opening: Public Record Office, 10 A.M.–5 P.M.; Provincial Office, Copenhagen, 11 A.M.–5 P.M.; Odense, 10 A.M.–4 P.M.; Copenhagen City Archives, 10 A.M.–4 P.M.; Viborg, 9 A.M.–noon and 2 P.M.–5 P.M.; Aabenraa, 9 A.M.–noon and 1 P.M.–4 P.M.; Army Archives, 11 A.M.–4 P.M. The genealogical researcher will, at any rate, for the dates up to 1863, be able to obtain the best genealogical material provided by the state and municipal governments. If anyone is unable to visit the particular office in which the documents required for his investigation are located, he can, under certain conditions, have these loaned at another office, or in a city or central library, which has fireproof storage space. Especially fragile or important records are, however, still excluded from this loan system. The latter category includes: parish registers, land registers, books of deeds and pledges, electoral and city hall registers, and census information. Formerly it was sought by law to regulate archive material in artificial systems, on the same lines as the arrangement of printed books in a library. It is now being realized in Denmark that the arrangement of archives should be the same as that adopted by France, that is, of preserving the archive ·material in its natural combinations. This principle is called the Native Principle, the Principle of Origin, or the Provenience Principle. This has now become the basis for all Danish record activity. The archives of any institution are held as a distinct stock. They are arranged as much as possible in accordance with their original layout, which as a rule will correspond with the procedure of the institution. After a register, or a series of registers, are placed the documents relating to it; after a series of land registers, similarly, are placed other documents pertaining to them. Thus, every document has its appointed or natural place where it will normally be found and where its contents and its importance are most readily understood.

## WILLS

These are found in the Record Office in Copenhagen, at least as regards the older wills. They formerly had to be confirmed by the king, and copies are entered in the Kancelliregistranter, one for each province. From 1849, wills have been registered by the Ministry of Justice. More modern wills are kept by the local notaries. In the provincial towns, the judge is the notary. There is in Copenhagen, with the notariate, a central index for all the wills drawn up by Danish notaries after 1932. Inquiries regarding wills should be addressed simply to: Rigsarkivet, Copenhagen.

## HERALDRY

There is nothing in Denmark which corresponds to the College of Arms. Those who are granted the principal Danish order, the Order of the Elephant, or the highest class (Knight Grand Cross) of the Order of Dannebrog, are supposed to have a coat of arms. This is to be put on their stall plate in the Chapel of the Danish Orders in the Castle of Frederiksborg in North Zealand. Copies of these coats of arms are found in the rolls of knights, kept by the

Ordenskapitul, of which Dr. Albert Fabritius is the historiographer.

There is not, however, a great interest in heraldry in Denmark, and there has never been a corporate body of Heralds as in England or Scotland. I am obliged to Dr. Ole Rostock for the following note, which sets out the position.

"Coats of arms in ancient days were either granted by the kings by patents in which was depicted the coat of arms. This was done in connection with ennobling, but some royal officials had letters patent confirming coats of arms without nobility. The letters patent were registered in ministries, "chanceries," and the granted arms were never duplicated, but there were never any visitations and no legal protection. However, some coats of arms were never granted, but simply taken. If "taken" coats of arms were duplicated, the oldest "owner" might appeal to the king, who decided to whom the arms "legally" belonged. Nowadays it is possible to have arms legally protected by registering them as a "trade-mark" for a family society in the *Official Gazette,* but that is the only way.

"Regarding the coats of arms for the knights of the Danish Orders of Chivalry, in fact nobody "grants" a coat of arms. When a person is appointed Grand Cross of Dannebrog, the Chapter of the Royal Orders asks for a coat of arms to be painted on the stall plate and hung in Frederiksborg Castle. If the person has an old family coat of arms he of course can use this, but if not, a request is made and an offer to let the painter of the Royal Chapter create one. The same applies for the Order of the Elephant, but since this order is principally not for commoners, the problem is not so real. In some cases, as in that of General Dwight D. Eisenhower, a coat of arms had to be created, and the same for General Dewing, but Sir Winston Churchill and Viscount Montgomery both have coats of arms in England, so they are shown on their stall plates at Frederiksborg."

## BOOKS

In this connection, the work *Danmarks Adels Aarbog* is particularly interesting. The 1958 issue was the seventy-fifth. This book, which is about the size of the *Almanach de Gotha,* or the *Libro d'Oro* of Italy, is a combination, as it were, of features which are found in *Burke's Peerage* and *Burke's Landed Gentry* (see chapter on England). In other words, families both titled and untitled are included. The nobility of Denmark are mentioned, with a list of the living members of the noble families. In addition, families are given which are extinct. Illustrations of family portraits are given, along with block illustrations of shields of arms.

The *Yearbook* is published by an association and is edited by Sven Houmøller and Albert Fabritius. The publisher is J. H. Schultz, Copenhagen. We learn from the book that there is a confederation of the Danish nobility. In the 1958 edition there is a list of the noble families whose arms and complete genealogical tables are found in the seventy-five issues; there is also a list of the families which have become extinct since 1884. Of genealogical tables, 724 have now been printed, in which 705 of the Danish noble families have been dealt with.

# ICELAND

## INTRODUCTION

Iceland was settled and colonized in the years 874–930 A.D. by Norwegians. A republic was established in 930, when a Central Parliament for all Iceland, the Althing, was established at Thingvellir. The Republic came to an end in 1262–64, when the Icelanders made a Treaty of Union with the Crown of Norway, in which they accepted its supremacy. In 1380 Iceland came under the Danish Crown. (see historical introduction to the Scandinavian countries, on page 45). Finally, in 1944, a plebiscite was held to determine the future form of government, and as a result, the Republic of Iceland was proclaimed on June 17, 1944.

## REGISTRATION OF BIRTHS, MARRIAGES, AND DEATHS

There has never been civil registration of births, marriages, and deaths in Iceland.

In 1735 a royal decree was issued to the two bishops of Iceland, commanding them to instruct the clergy in their dioceses to keep registers of births, christenings, confirmations, marriages, and deaths in their various parishes. The reaction to this decree was rather slow among the clergy, so another decree was issued, on July 1, 1746. This latter decree was more successfully enforced, and it may be said that there are now extant almost uninterrupted sets of parish registers from that time down to the present day.

An important point in the 1746 decree was that all these registers should remain in the parishes and not be removed by the incumbents when they left for other posts, as had very often been the case before. Another important item of the 1746 decree was that the vicars were instructed to superintend and report on the state of literacy or illiteracy of their parishioners, especially young people.

The registers of births, deaths, and marriages are still kept by the clergy, who send their annual returns to the Statistical Bureau of Iceland.

All parish records are deposited with the National Archives in Reykjavik.

The National Archives (Thjodskjalasafn Islands) was established in 1899 and became the depository for all state archives, both ecclesiastical and secular.

## COATS OF ARMS

There are no arrangements about coats of arms in Iceland. There is not and never has been any hereditary nobility in Iceland, and although we know that several Icelanders were knighted by the kings of Norway and Denmark in the thirteenth to sixteenth centuries, knowledge of their coats of arms is now very vague.

## WILLS

Wills may be registered with a notary public, always a government official in Iceland. In such cases, copies of the wills will ultimately be deposited in the National Archives together with that official's other documents.

## CENSUS

In Iceland a census took place a century earlier than in Britain. This was the 1703 census, and it was taken between December 1702 and June 1703 by sheriffs and clergymen. According to the letter of instructions, the census was to include all persons living in Iceland and to state their names, social status and occupation, place of residence, and their age. This census was published by the Statistical Bureau of Iceland under the title *Manntal á Islandi ário . . . 1703 . . .* (Reykjavik, 1924–47, XVIII, 650 pp., 4to). There is a copy of this census in the Icelandic Collection in the University College Library, Gower Street, London W.C. 1.

There still exist fragments from 1729 and 1762, and a complete general census of 1801. The latter two have not yet been published, whereas that of 1729, which is very incomplete, was printed with the 1703 census.

The 1816 census gives places of birth. This information was not given in any of the earlier censuses. This census is in process of publication, three out of four parts having appeared so far. The title is *Manntal á Islandi 1816 . . .* (Akureyri, 1947). Copy in University College Library (see above).

## ICELANDERS IN AMERICA

The following works are helpful in the above matter:

1. *Saga Islendinga i Vesturheimi (The History of the Icelanders in America).* Volume III and onward are compiled by Prof. Tryggvi Oleson of Winnipeg.

2. *Almanak Fyrir 1895,* I (published by Utgefandi), by Olafur S. Thorgeirsson of Winnipeg. This contains a wealth of personal historical and genealogical material about the first settlers in Canada and the United States.

3. Also, the following are useful as having an important bearing on the settlement of certain districts:

Thorleifur Jackson, *Brot of Landnáms Sögu Nýja-Islands (Brief History of the New Iceland Settlement)* (Winnipeg: The Columbia Press, Ltd., 1919).

Thorleifur Jackson, *Frá Aistri til Vesturs. Framhald af Landnáms—Sögu Nýja-Islands (From East to West. Continuation of the History of the New Iceland Settlement)* (Winnipeg: The Columbia Press, Ltd., 1921).

Thorleifur Jackson, *Framhald á Landnámssögu Nýja-Islands*

(*Continuation of the History of the Settlement of New Iceland*) (Winnipeg: The Columbia Press, Ltd., 1923).

Thorstína Jackson, *Saga Islendinga i Nordur-Dakota (History of the Icelanders in North Dakota)* (Winnipeg: The City Printing & Publishing Co., 1926).

# FINLAND

## INTRODUCTION

The Finns appear in the eighth century as a group under that name. For many centuries they were connected with the Swedes. It was by Sweden that they were conquered in 1157 and from Sweden they received Christianity and civilization. From the Swedes, the Finns received the same civil rights as they themselves possessed. In the sixteenth century Finland became Protestant, and today 95 per cent of the population belongs to the Evangelical Lutheran Church. The largest religious minority group, that of the Greek Orthodox Church, numbers only 70,000 out of a total population of 4½ million. The various Free Churches—Congregationalist, Methodist, and Baptist—number only about 19,000. It is important to remember this, as in Finland church registration is still as important as civil registration, and most people will find the records of their ancestors through the Evangelical Lutheran Church.

Finland remained united with Sweden until 1809, but in 1713–21 there was a Russian occupation. The whole century from 1710 to 1809 was a very troubled period for Finland, and this fact is reflected in the gaps in the records. In 1809 Finland was ceded by Sweden to Russia, becoming a grand duchy. It became a republic in 1919 and has so remained although much under Soviet influence since 1940. Both Swedish and Finnish are the official languages.

## REGISTRATION

Either church or civil registration is compulsory for every citizen of Finland. Since 1918 civil registration has been a possible alternative to church registration, but no one can be included in both registers. The Lutheran and Orthodox churches are state churches, but other congregations (Roman Catholic, Adventist, Mohammedan, and others) are also authorized to keep official registers. There is no central register for the whole country. Plans for a general reform of the registration system are ready, but final decisions have not yet been taken. Since the central register suggested will not contain information on persons deceased before the start of it, these plans are of little interest to the inquirer. The reform has been proposed for 1963.

Both church and civil registers contain (1) chronological lists (*historieböcker*) of births, marriages, deaths, and moves out of and into the register; and (2) lists of the members of the registers (*kommunionböcker*) by families (earlier, by households) in alphabetical or (earlier, exclusively) geographical order. The member lists are kept up to date and include the information in the chronological lists. In recent times at least, the larger registers have been kept on cards, but earlier the member-list books were rewritten approximately every ten years, which introduced many errors. They are the first source of the genealogist, but the data should be controlled in the chronological lists.

The oldest chronological lists preserved are from the middle of the seventeenth century, and the oldest member lists from the end of the seventeenth century. In many parishes, the older books have been destroyed by fire, etc. The oldest books have been partly transferred to the district archives (*landsarkiv*), but in several cases they are still in the parishes. Copies of all chronological lists before approximately 1850 and of a large part of the member lists have recently been prepared, and they are available at the Central Archives (Riksarkivet) in Helsinki. In order to find a person in these or more recent books, it is usually necessary to know the parish or (recently) commune where he lived.

## THE CENTRAL ARCHIVES

The name and address of the Central Archives is, in Finnish:

*Valtionarkisto*
*Rauhankatu 17*
*Helsinki*

and in Swedish:

*Riksarkivet*
*Fredsgatan 17*
*Helsingfors*

Either language can be used, and letters will reach their destination even without the street and number being mentioned.

Fairly detailed information on various series of older records kept in the Riksarkivet is given in *Oversiktskataog för Riksarkivet* (bilingual; Finnish name: *Valtionarkiston Yleisluettelo*), Vol. I (Helsinki, 1956). It contains information on fiscal records of various governmental bodies (which include the personal tax registers), court records, military records, and maps. Further volumes of the catalogue are being prepared.

## WILLS

Wills are fairly infrequent in Finland. Instead of these, the inquirer should use the "estate inventories" (*bouppteckningar*), which have to be delivered to the town or circuit courts before the widow or widower can be remarried, or the estate can be divided among the heirs. They include information not only on the property, claims, and debts of the estate but also on the heirs. The series of the inventories of towns (in the town archives, *stadsarkiv*, the older parts of which in some cases have been delivered to the district archives and in other cases are held by the towns) in some cases begin in the seventeenth century, but in most cases (including the circuit courts, the older documents of which are in the district archives) the series begin in the eighteenth century.

## THE GENEALOGICAL SOCIETY

The name and address of the Genealogical Society of Finland is:

*Genealogiska Samfundet i Finland*
*Snellmansgatan 9–11*
*Helsingfors*

This society was founded in 1917, and it publishes a yearbook (since 1917), a quarterly magazine called *Genos* (since 1930), and a series of irregular "Publications" (Vol. XXII is in print). From the above address, letters with questions which require research will be handed over to the (commercial) research agency authorized by the Society. The Genealogical Society owns a library (about 20,000 volumes), which contains most of the existing literature on Finnish genealogy, biography, and local history, and a foreign section, mainly containing genealogical periodicals obtained by exchange of publications. Consequently, publications of the Society are available in the libraries of various similar societies in the United Kingdom and the United States (for example, the Society of Genealogists, London, and several American societies; a fairly complete series is also available at the New York Public Library). The series of records owned by the Society consist only of copies, registers, and note collections. Most important are:

1. A complete set of copies of birth, marriage, and death registers of all parishes in Finland until about 1850. This collection is deposited at the Riksarkivet. It also includes copies of the corresponding registers of the Finnish congregation of Stockholm, and of the Swedish and Finnish congregations of St. Petersburg (the latter books are copied to the time of the Russian Revolution). The House of the Nobility owns similar copies of the registers of the German, Swedish, and Finnish congregations of Reval and Narva in Estonia.

2. A collection of cuttings of death notifications in the main daily papers since the beginning of the 1920s, arranged in alphabetical order (at Snellmansgatan 9–11). New notifications are added continuously. Various similar collections for earlier periods (collected by deceased genealogists for their own use) are available at the Riksarkivet.

3. A card register of sailors who died abroad since 1882, in al-

phabetical order, based on notifications in the periodicals *Merimie-
hen Ystävä* (Finnish) and *Sjömansvannen* (Swedish); both names
mean *The Sailor's Friend*.

4. Recently a registration of notes on appointments and other
biographical data in the official government paper has been started.
At present it covers only parts of the latter half of the nineteenth
century.

5. Collections of genealogical notes of deceased genealogists.
They are deposited at the Riksarkivet.

In addition to the above, there are two other series of basic documentary materials. The first is composed of yearly personal tax registers (*mantalslängder*), which give valuable information, particularly where church registers have been lost. These registers contain
at least the name of the head of every household (except the nobility)
and the number of other members over fifteen years old, separated
by kind (wife, brothers, sisters, sons, daughters, etc., and servants),
but also often the Christian names of these other members. At the
Central Archives in Helsinki there are such lists for the whole country since 1634, and other tax registers with less detailed information
since 1540. Since patronyms were widely used instead of family
names, they allow tracing of ascendants with reasonable certainty,
particularly among peasants, where sons usually inherited the farm
from their fathers.

The other set of materials is the court records. For seventeenth-
century, and sometimes eighteenth-century, genealogy, court records are often used when other sources are scarce or do not give
sufficient information. Fairly complete series of such records are
available from 1623. The study of them is time-consuming, but the
efforts are often rewarded by valuable information. The records of
the 1720s often give the only opportunity of bridging the gap in all
series of documents (even church registers) caused by the Russian
occupation in 1713–21, when considerable numbers of the population fled to Sweden or were killed or deported to Russia.

## COATS OF ARMS

There is no body which officially records coats of arms of families.
However, coats of arms are, with few exceptions, carried by noble
families only. These families are, with some exceptions, members

of the House of the Nobility, founded in 1812 in Helsinki. Complete agnatic genealogies of these families, including branches not living in Finland, are published in Carpelan, *Ättartavlor,* Parts I–IV (Part IV still in press). This work and other publications include information on coats of arms. Rights of nobility (and, consequently, coats of arms) are inherited agnatically by all sons. In a few exceptional cases, countship is inherited by primogeniture, but in these cases all younger sons are barons. For most nonmember families with coats of arms, printed genealogies are also available.

## LIST OF COMMUNES

A full list of the present communes in Finland is probably most easily available abroad in the *Statistical Yearbook of Finland* (Table 14 in the most recent issue, 1958), which contains Finnish, Swedish, and English text. There is usually one Lutheran congregation in each commune, but sometimes two or more. A full list of all congregations (also those other than Lutheran) is given in *Finlands Statskalender* (name of the corresponding book in Finnish: *Suomen Valtiokalenteri*), which is published yearly. Collected information on the years when birth, marriage, and death lists begin in various parishes is published in *Genos* (1943), pp. 16–31. However, these lists are often not complete for following years. This and a number of other articles in *Genos* on congregations and church registers are written by Mr. Osmo Durchman.

## THE HOUSE OF THE NOBILITY (RIDDARHUSET)

Address:

> *Riddarhusgenealogen*
> *Riddarhuset*
> *Helsingfors*

This was founded in 1812 (see above). A key to the genealogical literature of Finland is given in Gunnar Siven (Genealogiskt, Repertorium for Finland), *Genealogiska Samfundets i Finland Skrifter* (i.e., the series of "irregular publications" of the Society), Vol. XV

(Helsinki, 1943). It contains a list of family names in alphabetical order with references to publications, manuscripts, note collections, etc., which contain information on the families in question, of three consecutive generations or more.

All the families which could prove descent from any matriculated family in the Swedish House of the Nobility were automatically matriculated in the Finnish House of the Nobility. In this way, 3 counts, 22 barons, and 163 other noble families were matriculated. After this, the House of the Nobility was increased, because the Russian emperor, who was also Grand Duke of Finland, could confer nobility and also naturalize foreign nobles, so that they had the same rights as Finnish noblemen. In this way, new families were introduced into the House of the Nobility. Altogether there were one prince of the Holy Roman Empire, 11 counts, 63 barons, and 282 other noble families. Of them, there are now living in Finland 7 counts, 38 baronial families, and 144 other noble families, and besides them, 5 baronial and 23 noble families in foreign countries.

During the period 1818–1905, the Finnish Parliament consisted of four houses. The first of them was the House of the Nobility; the other three represented the priesthood, the burghers, and the peasantry. Since 1905, when the one-house parliament was founded, only one family has been matriculated at the House of the Nobility in Finland. When the Russian monarchy was abolished in 1917, the possibility of creating or naturalizing new noble families disappeared, and in the constitution of government of 1919 there was inserted a prohibition *de jure* against creation of nobility or any other hereditary rank.

### HERALDRY

Before noblemen were introduced into the House of the Nobility, their coats of arms were confirmed by the grand duke. Thus, all matriculated families have officially recognized coats of arms, which every member of the family has the right to use. No other coats of arms have been registered.

In the sixteenth and seventeenth centuries many commoners used so-called burgher's coats of arms. Likewise, coats of arms are now used by families who, in some cases with right, in other cases without any right, call themselves descendants of foreign noble families.

New civil coats of arms are drawn and accepted only in a very narrow sense. They are officially used only when Finnish citizens) are granted some foreign order, and a drawing of a coat of arms must be sent to the chapter of the order. Not even for persons in the uppermost class of society—for instance, the two latest Presidents of the Republic—is the matter taken under official consideration.

# GERMANY

## CIVIL REGISTRATION

Civil registration—called *Standesamt* (i.e., register office) *Reichspersonenstandsgesetz* (i.e., national law in respect to personal data)—was established on January 1, 1875. It became a reality by January 1, 1876, when every place in Germany had a *Standesamt* of its own or was assigned to one in the neighborhood. The law ordained the registration by an authority of births, marriages, and deaths.

Since that time official records such as those of birth, marriage, and death have been kept by the various local register offices. From these they are transferred once a year to the superior authorities (*Kreisverband*). These records are made out in duplicate in the original registers; the original remains with the certifying register office, and the duplicate is passed on to the superior authority.

When the records are made out by foreign representations—this presumably refers to particulars of Germans who are born, marry, or die abroad—the duplicate is retained by the Standesamt I (Register Office I) Berlin (Dahlem, Lentzallee 107).

Before the *Reichspersonenstandsgesetz* of 1875, the records of births, marriages, and deaths were kept by the ecclesiastical authorities in the respective parishes.

## ECCLESIASTICAL RECORDS

Here we find ourselves against the fact that Germany is very much divided in religious matters. Before going into research previous to 1875, it is essential to know the religion of the subject of your inquiry. Some parts of Germany, such as the Rhineland and Bavaria, are Roman Catholic; others, such as Brandenburg, are Lutheran, while Hessen and Lippe are Protestant but not Lutheran. The area called Niedersachsen has two state churches: a Lutheran in Hanover and a Reformed (that is, Protestant but not Lutheran) in the western part of Friesland.

Parish records were instituted earlier in the South than in the North. About 1550 there were already a large number of parish records along the river Saale in the so-called Mitteldeutschland. The parish records at Löberschütz, for instance, in the Grossherzogtum Sachsen begin in 1546 (this is the oldest in the area). In Brandenburg, the first *Kirchenbuch* (parish register) dates from 1566, in the town of Brandenburg, parish of St. Catherine. In Hanover, the first record is from 1562; for Schleswig-Holstein, that of St. Mary's Church of Flensburg begins in 1558; and in Mecklenburg, the oldest is of 1580. In each of these districts there is a catalogue of the records in the area.

## CENTRAL ARCHIVES

The centralization of documents in Germany has never been good, probably because of the numerous states into which Germany has been divided for the greater part of her history. Every city has archives of its own. This is, of course, a truism of every large city in the Western world, but in Germany it has reference to the type of archive which is useful to genealogists. Every province (that is, former state, like Bavaria) has its *Staatsarchiv*. Niedersachsen, for instance, has state archives at Hanover, Braunschweig, Oldenburg, Osnabrück, and Aurich. In these archives it is possible to find wills preserved. Generally wills are not kept for longer than thirty years; they are kept during that period by the lowest court of justice, the *Amtsgericht*.

## WILLS

In Germany, wills are not necessarily kept with a local authority. It is up to the testator to make arrangements to have his will filed with the local court if he so desires.

## GENEALOGICAL SOCIETIES

There is principally one society, which works all over Germany. This is: Der Herold, Verein für Heraldik, Genealogie und verwandte Wissenschaften. The chief of the Society is Dr. Ottfried Neubecker, and the address is:

*Westfälische Strasse 38*
*Berlin-Halensee*

Most of the German genealogical societies are regionally based, for example, for Bavaria, Württemberg, Hessen, or Niedersachsen. It should be observed that Hessen is a combination of three states, Hessen-Kassel, Hessen-Nassau, and Hessen-Darmstadt, as well as Frankfort. In the Rhineland, the Society is Westdeutsche Gesellschaft, in Köln. In Niedersachsen, Zentralstelle für Niedersächsische Familienkunde, in Hamburg. In connection with the later, a very useful source of inquiry is with:

*Herr Karl-Egbert Schultze, Genealoge*
*Papenhuder Strasse 36*
*Hamburg 22*

Herr Schultze is the manager, or secretary, of the Niederländische Ahnengemeinschaft E. V. This collects information about Dutch immigrants driven into Germany by the Duke of Alba in the persecutions in the sixteenth century in what were then the Spanish Netherlands. It corresponds thus to some extent to the Huguenot Society in England.

There is a kind of genealogical *Who's Who* for Germany. This is published by C. A. Starke Verlag, of Glücksburg/Ostsee. It is called *Wer Sucht Wen?* with a subtitle: *Verzeichnis der Familien-*

*Forscher und Verbande* (*Who Seeks Whom? A Record and Union of Genealogists*).

There is a society which unites all German genealogical societies. This is the Deutsche Arbeitsgemeinschaft Genealogischer Verbande (Union of German Genealogical Workers). This covers also German-speaking persons outside Germany, that is, in the Netherlands, Switzerland, and Austria.

## GERMAN NOBILITY

There are two collections which are of interest here. One is:

> *Deutsches Adelsarchiv*
> *Am Glaskopf, 21*
> *Marburg an der Lahn 16*

This deals with information on the genealogical collections of the German Union of Nobility. The Direktor des Archivs is H. F. v. Ehrenkrook. A good deal of information has been accumulated on German families of noble origin. It produces the *Genealogisches Handbuch des deutschen Adels* (*Genealogical Handbook of the German Nobility*). This handbook is frequently referred to as the continuation of *Gotha*. It is printed by C. A. Starke, who is publishing also the *Deutsches Geschlechterbuch* (*German Family Book*). In addition, there is also the *Handbuch des in Bayern immatrikulierten Adels* (*Handbook of Nobility in Bavaria*), by Herr Nebinger, Stadtarchiv Neuberg/Donau. The publishers are Verlag Degener & Co., Neustadt/Aisch.

## HERALDRY

In modern times there is the Deutsche Wappenrolle (German Roll of Arms), kept by Der Herold (see above). There is also a printed register of all known German arms, the *Kenfenheuer,* which is compiled from all known collections of books of arms.

## ADDRESSES

A very useful book is the *Taschenbuch für Familien Geschichts Forschung* (*Pocketbook for Family History Research*). This contains details of all manner of genealogical information, including details of handwriting (in the old German script) and private family histories. The following addresses as given in the book are particularly useful.

*Arbeitsgemeinschaft der genealogischen Verbände in Deutschland* (*Working Association of Genealogical Societies in Germany*), *Hanover, Am Markt 4.*

*Niedersächsische Landesstelle für Familienkumde, Hanover, Am Markt 4.*

*Standesamt* (*Registry Office*) *Berlin-Mitte* (*Middle*), *Berlin C.2, Elisabethstrasse 28–29.*

*Standesamt I Berlin* (*West*), *Berlin-Wilmersdorf, Fehrbelliner Platz 1.*

*Standesamt I Berlin* (*East*), *Berlin C.2, Stralauerstrasse 42–43.*

*Hauptstandesamt Hamburg* (*Chief Registry Office*), *Hamburg 1, Johanniswall 4.*

*Sonderstandesamt Arolsen* (*Kr. Waldeck*).

*Berliner Hauptarchiv, Berlin-Dahlem, Archivstrasse 12–14.*

*Archivamt der Evangelischen Kirche Deutschland, Hanover, Militarstrasse 9; and Marinegeminden in Wilhelmshaven, Kirchplatz 5.*

*Kirchenbuchamt für den Osten, Hanover, Militarstrasse 9.*

*Bischöfliches* (*Episcopal*) *Generalvikariat, Abt. für Ostvertriebene, Limburg/Lahn.*

*Deutsche Dienststelle für die Benachrichtigung der nächsten Angehorigen von Gefallenen der ehemaligen deutschen Wehrmacht, Berlin-Wittenau* (*Wast*), *Eichhorndamm 167–209* (*Postfach*).

*Personenstandsarchiv II, Dortmund-Lütgendortmund.*

*Kirchenbücher katholischer Militargemeinden—Historischen Archiv des Erzbistums Köln, in Köln/Rhein, Marzellenstrasse 32. (For Protestant particulars see Kirchenbuchamt für den Osten, above.)*

A SPECIAL NOTE ON THE ARCHIVES OF THE GERMAN NOBILITY IN SCHÖNSTADT (THE FOLLOWING IS A TRANSLATION FROM NOTES SUP-PLIED):

"After the collapse of 1945, in the autumn of the same year H. F. v. Ehrenkrook together with J. von Flotow, both of them refugees from the East, decided to publish refugee lists of the German nobility, giving the addresses and the facts of the nobility who were pouring in from the East. This material appeared first in typescript and was eventually printed. The *Adelsarchiv* thus formed grew into a central office for the affairs of the entire German nobility with three business addresses:

*In Westerbrak, Kr. Holzminden, Jurgen von Flotow (the editorial office of the journal* Deutsches Adelsarchiv).

*In Melle, Bex. Osnabrück, Baron Detlev von Hammerstein-Retzow (charitable center of the Deutsches Adelsarchiv, now recognized as a charitable organization and office dealing with persons missing).*

*In Schönstadt, near Marburg/Lahn, H. F. v. Ehrenkrook (the genealogical section).*

"In the archives in Schönstadt (center of the fight against usurpation of noble names, now also office of the committee for questions dealing with the law pertaining to the nobility) a library has been assembled, belonging to H. F. v. Ehrenkrook, of about 1600 volumes and a manuscript collection with more than 300 headings which also contains a number of smaller collections (e.g., Bylburg, etc.). Various families have lent material dealing with their family history. Also the records of the *Edda (Iron Book of the German Nobility)*—now deposited with the state archives in Marburg—are today under the supervision of the Deutsches Adelsarchiv in Schönstadt.

"This extensive and still increasing library forms the basis for the publication of the *Genealogical Handbook,* published by the firm C. A. Starke, which after its flight from Görlitz found a second home in Glücksburg/Ostsee. Some fourteen or fifteen volumes had been published by 1957."

# AUSTRIA

## INTRODUCTION

The earliest records in Austria, as elsewhere for the majority of the population, are ecclesiastical. This stemmed from the Council of Trent (1545–63), and as stated in the Introduction to this volume, there was during the period 1530–70 a movement in western Europe generally to keep parish records. The enormous importance of church records in Austria can be realized, however, when it is understood that civil registration in the American or British sense is a matter of little over twenty years standing. For periods before 1939, it is of paramount importance to know a person's religious denomination in order to have the key to his genealogy.

The expression "register books" occurs for the first time in an Austrian court decree of February 22, 1722; the control of ecclesiastical registration was through an imperial patent of February 20, 1784. But as far back as 1523–29 there was a burial register in St. Stephen's Cathedral in Vienna, and in the same church a marriage register of 1542–56. According to Dr. Hanns Jäger-Sunstenau, there is a phenomenon common, he thinks, in the whole of Europe, but observable in Austria, "that the age of records decreased from the West toward the East; Tyrol and Vorarlberg are thus the best documented. The books preserved today in the most ancient parishes date only from the end of the Thirty Years' War (1648), and in the neighborhood of Vienna, for the most part, only from 1684, after the second siege by the Turks. The oldest parish register in the old monarchy was the baptismal register, beginning in 1457 at the parish of Pirano, in what was originally Venetian Istria." (See Introduction.)

## ROMAN CATHOLIC CHURCH RECORDS

Austria being predominantly a Roman Catholic country, the most prolific records are those of the Roman Catholics. About the period of the Thirty Years' War (ended 1648 by the Peace of Westphalia), the Protestant church records were merged with those of the Catholic parishes. The one exception to this rule was in the case of Protestant diplomats and their staffs, whose records are found in the books of the Danish, Swedish, and Dutch embassies in Vienna in the eighteenth century. True, on October 13, 1781, a patent of toleration from the Austrian emperor allowed the keeping of private records as distinct from Catholic parochial records, but even so, right up to January 20, 1849, all such cases had to be included in the appropriate Catholic parish. A list of the several provinces of Austria is given below, under "Records of the Provinces." In order to understand this more easily, it may be noted that the Catholic Church organization is divided into the following dioceses. The archbishoprics of Vienna (for Vienna and eastern Lower Austria) and Salzburg (for the province of Salzburg and five judicial districts of the Tyrol); the bishoprics of St. Pölten (for western Lower Austria), Linz (for Upper Austria), Seckau-in-Graz (for Styria), and Gurk-in-Klagenfurt (for Carinthia); and also the apostolic administratures of Burgenland at Sauerbrunn (created from the dioceses of Raab and Steinamanger) and of the Tyrol and Vorarlberg at Innsbruck (created from the diocese of Brixen, or Bressanone). For Vorarlberg, there has existed since the transfer, effected in 1816, of the dioceses of Chur and Constance (in Switzerland) to Brixen (or Bressanone), a special Vicariate General at Feldkirch. Particulars of the division into parishes will be found in the *Austrian Official Calendar* and in the numerous diocesan directories.

## RECORDS OF THE PROVINCES

In the following list, the name of the province is followed by the name of the place where the records are kept, then by the dates when the records begin or by inclusive dates.

*Burgenland.* Ordinary Office: Sauerbrunn, 1922. County Archives: Eisenburg, Odenburg, and Wieselburg, 1827–95. Ordinary Offices: Raab and Steinamanger, 1896–1921.

*Carinthia.* Ordinary Office: Gurk-in-Klagenfurt, 1840.

*Lower Austria.* Ordinary Office: Vienna, 1797. Ordinary Office: St. Pölten, 1785.

*Upper Austria.* Ordinary Office: Linz, 1819.

*Salzburg.* 1816.

*Styria.* Ordinary Office: Seckau-in-Graz, 1835 (a few copies were destroyed by a bomb).

*Tyrol.* Ordinary Office: Innsbruck, 1921 (copies previously at Brixen). Ordinary Office: Salzburg, 1816.

The following list states in which volume of the *Accounts of Records in the Tyrol* the present seventeen Tyrolean judicial divisions appear. An (S) suffixed signifies that the division belongs to the archdiocese of Salzburg.

| | | | | |
|---|---|---|---|---|
| Hall .. .. .. .. .. 3 | Rattenberg (S) .. .. .. .. 4 |
| Hopfgarten (S) .. .. .. 4 | Reutte .. .. .. .. .. .. 2 |
| Imst .. .. .. .. .. 1 | Ried .. .. .. .. .. .. 1 |
| Innsbruck .. .. .. .. 2 | Schwaz .. .. .. .. .. .. 3 |
| Kitzbühel .. .. .. .. 4 | Silz .. .. .. .. .. .. 1 |
| Kufstein (S) .. .. .. 4 | Steinach .. .. .. .. .. 2 |
| Landeck .. .. .. .. 1 | Telfs .. .. .. .. .. .. 1 |
| Lienz .. .. .. .. .. 4 | Zell-am-Ziller (S) .. .. .. 3 |
| Matrei .. .. .. .. .. 4 | |

*Vorarlberg.* Ordinary Office: Feldkirch, 1839.

*Vienna.* Copies: City districts I–IX, 1812. City districts X–XXVI, 1797. There are also the registers of deaths, kept by the municipal coroners and preserved since 1648 (in the archives of the city of Vienna), which have only three gaps—1657–58, 1663, and 1676–77 —which constitute about 1.7 per cent of the whole. For the years 1648–72, an annotated index has been prepared.

# THE EVANGELICAL CHURCH RECORDS

The supreme authority is the High Church Council. There are two main Protestant Churches, that of the Augsburg Confession and the other of the Helvetian (that is, Genevan), being Lutheran and Calvinist, respectively. The Augsburg denomination is organized under three superintendencies: (1) for Vienna, Lower Austria, Styria, and Carinthia; (2) for the Burgenland; and (3) for Upper Austria, Salzburg, the Tyrol, and Vorarlberg.

The Helvetian denomination has only one superintendency. In 1938 there were 120 parishes in the Augsburg denomination and 6 of the Helvetian denomination (three of these being in Vienna and two in Vorarlberg). There are very few Evangelical records preserved in Austria from the time before the Counter Reformation (mid-sixteenth–seventeenth centuries). Of those which remain there is an incomplete volume in Graz, 1567–98; and some records in Linz, 1576–81 and 1608–17. After 1648, as stated above, Protestant records tended to be merged with those of the Catholics. Since 1878 it has been obligatory to send copies of all records to the High Church Council in Vienna (Vienna I, Schellinggasse 12). They are still kept there today, and, certainly up to 1917, so were those of most of the Evangelical parishes of those kingdoms and provinces which were formerly represented at the Council of the Empire (of Austria-Hungary) but which are not now in Austria. Besides the *Austrian Official Calendar,* information on the parishes and their age is obtainable from the *Directory of the Evangelical Church,* published in Vienna (1875), and from Heinrich Liptak's *Evangelical Austria* (Vienna, 1935). A valuable guide, for descendants resident in Austria, is provided by the little book by Gustav Arz, *The Records of the Evangelical Communities in Transylvania* (Berlin, 1939).

# THE OLD CATHOLIC CHURCH

This is a small body which dissented from the Catholic Church after the Vatican Council had in 1870 declared that the infallibility of the Pope was a doctrine of the Christain Faith. From 1877 the

Old Catholics had the right to keep records publicly, and copies were taken to the district captaincies, that is, to the city councils of Vienna and Linz. There are nine parishes of this Church, as follows, with the dates of the beginnings of their records.

| | | | | | | | | | | |
|---|---|---|---|---|---|---|---|---|---|---|
| Vienna I | .. | .. | .. | 1872 | Graz | .. | .. | .. | .. | 1899 |
| Vienna III | .. | .. | .. | 1935 | Klagenfurt | .. | .. | .. | 1932 |
| Vienna X | .. | .. | .. | 1934 | Linz | .. | .. | .. | .. | 1878 |
| Vienna XV | .. | .. | .. | 1923 | Salzburg .. | .. | .. | .. | 1922 |
| Vienna XVI | .. | .. | .. | 1921 | | | | | | |

## THE GREEK ORTHODOX CHURCH

This Church has four parishes in Vienna: (1) Holy Trinity, for Austrian nationals (records from 1790); (2) St. George, for foreigners of Greek and other non-Slavonic nationalities (from 1775); (3) the Serbian Church community, for those of Slavonic nationality (from 1893); (4) the Rumanian Orthodox Church community (from 1929).

## THE JEWISH COMMUNITY

In 1938 there were thirty-four Jewish communities in Austria, whose records had to be delivered to the district captaincies (that is, to the councils of the county boroughs, earlier known as the self-governing cities). At these centers copies existed from an early date. This provision no doubt accounts for the fact that the longest Jewish pedigrees I have seen are those of the Viennese Jews, going back in some cases to the fifthteenth century. When the Germans annexed Austria to the Third Reich in 1938, they removed many original Jewish records to Berlin, then to a salt mine near Hettstedt-am-Ilm in Thuringia. It is reported that these records were destroyed in April 1945.

The Viennese Jewish records were, however, preserved and are now stored with others at the Jewish religious center. The address is: Vienna I, Schottenring 25. The dates of these records are as follows:

| | | | | | | | | |
|---|---|---|---|---|---|---|---|---|
| Baden | .. | .. | .. | 1874–1938 | Klosterneuburg | .. | | 1868–88 |
| Gross-Enzersdorf | .. | | 1907–35 | Mödling | .. | .. | .. | 1868–1935 |
| Hollabrunn | .. | .. | 1902– | St. Pölten | .. | .. | | 1863–1938 |
| Horn | .. | .. | .. | 1874–1937 | Stockerau-Korneuburg | 1872–1937 |
| Vienna | .. | .. | .. | 1784– | | | | |

In addition, there are records at the provincial government offices in Linz, Graz, Salzburg, and Innsbruck.

## RECORDS OF OTHER COMMUNITIES AND FOR UNDENOMINATIONAL PERSONS

Since 1870 certain records have been kept in the district captaincies and councils of self-governing cities. These are for undenominational persons, for those belonging to state-recognized religious communities which do not possess their own official community center (the members of the Armenian Orthodox Church, the Lippowaner, Mennonites, Herrnhuters, and Mohammedans), and also for those belonging to religious denominations not recognized by the state. Also, the so-called "dispensed marriages" were recorded and the records kept at the same place. The copies from the district captaincies are lodged with the provincial governments. The books of the Vienna City Council (1867–1938) and the separate district captaincies of Sechshaus (1869–91), Hernals (1868–91), Hietzing (1890–1938), Floridsdorf (1874–1938), and Mödling (1897–1938) are kept at the Record Office of Vienna-Alsergrund (Vienna IX, Währingerstrasse 39).

## AUSTRIANS RESIDENT ABROAD

Volumes of records made at legations are kept in the Vienna House, Court and State Archives. These include those from Barcelona (from the eighteenth century), Bursa, Turkey (1901–18), and Paris (1904–10).

## MILITARY PERSONNEL

Up to 1919 a special system existed for keeping the records of military personnel. The records of the chaplains' departments for the Army and Navy cover not only the Catholics but also the Protestants, the Greek Orthodox, and the Moslems. The records of the various bodies of troops, which begin in 1816, were kept by the Field Consistory, as the highest military clerical authority; under the Field Consistory were Field Superiors, in each of the fifteen corps and in the Zara detachment, and these latter kept the older original records before 1816. On March 1, 1919, the keeping of special records for members of the existing Royal and Imperial Army in Austria was abolished. The local chaplains have always been the record keepers for the former frontier regiments, for the Royal and Imperial Territorial Reserve, and for the Home Guard, which was instituted in the autumn of 1918. Since May 1, 1923, special records have again been kept for those in the Austrian Federal Army, and this was carried out from 1938 onward by a chaplain in each of the seven existing divisions. Today the military records are grouped together in Department 9/m of the Federal Ministry for the Interior, Vienna VII, Karl-Schweighofer-Gasse 3.

## CIVIL REGISTRATION

From the above it will be clear that, until very recent times, record keeping in Austria has been a matter for the religious organizations, more especially, the Roman Catholic Church. There was, from 1870, a form of civil registration (see above) for the few people who were without a religion or at least a recognized one. Civil registration of birth, marriage, and death began in 1938, when Austria came under the rule of Hitler. Marriage registration records date from August 1, 1938; birth and death registrations from January 1, 1939.

The only exception to this is in the area of the Burgenland, which was formerly part of Hungary and only became Austrian in 1920. Under a Hungarian law, state (that is, civil) records were introduced on October 1, 1895. This was continued by the Austrian legislature with an order of May 29, 1922. The registrars are employed there in an official capacity as record keepers, to the number of 118. The copies of the state records of Burgenland date from 1921 and are preserved at the provincial headquarters at Eisenstadt. The records before 1921 were not transferred by the Hungarian authorities.

The total number of Austrian register offices existing on January 1, 1948, amounted to 1524, divided among the various provinces as follows:

| | | | | | | | |
|---|---|---|---|---|---|---|---|
| Burgenland .. | .. | .. | .. 118 | Styria | .. | .. | .. 282 |
| Carinthia .. | .. | .. | .. 238 | Tyrol | .. | .. | .. 172 |
| Lower Austria .. | .. | .. | 175 | Vorarlberg .. | .. | .. | .. 46 |
| Upper Austria .. | .. | .. | 381 | (Greater) Vienna | | .. | .. 23 |
| Salzburg .. | .. | .. | .. 89 | | | | |

The Central Statistical Office, Vienna, published a list of parishes in Austria, and opposite the name of each parish is given the register office appropriate to it. The copies of the marriage registers are in the provincial government offices; those of the register-office books are in the council offices of the chief town of the district.

## WILLS

Will making, or keeping, in Austria begins with the reception of the Roman system of law at the end of the fifteenth century. ("Reception" here means the acceptance by the Austrian state of the old Roman law in place of its old feudal and customary law.) Wills were then preserved in the archives of the seigneurs, the monasteries, or the towns. Since about 1900, wills have been kept in the law courts. For wills of the earlier periods, search must be made in the archives of the following cities:

| Province | City or Town | Province | City or Town |
|---|---|---|---|
| Vorarlberg | Bregenz | Burgenland | Eisenstadt |
| Tyrol | Innsbruck | Lower Austria | Vienna |
| Carinthia | Klagenfurt | Styria | Graz |
| Upper Austria | Salsburg and Linz | | |

## PUBLIC RECORDS

The archives of the state are in four parts: (1) The Haus-, Hof-, and Staatsarchiv, which give the records of the Habsburg and Lothringen family, which for so long ruled Austria. (2) The Austrian state records. (3) The Holy Roman Empire, from the thirteenth century to 1806, when it was abolished by Napoleon. The oldest charter in the state archives is from about the year 870. (4) The Kriegsarchiv, the military records from about 1500. In addition, in each of the nine Austrian Bundesländer, or provinces, there are archives. The main center is Vienna, where the head of the organization is Dr. Hanns Jäger-Sunstenau, Vienna III, Landstrasser Haupstrasse 140.

## HERALDRY

In Austria there never was an official place for recording armorial bearings. In the public records (see above) can be found all papers about granting coats of arms, whether the grant was with or without nobility. From about 1760 it was forbidden for a family which was not noble to bear a coat of arms without a specific grant from the emperor. Such grants were few. In 1919, when the Austrian Republic was set up, a law was made by which the use of coats of arms in any official sense was forbidden. The Heraldisch-Genealogische Gesellschaft *Adler* (founded 1870), Vienna II, Haarkof 4a, began in 1950 the private registration of coats of arms in the Oster- reichische Wappenrolle (Austrian Roll of Arms).

# THE NETHERLANDS

## CIVIL REGISTRATION

Civil registration of birth, marriage, and death began in the Netherlands when the country had been conquered by Napoleon and incorporated into French territory. This was in 1811, and the French Code Napoléon (Civil Code), which ordered this registration, was adopted in the same year. The Code Napoléon was replaced in 1838 by the Dutch Civil Code, but the system of registration introduced in 1811 was taken over by the Dutch. Thus, the origin of the registration system in Holland is the same as in Belgium, though some years later in date. The records are kept by the local registrars of each municipality where the births, marriages, or deaths take place.

## CHURCH REGISTRATION

Before the introduction of the civil registration, recording took place in the registers of the churches. These registers have been transferred to the national archives, located in the capitals of the provinces. However, in the large municipalities, which have the disposal of archives which reach certain requirements, registration has been transferred to the local archives.

## SITUATION OF THE ARCHIVES

Holland has eleven provinces. Their supervision is under the Algemeen Rijksarchief, 7 Bleÿenburg, The Hague. At this supervisory center at The Hague are kept the archives of the central government and the archives of the province of Zuid-Holland. As mentioned above, the more important towns have their own archives apart from the provincial archives. Foreigners are advised to apply to the Algemeen Rijksarchief, which will forward questions to the provincial or town archives concerned.

In the archives are kept, in addition to the church registers before 1811, the court archives (transfer of immovables, etc.) and the archives of the notaries public (wills, etc.). Duplicates of the civil registers from 1811 to 1883 are kept in the provincial or town archives, and from 1883 in the court.

A Public Record Office or the like does not exist in the Netherlands, in any case not in the field of civil registration. In this connection it may be observed that in each municipality a so-called population register is also kept, giving details about persons belonging or having belonged to the resident population of the municipality. However, this registration only began in 1850 and, consequently, for inquiries about ancestors, this is less important than the civil registration and church registration. As regards the population registers, there is a Public Record Office, the Rijksinspectie van de Bevolkingsregisters (State Inspection of the Population Registers), located at The Hague.

## WILLS

For the legal validity of a will in the Netherlands, it is prescribed by law that the will be drawn up by a public servant, the notary, appointed by royal decree. The number of notaries is about 900. The will is generally drawn up by the notary of the district where the person who wishes to make a will lives, and it is kept by the notary in his files (his so-called repertorium).

In The Hague there is the Central Testamenten Register (Central Register of Wills), containing all testaments drawn up in the

Netherlands during the last fifty years. It does not, however, give information on wills drawn up in former centuries. For investigation into ancestry, old wills will be needed, and those drawn up before 1840 have been transferred to the government archives mentioned above.

## SOCIETIES

There are several genealogical societies in the Netherlands.

1. Koninklijk Nederlandsch Genootschap voor Geslacht en Wapenkunde (Royal Society for Genealogy and Heraldry). Founded in 1883, it has very fine collections. It issues a monthly periodical, *De Nederlandsche Leeuw.* ADDRESS: 5 Bleijenburg, The Hague. PRESIDENT: Jhr. Dr. D. P. M. Graswinckel. SECRETARY: Mr. C. M. R. Davidson.

2. Nederlandse Genealogische Vereniging. Founded in 1946, it has about 1300 members. It has no office or library but publishes a periodical, *Gens Nostra,* about every two months. ADDRESS: Post Box 976, Amsterdam.

3. Central Bureau voor Genealogie. Founded in 1945. It supervises the genealogical collections of the state. It has a large library, many manuscripts, and special collections, such as notices of birth, marriage, and death in the newspapers from 1790 to the present. It has also the famous heraldic collection known as Muschart and an iconographical collection. There is a staff of ten and about twenty assistants. It publishes a yearbook called *Central Bureau voor Genealogie,* and another, *Nederlands Patriciaat.* It provides the secretariat for the *Nederlands Adelsboek* (*Yearbook of the Dutch Nobility*). ADDRESS: 18 Nassaulaan, The Hague.

## HERALDRY

There is no legislation as to armorial bearings in Holland. Everyone may have a coat of arms or take one if he wishes. There is no official registration of arms, with the exception of those granted to the nobility. In the latter connection, there is the Hoge Raad van Adel (Supreme Court of Nobility) 71b Zeestraat, The Hague. It consists of a president and four members, all appointed by the

Queen. The Hoge Raad has a secretary and further staff. It advises the Queen in matters of (1) nobility, (2) flags and coats of arms of provinces, towns, villages, etc., (3) emblems of units of the Navy, Army, and Air Force, (4) admission to the Teutonic Order and the Order of Malta. The Hoge Raad van Adel has an extensive documentation about the Dutch nobility but does not undertake paid genealogical research.

# BELGIUM

## INTRODUCTION

It must first of all be understood that both French and Flemish are used in Belgium. In books which deal with Belgian records, the text is usually given in both languages. For this reason I have, in many cases, given the terms used in both languages.

## PARISH REGISTERS

Before the French Revolution the parish registers were kept by the Catholic curés (pastors) and their beadles in the different parishes. Most of these old parish registers have been transferred to the local provincial capitals. For instance, the parish registers of the communes of Bassevelde, Watervliet, and Waterland-Oudeman in East Flanders have been concentrated in Ghent, the capital of East Flanders, at the Archives du Royaume (Ryksarchief). Consequently, the parish registers are kept now in the state archives and also in the town or commune halls (*hôtel de ville or hôtel communal—stadhuis* or *gemeentehuis*). In a very few cases they are still kept by the parish priests. Some of the old registers were also kept by a few Protestant clergymen (in Brussels).

The addresses of the various state archives are as follows:

*Antwerp: 5 Door Verstraeteplaats*
*Arlon: Place Léopold*
*Bruges: 14–18 Akademiestraat*

*Ghent: Geeraard Duivelsteen*
*Hasselt: Bampslaan*
*Liége: 8 Rue Pouplin*
*Mons: 23 Place du Parc*
*Namur: 45 Rue d'Arquet*

## CIVIL REGISTRATION

This began in 1795, when the forces let loose by the French Revolution overran Belgium. The French occupied the country, and civil registration began. The records of births, marriages, and deaths are now kept in the town and commune halls of Belgium. The best course is to apply to M. l'Officier de l'Etat Civil (M. Officier van de Burgerlyke Stand) of the town or commune concerned.

## WILLS

Those made before the French Revolution have usually been deposited in the state archives in the provincial capitals in Belgium (for list, see above). It may happen that the original acts (*protocoles*) of the notaries of the pre-Revolutionary period are nowadays in the possession of the present-day notaries who hold these offices. As a general rule, the Chambers of Notaries publish an index of the original acts of notaries kept per district (*arrondissement*), while mentioning the place where they are kept; for instance, the lists for the districts of Antwerp and Malines are at the State Archives, 5 Door Verstraeteplaats, Antwerp.

## GENERAL ARCHIVES

*M. E. Sabbe, L'Archiviste Général*
*Archives Générales du Royaume*
*78 Galerie Ravenstein*
*Brussels*
(*Open weekdays 9* A.M. *to 6* P.M.)

A full account of the archives is given in *Les Archives Générales du Royaume (Het Algemeen Rijksarchief)*, by M. Van Haegendoren

(Brussels, 1955). This work contains a very great deal of valuable information on the various Belgian records, and is preceded by a historical sketch which is, as the author says, useful to researchers as well as to students, because they will then know why some materials are found dispersed and in disorder. At first, in the Middle Ages, the princes kept their records in various places, such as their castles and abbeys. Only with the Burgundian era (see Introduction to this volume) did centralized archives begin to exist. The various Fiscal Chambers had settled headquarters at Lille in 1386 and at Brussels in 1404. The archives of the other departments of the government were generally deposited at Lille. The Chambre des Comptes at Lille may be considered as the depot of the archives of the Low Countries for the period previous to 1530–31. The troubles of the sixteenth century (the wars of religion) caused the displacement of various records, many of the government archives being removed to Holland. Under the Treaty of Münster, the archives which concerned the United Provinces were ceded to Holland in 1666. Again, in the seventeenth century, the French invasions of the Spanish and Austrian Netherlands caused grave disorder in the archives. In 1667, when Lille fell into the hands of the French, only a small part of the archives were saved. This was only one of the many vicissitudes in the history of the Belgian annals, some of which had to be ceded to France. All those which were reclaimed from the French were deposited at Brussels in 1769–71. There was not, however, a central depot before the French Revolution; the different sets of archives were preserved by the authorities which had formed them. The bombardment of Brussels in 1695 and the fire of 1731 caused the loss of the archives of the town, and also most of the archives of the states of Brabant. The French Revolution caused further trouble in the archives. Some were saved when the Belgian Government withdrew from Brussels, and some collections went actually as far as Vienna. Many were lost by passing into the hands of individuals.

After 1815 two central depots of archives were organized, one at Brussels and the other at The Hague. During the period immediately following the Napoleonic Wars, many documents were reclaimed from France and Austria. In 1859 a better organization of the archives was introduced.

During the two world wars, the Belgian archives were in great danger. The Germans had schemes for the reorganization of European records as well as of everything else. Fortunately, the Belgian archives have recovered from these dangers. The records are divided into three parts.

### Printed Records

These include the records of the following:

The Council of State

The Royal Council of Philip V

The Council of State of Regency

The Council of State of Maximilian Emanuel

Privy Council

Council of Finances

Secretariat of State and of War

The Board of Maritime Commerce

The Secretariat of the German State

Spanish Embassy at The Hague

Chancellery of the Netherlands at Vienna

Contradorie et Pagadoire des Gens de Guerre

Monts de Piété

Articles regarding contested lands, moneys, redemptions, administrations, and subsidies

Committee for the census of Luxembourg

Jesuit Committee

Royal Commission for Studies

Many other items which relate to various government bodies

### Modern Records Not Printed

These cover the Chamber of Accounts and many manuscript volumes of charters of the various cities of Belgium. There are also the Chancellery of Mary of Hungary, of the Count Charles of Lorraine and many others.

### Ancient Collections

These include many interesting documents, such as those relating to heraldic processes and the Aulic Tribunals, which exercised jurisdiction over the personnel of the court, especially over inferior personnel, and by extension over certain inhabitants neighboring on the palace.

Parish registers are included here (see above), and below is given a list of the communes in the province of Brabant which have confided their parochial registers to Brussels:

| | |
|---|---|
| Archennes .. .. .. .. .. .. | 1794, 1795, 1797 |
| Beersel .. .. .. .. .. .. | 1664–1797 |
| Bierges .. .. .. .. .. .. | 1605–1796 |
| Bierk (Hal) .. .. .. .. .. .. | 1659–1813 |
| Brainé-le-Château .. .. .. .. | 1609–1804 |
| Chastre-Villeroux-Blanmont .. .. | 1600–1797 |
| Corry-le-Grand .. .. .. .. .. | 1682–1803 |

| | | |
|---|---|---|
| Couture-St.-Germaine | .. .. .. | 1628–1641 |
| Glimes .. .. .. | .. .. .. | 1622–1796 |
| Hamme .. .. .. | .. .. .. | 1592–1796 |
| Hévillers .. .. .. | .. .. .. | 1724–1797 |
| Incourt .. .. .. | .. .. .. | 1726–1812 |
| Ittre .. .. .. | .. .. .. | 1709–1749 |
| Kortenberg .. .. | .. .. .. | index |
| Marilles .. .. .. | .. .. .. | 1683–1812 |
| Mont-St.-Guibert .. | .. .. .. | 1692–1822 |
| Oórbeek .. .. .. | .. .. .. | 1713–1796 |
| Ophain .. .. .. | .. .. .. | 1612–1667 |
| Opprebais .. .. | .. .. .. | 1789–1870 |
| Orp-le.-Grand .. | .. .. .. | without index |
| Orsmaal-Gussenhoven | .. .. .. | 1610–1650 |
| Overijse .. .. .. | .. .. .. | 1626–1795 |
| Rosières .. .. .. | .. .. .. | 1678–1796 |
| Ruisbroek .. .. | .. .. .. | 1679–1803 |
| Scherpenheuvel .. | .. .. .. | 1610–1805 |
| St.-Gery .. .. .. | .. .. .. | 1687–1797 |
| Thorembais-St.-Trond .. | .. .. | 1754–1757 |
| Vertrijk .. .. .. | .. .. .. | 1782–1798 |
| Wauthier-Braine .. | .. .. .. | 1606–1796 |
| Walhain-St.-Paul .. | .. .. .. | 1754–1765 |
| Winksele .. .. | .. .. .. | 1613–1797 |
| Zellik .. .. .. | .. .. .. | 1655–1832 |
| Zetrud-Lummen .. | .. .. .. | 1710–1778 |

Family archives exist in this section in large numbers. There is also a fourth section, containing such matters as the genealogical collections associated with the names of Em. de Borchgrave and the Poullet family.

To the above account of the Archives Générales du Royaume may be added the following note, which is taken from the catalogue of the Genealogical and Heraldic Exhibition at Brussels in 1958. In this exhibition, some splendid examples were shown of patents of nobility, grants of arms, and genealogical trees. Most of the families mentioned were noble houses, but, as I shall show further on, many lines of the modern period which do not possess titles can trace their ancestry to a noble family.

## SOCIETIES

*1. The 4th International Congress of Heraldry and Genealogy* was held in Brussels in May 1958 and the results published in

*Recueil du IV Congrès International des Sciences Généalogique et Héraldique,* issuing from L'Office Généalogique et Héraldique de Belgique. The Secretary General of the Office is:

> *Le Chevalier Zavier de Ghellinck Vaernewyk*
> *L'Office Généalogique et Héraldique de Belgique*
> *37 Rue Bosquet*
> *Brussels*

The publication of the Society is *Le Parchemin,* founded in 1936, a monthly bulletin in which various matters of genealogy and heraldry are put forward and discussed. Questions can be put into this magazine, and the answers sent in by readers are printed.

**2.** *Le Conseil Héraldique.* Full particulars can be had from:

> *M. le Vicomte Charles Terlinden*
> *President, Le Conseil Héraldique*
> *85 Rue du Prince Royal*
> *Brussels*

This Heraldic Council was set up under a decree, dated February 6, 1844, of King Leopold I of the Belgians, following a resolution of 1843 that a consultative commission should be established for the purpose of verifying titles and examining requests for recognition of nobility. There are seven members and a registrar. The Council is consulted each time that the Ministry of Foreign Affairs presents a report to the sovereign on a request for recognition or confirmation of nobility or of title. It is required to agree on the noble status of everyone who requires an elevation in rank, extension of his titles to other members of his family, a change in his arms, or the recognition or confirmation of letters patent which have been granted by a foreign sovereign. The Minister of Foreign Affairs sends to the Council a dispatch concerning the decrees by which the sovereign grants titles of nobility, in order that the commission may submit its observations on the proposal for letters patents, arms, and other details of the order. The Council holds the roll of nobility and the register of letters patent. The Council can deliver attestations of affiliation and can certify the possession and use of arms. The Council keeps duplicate copies of genealogies, of blazons, and of all matters produced in support of favorable decisions taken by the Council. The copies are kept by the Registrar in a special register, and copies may be obtained from him at the expense of those requiring them.

Thus the Conseil Héraldique corresponds in its main functions to those of the Committee of Privileges of the House of Lords in England, and in others to the College of Arms.

A work published in 1896 by MM. Arerdt and De Ridder, entitled *Législation Héraldique de la Belgique 1595–1895, Jurisprudence du Conseil Héraldique 1844–1895,* gives an account of Belgian nobility legislation, old and new. The Conseil Héraldique thus keeps records of the noble coats of arms, that is, those belonging to the Belgian nobility. In Belgium (and in Holland) everyone has the right to choose a coat of arms, except that no noble emblems may be used unless one is entitled to a title of nobility. The coat of arms of another family (even though extinct) may not be adopted except on authority.

*3. L'Association de la Noblesse du Royaume de Belgique,* 96 Rue Souveraine, Brussels. (Letters should be addressed to M. le Secrétaire.) Office hours: 9 A.M.–noon and 3 P.M.–5 P.M. on Wednesdays and Fridays.

*4. Antwerpsche Kring voor Familiekunde* (Antwerp Society for Family Researches). ADDRESS: 25 Moonsstraat, Antwerp.

This society is dedicated to genealogical and heraldic researches. It publishes a review, *De Schakel,* which means *The Link.* Contributions to this periodical may be in Flemish or in French.

*5. Service de Centralisation des Etudes Généalogiques et Démographiques de Belgique.* The Secretary is M. P. E. Claessens, 26 Rue aux Laines, Brussels.

This service publishes some very useful notes. For example, in their publication, *L'Intermédiaire des Généalogistes,* Number 60 (November 1955), there is a very long article, "The Bastards of the House of Burgundy and Their Descendants." It appears that the dukes of Burgundy, the ancient possessors of Belgium, were particularly active in mingling with their people. The writers observe: "The most virtuous dukes made proof of a very relative chastity. Philip the Brave seems to have left only two bastards. John the Fearless had four, but one of these, John, Bishop of Cambrai, had seventeen. Philip the Good bid higher, but his thirty-three mistresses gave him only twenty-six children. Charles the Brave, called in the last century the Bold or the Rash, despite his proverbial continence, abandoned it many times in Lorraine. Thus, it is not astonishing that the blood of Burgundy has perpetuated itself to our times, surviving through five centuries the happenings which brutally put an end to the legitimate branch." No disgrace attached to these illegitimate offspring. In fact, as in the England of Charles II, noble ladies were proud to be the recipients of their sovereigns' transient affection. A lady of the house of Croy allowed herself to be debauched very joyously at a ball, by her duke, and the descendants were proud of the alliance.

As the house of Burgundy gradually declined in importance with the extinction of the legitimate male line, the bastard lines lost some of their social position. The writers of the article add: "In the regions of Lille, Vilvorde, Enghien, or Courtrai, the Bourgognes, though bearers of an illustrious name, lost their family tradition to the extent that some forgot their origin. They abandoned the particle [i.e., "de"], which was often omitted in the old documents, and submitted to the mutilations of their patronymic which were due to the negligence or ignorance of clergy and clerks. We find them in the male and female line at all levels of society, to the extent that today there can be few Belgian families which do not share in their blood, a fact which verifies a maxim of Plato, 'Each king descends from his subjects, and each subject draws his origin from kings.'" To drive home their point, the authors go so far as to show, at the end of their article, some families of Bourgogne which have not (as yet) been attached to the ducal pedigrees.

I do not seriously suggest that an American citizen should be rapturously enchanted at the prospect of being twenty-fifth in descent from some Duke of Burgundy. I cannot help recalling the amusing circumstances in which I came across Number 60 of *L'Intermédiaire des Généalogistes*. While I was at the 4th Congress in Brussels in 1958, referred to above, I went on a tour of some historic record centers, and while I was traveling in the coach copies of the booklet were handed around. I was interested in the touching solicitude of our Belgian colleagues in desiring to make us acquainted with the bastards of Burgundy. One of the latter is known in history as Le Grand Bâtard (Big Bastard), and certainly from him descended many notable lines. Certainly, in more serious vein, the great care which the Belgians have bestowed upon such a genealogical watershed as the dukes of Burgundy, and the skill which has attended their researches, does serve to show the likelihood of success in seeking for Belgian ancestors.

Indeed, in the same number of *L'Intermédiaire* which I have quoted, an account is given of the Belgian origins of the Delano (De Lannoy) family of the United States. This family is traced from one John de Lannoy, born at Turcoing toward 1570, married at Tournai, January 13, 1596. His son Philip went to America, and from him descended Warren Delano, whose fifth child, Sarah, married James Roosevelt in 1880; the latter, James and Sarah, were the parents of Franklin Delano Roosevelt.

To all of which may be added the fact that Jean de Lannoy of 1570 was fourth in descent from Bauduin de Bourgogne, Seigneur de Fallais-Oba-Bredame.

Another very interesting example of a pedigree which is traced from sources in Belgium is that of the British peer Lord Baillieu, whose family originated in Belgium in the sixteenth century, came to England at the time of the French Revolution, and later went to Australia.

# LUXEMBOURG

## INTRODUCTION

Luxembourg is a small independent state between Belgium, France, and Germany. It is a grand duchy ruled by its sovereign, the Grand Duchess Charlotte. It has been a grand duchy since the Congress of Vienna (1814–15) but has been independent only since 1867, when its neutrality was guaranteed by the principal European powers. In 1890 the rule over it passed to the Walramian branch of the Orange-Nassau family; its history in the Middle Ages and right until the Napoleonic Wars was very checkered, and Luxembourg has been the property of Burgundy, France, Austria, and Spain. This historical note is necessary because of the difficulty which might otherwise ensue in understanding the genealogy of Luxembourg. Although it is only a small state, it is important to many whose ancestors have come from there. The French Revolution made a great change in the keeping of archives in Luxembourg, for it was at the time of the Napoleonic invasion of Luxembourg that civil registration of births, marriages, and deaths began.

## CIVIL REGISTRATION

This began in 1796, when the French controlled the area. These registers are deposited with the communal administrations. The main source of information on this part of the subject is to be found with:

*M. Léon Zettinger, Archiviste de la Ville de Luxembourg*
*Hôtel de Ville*
*Place Guillaume*
*Luxembourg*

There are 126 municipalities in Luxembourg, each with an office in which documents relative to the citizens are written twice in the original. One copy remains in the municipality; the second is sent to the competent tribunal in Luxembourg or in Diekirch. Every ten years *Tables Décennales* (Decennial Tables) are made, in which names in connection with births, marriages, and deaths are arranged in alphabetical order with the dates. These tables are preserved in the Public Record Office of Luxembourg and run from 1793 to 1952 inclusive.

## PARISH REGISTERS

These exist in the more ancient parishes from the seventeenth century. The registers of the town of Luxembourg will be found in the archives of the town (see address given above). They are kept either in the local parish, the appropriate municipal office, or in Luxembourg or Diekirch. In the eighteenth century there were about 166 parishes.

The town of Luxembourg has in its possession the parish registers of the old parishes of the town, and these are partly from 1601 (with gaps) and partly from the beginning of the eighteenth century.

## RELEVES DES PROTOCOLES NOTARIAUX

These are records of proceedings before the public notaries which deal with various matters of property, and they are especially valuable as regards marriage settlements. The oldest go back to the year 1612, and the most recent to 1893. By a grand-ducal decree of 1951, these documents, when more than sixty years old, must be deposited in the Government Archives. Particulars of these documents can be obtained from:

*M. Antoine May, Conservateur aux Archives du Gouvernement*
*4 Boulevard Roosevelt*
*Luxembourg*

By the courtesy of M. May, I am able to give a list of notaries and their records, and although this is incomplete, it is of the greatest value (see at end of chapter).

In addition, there are in the Government Archives many census returns and other matters of importance; they give valuable details about the births, marriages, deaths, alliances, etc., and also sometimes include original copies of letters patent with description of arms.

## COATS OF ARMS

The modern position is that arms grants are in the province of the Grand Duchess but that they are seldom made. There are no Heralds in Luxembourg, but the sovereign acts in such matters on the advice of the Council of Ministers. In the Government Archives there is a registry of arms and titles of nobility which give the texts of the decrees with reproduction of the arms. This goes back to the period when the King of Holland was also sovereign of the grand duchy. For the period before this time (of the Dutch rule), reference must be made to the Registry of Patents of the Provincial Council for Commissions and Declarations from 1544 to 1791 (*The Inventory of the Archives of the Government—Inventaire des Archives du Gouvernement*—by P. Rapport, 1910). In this collection are often found concessions or grants of arms which are not preserved in Luxembourg but which are found in Brussels in the Archives du Royaume, Département de la Noblesse. This last case is an example of the way in which the affairs of Luxembourg are bound up with those of other countries.

## HERALDIC SOCIETIES

There was formerly a Luxembourg Heraldic Society, founded in 1947, from which was afterward formed the Association of Friends of History (Les Amis de l'Histoire, or Letzeburger

Geschichtsfrenn), which has for its object to propagate and to popularize the study of national history in the widest sense. One of the sections of the Association is Le Conseil Héraldique. This latter deals with matters specializing in heraldry, sigillography, and symbolism. Further information on this subject can be obtained from M. Robert Matagne, membre corr. Institut Grd. Ducal, sect. histor., Délégué aux Relations Extérieures du Conseil. Héraldique du Luxembourg. His address is 25 Rue Bertholet, Luxembourg.

## PUBLICATIONS

*La Noblesse au Grand-Duché de Luxembourg.* This work is by M. Jean-Robert Schleich de Bossé, and the second volume was published in 1957. It has pedigrees and coats of arms and much genealogical information.

*Bourses d'Etudes.* This work is by Aug. Bruck, Chef de Division au Gouvernement, and its full title is *Fondations de Bourses d'Etudes Instituées en Faveur des Luxembourgeois, 1882–1907.* The *bourses* are scholarships, or, as is said in England, exhibitions. The amount of genealogical information given in this work, of which the second edition is accessible to me, is very considerable. The book runs to over a thousand pages, and there is an index of twenty-five pages giving the names which are mentioned in the genealogical outlines. From this it can be gathered that the amount of genealogical material preserved in Luxembourg, in the archives of the various towns of this small state, is considerable.

NOTE: I am much obliged for assistance in preparing the above account to M. Emile Erpelding, 23 Rue de Rochefort, Luxembourg-Beggen, Luxembourg. M. Erpelding is an experienced genealogist whose researches have been of great assistance to American inquirers. He is particularly interested in tracing families with the name of Erpelding; he has traced the Erpelding genealogy to 1650.

## ROSTER OF NOTARIZED REGISTRARS—
## DIEKIRCH

(issued by the Record Office of the Courts of the District of Diekirch
and filed in the Government Archives)

The references to Roman numerals in the years in some cases below are to the new era calendar instituted by the French revolution-
aries.

| NAME | RESIDENCE | DATE OF RECORDS FILED |
|---|---|---|
| Adami, Jean-François | Vianden | 1712–1740 |
| Adolphi, P. J. | Vianden | 1671–1707 |
| André, Damian | Vianden | 1726–1770 |
| André, Julien-Louis | Vianden | 1802–1820 |
| Arendt, Michel | Diekirch | 1795–1819 |
| Atten, A. | Wiltz | 1818–1849 (with index) |
| Augustin | Vianden | 1763–1775 |
| Balthasar | Diekirch | 1637–1682 |
| Becker, Jean-Nicolas | Useldange | 1801–1841 |
| Becker, Tilmanni | Capweyler (Saeul) | 1732–1778 |
| Berg, Jean | Wiltz | 1678–1704 |
| Berg, J. P. | Wiltz | 1716–1727 |
| Bernard, Gilles | Wiltz | 1684–1747 |
| Bernard, Jean-Georges | Wiltz | 1725–1769 |
| Bernard, Charles-Théodore, père | Wiltz | 1781–1813 |
| Bertrand | Wiltz | 1760–1781 |
| Beschmont, Pierre | Weiswampach | 1810–1838 (with index) |
| Bian, Félix | Echternach | 1845 |
| Blum, Michel | Ettelbruck | 1804–1822 |
| Brassel, J. J. | Arsdorf Rambrouch | 1792–1819 |
| Brimeyer, Christophore | Greisch | 1756–1786 |
| Buttgenbach, père | Diekirch | 1679–1715 |
| Buttgenbach, J., fils | Diekirch | 1760–1781 |
| Claudon, J. H. | Ettelbruck | 1754–1780 |
| Clomes, J. B. | Bastogne | 1781–1788 |
| Cuno, A. | Echternach | 1755–1791 |
| Declay, J. | Diekirch | 1749–1777 |
| Defer, F. A. | Echternach | 1767–1811 |
| Delahaye, Charles | Wiltz | 1733–1780 |
| Dengler, J., père | Clervaux | 1760–1807 |

| NAME | RESIDENCE | DATE OF RECORDS FILED |
|------|-----------|------------------------|
| Dengler, C., fils | Clervaux | 1809–1817 |
| Didier, J. B. Ant. Charles Constantin | Diekirch | 1821–1859 |
| Didier-Hollenfeltz Didier, Pierre-Jules | Diekirch | 1860–1872 |
| Du Pont, H. | Basbellain | 1688–1741 |
| Dupont, Ant. | Dasbourg, Hosingen, and Weiswampach | 1780–1809 |
| Ensch, A. | Clervaux | 1777–1811 |
| Ensch, Martin | Echternach | 1770–1797 |
| Everling, A. | Grosbous | 1765–1794 |
| Felten, P. | Ettelbruck | 1710–1748 |
| Feyder, V. J. M. | Vianden | 1842–1857 |
| Franck, J. P. | Bellain | 1731–1773 |
| Giebel, J. | Vianden | 1761–1775 |
| Gobaud, Jean-Charles | Vianden | 1778–1795 |
| Guillaume, Paul | Wiltz | 1791–*an* XIII |
| Hanff, Jean-Joseph | Echternach | 1820–1841 (with index) |
| Hartmann, W. | Echternach | 1718–1757 |
| Hartmann, Antoine | Echternach | 1764–1794 (with index) |
| Herweg, J. B. | Echternach | 1800–1828 |
| Hippert, N. | Vianden | 1831–1839 |
| Hormann, J. | Wilwerdange | 1782–1794 |
| Hourst, J. B. | Ettelbruck | 1741–1745 |
| Huberty, Théodore | Beckerich | 1770–1792 |
| Jommes, C. | Ettelbruck | 1752–1787 |
| Juttel, Nicolas | Diekirch | 1793–1796 |
| Knaas, A. | Luxembourg | 1786–*an* VIII |
| Krell, Michel | Echternach | 1786–1803 |
| Laplume, J. | Colmar-Berg | 1693–1734 |
| Leibfried, André | | 1803–1831 (with index) |
| Limpach | Ettelbruck | 1783–*an* VIII |
| Loser, J. M. | Rosport | 1775–1788 |
| Loutsch, N. | Heinstert | 1730–1751 |
| Maes, Jean-Joseph | Echternach | 1806–1850 |
| Marnach | Marnach | 1776–1779 |
| Martiny, M. | Clervaux | 1760–1769 |
| Martiny, Michel | Wiltz | 1770–1795 |
| Mercatoris, Jean | Diekirch | 1624–1663 |
| Merck, J. | | 1622–1684 |
| Meirfeld | Vianden | 1631–1674 |
| Mergay, J. M. | Echternach | 1752–1754 |
| Meyer, Willibrord | Vianden | 1869–1874 |

| NAME | RESIDENCE | DATE OF RECORDS FILED |
|---|---|---|
| Michaelis, J. P. | Weiswampach | 1764–1792 |
| Piraux, Pierre | Diekirch | 1774–1795 |
| Printz, A. | Vianden | 1738–1764 |
| Promenschenkel, P. J. | Diekirch | 1724–1753 |
| Promenschenkel | Diekirch | 1754–1778 |
| Reding, N. | Befort (château) (1781–1784) Esch/Sûre (1785–1789) Ettelbruck (1794–an IV) | 1781–an IV |
| Reding, N. | Beckerich | 1791–1819 |
| Reding, N. | Beckerich | an IV–1852 (with index) |
| Reuter, W. | Luxembourg (1782–1783) Useldange (1784–1792) | 1782–1792 |
| Rischard, Philippe | Esch/Sûre | 1779–1795 |
| Rischard, Martin | Esch/Sûre | 1795–an V |
| Rousseau, Auguste | Wiltz | 1796–1813 |
| Schaack, Arnold | Vianden | 1898–1901 |
| Schmit, Martin | Vianden | 1876–1882 |
|  | Vianden | 1796–1799 |
| Seyler, J. P. N. J. | Ettelbruck (1841–1855) Diekirch (1855–1875) | 1841–1875 |
| Springenfeld | Diekirch | 1718–1731 |
| Suttor, Jos. Guillaume | Dasbourg (1809–1814) Ettelbruck (1814–1831) | 1809–1831 |
| Thilmany, J. N. | Boulaide | 1752–1781 |
| Thren | Wiltz | 1778–1782 |
| Thull, Nicolas | Wiltz | 1782–1793 |
| Vannerus, Simon, père | Diekirch | 1773–1792 |
| Vannerus, François Julien, fils | Diekirch | 1804–1850 |
| Veydert, J. M., père | Vianden | 1733–1773 |
| Veydert, J. N., fils | Vianden | 1773–1823 |
| Victor, N. | Ettelbruck | 1711–1755 |
| Watlet, C. | Diekirch | 1783–1793 |
| Welter, D. | Diekirch | 1695–1725 |
| Witry, Auguste | Vianden | 1883–1890 |
| Witry, Michel | Echternach | 1828–1868 |
| Wolf, Charles, Marcel, Alphonse, Nicolas | Vianden | 1857–1868 |

# ROSTER OF NOTARIZED REGISTRARS— LUXEMBOURG

(issued by the Courts of the District of Luxembourg and presently filed in the Government Archives)

| NAME | RESIDENCE | DATE OF RECORDS FILED |
|---|---|---|
| Adami, Guillaume | Luxembourg | 1696–1709 |
| Alberti, Nic. | Luxembourg | 1680–1695 |
| Aldring, J. | Luxembourg | 1629–1639 |
| Arend, J. P. | Luxembourg | 1729–1744 |
|  | Dudelange | 1745–1748 |
| Barthels, Christophe | Luxembourg | 1722–1776; 1782–1791 |
| Bartholet, J. Th. | Luxembourg | 1736–1744 (index: 1736–1741; see Klepper) |
| Bassompierre, Jean-Mathias | Luxembourg | 1677–1688 |
| Beer, N. | Luxembourg | 1754–1761; 1766–1770 |
| Behm, Jean-Nicolas | Luxembourg | 1771–1779; 1781–1782; 1784–1789; 1792–1793 (index: 1766–1788) |
| Bernard, Jean, Richard | Wiltz, | 1757 |
|  | Château de Sanem | 1758–1759; 1762–1763 |
| Beyser, Maximilien | Luxembourg | 1769–1775; 1778; 1781–1784; 1787–1788; 1790–1792 |
| Bofferding, Corneille | Luxembourg | 1755–1780 |
| Brabender, J. P. | Luxembourg, | 1763–1764; 1767–1776; 1780–1786 (index: 1763–1789) |
| Bracht, J. B. | Remich | 1785–1788; 1791–1796; 1798–1802; 1805–1811 |
| Braun, Dom. | Grevenmacher | 1755–1761; 1764–1765; 1768–1769 |
| Braun, Fred. | Grevenmacher | 1716–1754 |
| Brincour, Dominique | Luxembourg | 1742–1787 |
| Brosius, H. | Luxembourg | 1767–1790 (index: 1765–1790) |
| Broucq, J. P. Auguste | Luxembourg | 1721–1733; 1735–1739 (index: 1721–1738) |

| NAME | RESIDENCE | DATE OF RECORDS FILED |
|---|---|---|
| Burgruetgen, Guill. Alex | Luxembourg | 1747–1753; 1755–1757; 1759–1761; 1763; 1765–1767; 1769– 1770; 1772–1777; 1779–1783 |
| Collignon, Jean | Mussy-la-Ville | 1712–1722 |
| Collignon, P. | Luxembourg | 1732–1752  (index: 1731–1752; see Klepper) |
| Collignon, Joseph | Grevenmacher | 1773–1780 |
| Conter, J. | Remich | 1736–1740; 1746–1759; 1761–1762; 1767–1771; 1773–1775;1779 |
| Conter, Jean-Jacques | Luxembourg | 1767–1770; 1773–1775; 1785–1796 |
| Conter, Pierre | Remich | 1775–1776; 1780; 1782–1785;1787–1795 |
| Crocius, Charles | Luxembourg | (index: 1878–1905) |
| Crocius, Philippe, Jacques | Remich | 1755–1764; 1766; 1768–1769;1771; 1774–1778; 1781–1784; 1787–1795 |
| Cuno, Fr. | Luxembourg | 1808–1820; 1829–1836 |
| Dangler, François | Luxembourg | 1778–1781; 1786–1791; 1794–1795; *an* IV, V, VI, VII, VIII, IX, X, XI, XII |
| Defresne, Jos. | Bettembourg | 1786–1796; *an* V, VI, VII, VIII,XI |
| Degen, Fred. Mathias | Mondercange | 1688–1717 |
| Deleau, H. | Luxembourg | 1732–1743; 1751–1754 (index: 1725–1754; see Hartmann, B.G.) |
| Denis, J. B. | Luxembourg | 1728–1739; 1741; 1743; 1755–1761 |
| DeWald, J. Ch. | Luxembourg | 1768; 1770; 1772–1790; 1799–*an* VIII |
| Donlinger, Jean-Adam | Luxembourg | 1698–1725  (index: 1698–1728; see Klepper) |
| Eichhorn, Théodore | Wormeldange | 1820–1839 |
| Erpelding, Alexandre | Luxembourg | 1769–1771; 1776–1779; 1790–1791 |
| Fischer, J. | Luxembourg | 1762; 1765–1773 |
| François, Frédéric | Luxembourg | 1772–1774; 1780–1781; 1783–1787; 1789; 1795; *an* VII, X, XIII, 1806–1807; 1810  (index: 1772–1796) |
| François, Frédéric, père | Luxembourg | (index: 1772–1812) |

| NAME | RESIDENCE | DATE OF RECORDS FILED |
|---|---|---|
| François, Jean-Joseph | Luxembourg | 1812 (index: 1806–1810; 1814–1821) |
| François, Jean, le jeune | Luxembourg | 1813–1830 (index: 1813–1833) |
| Funck, Jean-Baptiste | Grevenmacher | 1838–1839 |
| Henri, Melchior | | |
| Gattermann, J. H. | Grevenmacher | 1709–1714 |
| Gebhardt, François Maximilien | Differdange, | 1817–1827; 1829–1835 |
| | Bascharage | |
| Gemen, J. B. | Larochette | 1763–1791 (index: 1763–1791) |
| Gerber, Jean | Luxembourg | 1667–1669; 1678; 1691–1700 |
| Gilles, Mathias Ernest | Luxembourg | 1669–1680; 1684–1694 |
| Gindt, J. F. | Grevenmacher | 1701–1706; 1791–1796; *an* IV,V, VI |
| Godtfrien, A. | Luxembourg | 1807–1809; *an* XI, XII |
| Groff, Jean Nic. | Luxembourg | 1629–1633 |
| Guilleaume, Jean François | Luxembourg | 1767–1774; 1788–1794 (index: 1766–1796) |
| Hartmann, Bernard Godefin | Luxembourg | 1732–1752 (index: 1728–1752) |
| Hencques, J. M. | Echternach | 1753–1760; 1766–1778 |
| | Larochette | (index: 1777–1796) |
| Haagen | Luxembourg | (index: 1777–*an* VIII; see Nauw) |
| Haagen | Luxembourg | 1739–1778; 1780–1785 |
| Hermann, Paul | Luxembourg | 1774–1780; 1782–1786 |
| Herneupont, Fr. St. | Grevenmacher | 1774–1779; 1781–1789 |
| Herneupont, L. | Luxembourg | 1709–1711 |
| Henn, P. | Luxembourg | |
| Hess, Jean-Jacques | Grevenmacher | 1789–1796; *an* VI, VII, VIII,IX, X, XI, XII, XIII, XIV, 1807–1826 (index: 1789–1810) |
| Hess, Jean-Charles | Grevenmacher | 1827–1856 |

| NAME | RESIDENCE | DATE OF RECORDS FILED |
| --- | --- | --- |
| Heuschling, François-Xavier | Luxembourg | 1807–1829 (index: 1795; 1807–1818) |
| Heuschling, H. | Bettembourg | 1733–1757 |
| Heuschling, J. | Luxembourg | 1752–an IV |
|  | Bitbourg | (index: 1752–1789) |
| Hormann, Jean Adam | Luxembourg | 1736–1744 |
| Huberty, Jean-Pierre | Grevenmacher | 1785–1795; an IV, VII, VIII,IX, X, XI, XII, XIII, XIV; |
|  | Luxembourg | 1807–1834 (index: 1785–an XIII; 1813–1834) |
| Jost, Baptiste | Esch/Alzette | An IV, V |
| Jungers | Luxembourg | 1740–1755 |
| Kieller, Sébastien | Mondercange | 1717–1720 (Dickes Th. greffier); 1721–1727; 1730–1734; 1737–1743 |
| Kleber, F. | Luxembourg | 1733–1759; 1761–1764 (index: 1733–1764) |
| Klein, François | Wormeldange | 1786–1796; an VI, VII, VIII,IX, X, XI, XII, XIII, 1806–1820 |
| Klein, François | Luxembourg, | 1793–1796; an IV, VI, VII, VIII |
|  | Dalheim | 1778–1779; 1782–1791; |
| Klein, Jean-Nicolas | Junglinster | 1814–1860 (index: 1814–1860) |
| Kellner, W. | Luxembourg | 1708–1732 |
| Klensch, Jean | Luxembourg | 1624–1647 |
| Klepper, D. | Luxembourg | 1739–1744 (index: 1734–1744) |
| Kneip, Pierre, François Joseph | Luxembourg | 1810–1820 (index: 1811–1818) |
| Krell, Damien Henri | Luxembourg | An IV, V, VI, VII, IX, X, XI |
| Lambert, J. | Luxembourg | 1721–1723 (index: 1721–1723; see Klepper) |
| Langers, Louis | Luxembourg | 1783–1796 |
| Leclerc, Pierre | Luxembourg | 1695–1712; 1716–1719 (index: 1707–1719) |

| NAME | RESIDENCE | DATE OF RECORDS FILED |
|---|---|---|
| Leclerc, Jacques Théodore Jos. | Mersch | 1814–1819; 1821–1823; 1826–1831 |
| Ledure, Jean Nic. | Altwies | *An* IX, X, XI, XII, XIII, XIV, 1807–1822 (index: 1811–1822) |
| Ledure, J. P. | Grevenmacher | 1840–1841 |
| Witry, Michel | Grevenmacher | 1840–1841 |
| Lorent, J. P. | Remich | 1711–1725; 1727–1733 |
| Majerus, Nic. | Luxembourg | 1784–1790; 1824–1835 (index: 1784–1796; see Nauw) |
| Mannart, Jean-Paul | Luxembourg | 1670–1685 |
| Mathieu, R. J. | Luxembourg | 1749–1750; 1752–1769; 1775; 1777; 1784–1789 |
| Meyer, H. | Messancy | 1776–1785 |
| Mitz, David | Grevenmacher | 1714–1741 |
| Moris, Antoine | Luxembourg | 1746–1756; 1761–1763; 1766–1786 |
| Moris, Jacques | Wormeldange | 1774–1788 (index: 1787–1788) |
| Moris, Maurice | Grevenmacher | 1806–1829 |
| Mothe, H. | Mondercange | 1781–1807 |
| Naey, Pierre | Luxembourg | 1659–1689; 1691–1707 |
| Nauw, Jean-Baptiste | Luxembourg | 1728–1730; 1733–1738 (index: 1728–1742) |
| Niederprum, M. | Luxembourg | 1786–1789; 1791–1793 |
| Nockin, F. H. père | Belvaux | 1731–1758; 1761–1781 |
| Nockin, J. B. fils | Belvaux | 1782–1796; *an* IV–XI |
| | Esch | (index: *an* IV–X) |
| Nothomb, Pierre | Luxembourg | 1804–1807; *an* XI |
| | Bettembourg | |
| Oblet, Charles Alex | Luxembourg | 1698–1719 (index: 1686–1725) |
| Oms, J. P. | Bettembourg | 1809–1818 |
| Ordt, Wolfgang Henri | Luxembourg | 1698–1702; 1704–1706; 1708–1714; 1717–1719 |

| NAME | RESIDENCE | DATE OF RECORDS FILED |
| --- | --- | --- |
| Ordt, Pierre-Paul | Luxembourg | 1726–1730 |
| Outremont, N. | Remich | 1785–1796; *an* IV, V, VI, VII |
| Pegora | | (index: 1785–1788. index: 1762–1764; see Klepper) |
| Philippe, Pierre, père | Mersch | 1782–1793; 1795; *an* IV, V, VI, VII, VIII, IX, X, XI, XII, XIII, XIV; 1806–1811 |
| Philippe, Pierre, fils | Mersch | 1814–1817 |
| Pierret, François | Luxembourg | 1693; 1699–1700; 1708–1738 |
| Rang, Georges | Luxembourg | 1631–1633 |
| Reding, J. N. | Luxembourg | 1715–1743 |
| Reding, J. F. | Luxembourg | 1681–1691 |
| Reuter, Dominique | Luxembourg | 1792 |
| Ritter, Jean Henri | Grevenmacher | 1787–1796; *an* V, VI, VII, VIII, IX, X, XI, XII, XIII, 1806–1820 (index: 1786–1796) |
| Ritter, Joseph | Grevenmacher | 1820–1836; 1839–1840; 1842–1857; 1859–1864 (index: 1831–1856; 1858) |
| Sassenheim, Jean-Pierre | Sanem | 1678–1690 |
| Schanus, J. M. | Grevenmacher | 1778–1790; 1793–1796 |
| | Clemency | |
| | Luxembourg | |
| Schmit, Jean-Pierre | Luxembourg | 1776–1781; 1784–1788; 1792–1794 |
| Schwind, Nicolas | Septfontaines | 1783–1786 |
| Schwab, J. G. | Luxembourg | 1740–1775 (index: 1740–1775) |
| Schwartz, Jean-Baptiste | Luxembourg | 1784–1787; 1789–1790; 1794–1796 (index: 1784–1795) |
| Schumacher, Nic. | Bettange | 1819–1834 |
| Servais, P. | Mersch | 1763–1786; 1788–1790 |
| Sparnagel, Salomon | Luxembourg | 1612–1613 |

| NAME | RESIDENCE | DATE OF RECORDS FILE |
|---|---|---|
| Spranck, Michel | Luxembourg | 1758–1764; 1769–1788 (index: 1760–1787) |
| Spyr, Pierre | Luxembourg | 1724–1759 (index: 1756–1761; see Kleber) |
| Stephany, J. | Remich | 1726–1740 |
| Strabius, J. | Luxembourg | 1673–1687 |
| Taffler, J. | Luxembourg | 1698–1720 (index: 1706–1719; see Leclerc,P., Lux.) |
| Thiry, Claude | Luxembourg | 1784–1789; 1794 (index: 1784–1793) |
| Thomas, P. | Luxembourg | 1767–1775 (index: 1754–1781; see Kleber) |
| Thorn, Jean-Pierre | Remich | 1783–1797; *an VII, VIII, IX, X, XI, XII* (index: 1783–1796) |
| Thorn, F. M. | Remich | 1805–1835 (index: 1805–1832) |
| Ungeschickt, Jean Guill. | Wellen (Grevenmacher) | 1724–1769 |
| Wenger, Jean-Henri | Luxembourg | 1776–1796; *an IV, X, XI, XIII,* 1805–1825 |
| Wenger, J. B. | Luxembourg | 1816–1823 |
| Weydert, André | Grevenmacher | 1830–1839 |
| Winckell, F. | Remich | 1693–1699; 1704–1707; 1714–1716 |
| Winckell. Jean-Paul | Remich | 1727–1776 |
| Winckell. J. P. | Altwies | 1781–1788 |
| Winckell, Jean-Nic. | Remich | 1754–1761; 1763–1781 (index: 1754–1770) |
| Winckell, Paul-Fréd. | Remich | *An IV, X, XIII,* 1806–1815 |

# FRANCE

In France, not only are there vast stores of records which bear on genealogical research, but there is also the immense advantage that everything is organized in a most efficient manner.

## ECCLESIASTICAL REGISTERS

As in other western European countries, the keeping of registers of baptisms, marriages, and burials was made obligatory in France from the sixteenth century and was confided to the parish priest (the curé). Two copies were made; the one remained in the parish, the other was sent to the office of the judicial organism (*le greffe*) with which the parish, seneschal's court, or bailiwick was connected.

In 1792 (the era of the French Revolution) the parish registers which were found in the parishes were turned over to the archives of each municipality, and the copy of the archives of the *département*.

From 1792 the documents of the civil status (*l'état civil*) have been kept by the state in each commune (that is, township or parish), in two copies. One stays in the commune, the other goes to the office (*le greffe*) of the Tribunal of First Instance. If, therefore, you wish to study the ancestry of a family, you must know the *département* where it originates. Then you must write to the archivist of the *département*, who will give you information and indicate the commune or communes of origin as well as the records which he has in his own depot. A list of the depots of the departmental archives with their addresses is given at the end of this account.

Since 1792, the parishes have continued to keep two copies of their entries of baptism, marriage, and burial. These include the great bulk of the population, as the majority of French people are Catholics, to the extent at least that they are baptized, married, or buried with religious rites.

One set of these registers remains in each parish; the other is sent to the archives of the bishopric to which the parish belongs.

These parochial registers are somewhat incomplete, often omitting the patronymic and some of the Christian names. They are, however, very useful for Paris, where the old archives of the civil state were destroyed up to 1871 in the course of the fighting with the Communists during the disorders of that year. At that time the Hôtel de Ville was burned and with it was destroyed a magnificent collection of parochial registers.

It may be noted in this connection that for Parisian families you must have recourse to the minutes of Parisian notaries. This great loss of the parish registers and other documents burned in 1871 is comparable to the destruction of the Irish records in 1922. It has put a stop to many researches concerning Parisian families. However, as M. Jacques Meurgey de Tupigny (see below) remarks, happily Paris is peopled with provincials and there are many chances that the grandfather whom you seek may have been born in a province.

## WILLS

Wills are found in the archives of the notaries, whose property they remain. You must then know the name of the notary who drew the will, to have the chance of finding it. For the Département de la Seine, the 144 surveys (*études*) of the notaries have been deposited in the National Archives. For the other *départements,* the matter varies very greatly, but the archivist of the *département* cannot fail to give you information. For the eighteenth century, there exists, in the Archives de la Seine, a *fichier* (card index) of wills which have been registered by the administrative authority and which have a great interest.

## HERALDRY

The French state ignores the arms of families except in cases of litigation; for example, if anyone takes the arms of a family to put them on the labels of bottles. This happened to a merchant who had bought a property and who had put on his bottles the arms which he had found on the gate of the château. He lost his case and was ordered to remove the arms from the labels. On the other hand, the arms of towns are controlled by the ministries of the Interior and of National Education. (The Direction of the National Archives comes under the latter ministry.) Thus heraldry is a simple matter, a kind of customary right, and no documents or payments are required.

In other words, with the exception of the arms of towns, the French law does not recognize arms or their use. Anyone can take what arms he pleases. But the law does recognize the theft of arms, as of any other possession. Arms and automobiles are on a level, as in the case cited above.

There are, of course, many thousands of coats of arms in France, which gave to heraldry its original language. The best French armorial (corresponding to *Burke's General Armory*) is the *Grand Armorial de France,* in seven volumes, the last of which appeared several years ago. There are about 40,000 coats of arms mentioned in these volumes. They can be procured from, La Société du Grand Armorial de France, 179 Boulevard Haussmann, Paris. The price is about 100 livres.

There is a Société Française d'Héraldique et de Sigillographie, 113 Rue de Courcelles, Paris 17. The President is M. Jacques Meurgey de Tupigny (Conservateur aux Archives Nationales).

## THE NATIONAL ARCHIVES

These must be distinguished from the archives of the *départements.* The Archives Nationales keeps all documents from the government ministries and the great organizations of the state. There is a very valuable guide to these archives, as follows: *Guide des Recherches Généalogiques aux Archives Nationales,* by M. Jacques Meurgey de Tupigny. This work is very good, not only in the subjects covered by its title but also in the advice given by M. De Tupigny on the subject of genealogical research. Much of this advice would be applicable in any country. There is also a study on biographical researches in the Archives de la Seine by François de Vaux de—Foletier.

In the National Archives the sections are arranged under the headings of: (1) *Section ancienne,* (2) *Section moderne,* (3) *Sous-section des archives priveés, economiques, et du microfilm,* (4) *Minutier central,* and (5) *Sceaux.* We will deal with these sections in detail.

*1. Section ancienne* (Old Section). This has documents on genealogical titles, information on the civil status (notarial archives, legitimizations, naturalizations); heraldry; royal lines; the royal household; the offices of administration, finance, and justice; particulars of the Army, Navy, colonies, the clergy, the nobility, and the orders of chivalry. The genealogical titles cover a vast range and include much that is concerned with the nobility of the various provinces.

*2. Section moderne* (Modern Section). This deals with information from the Revolution onward, through all the political vicissitudes of France up to the Second Empire. There is an interesting section under the heading of *Cultes* (religions). There are many dossiers on individual Catholic priests, Protestant clergy, and Jewish rabbis.

*3. Sous-section* . . . (Subsection of Private, Economic, and Microfilm Archives). It is expressly stated in the *Guide* that some of these documents can be profitably consulted on genealogical researches. Many family archives are deposited in this section (as in the Manuscript Department of the British Museum). A full list of these decuments is given in M. De Tupigny's *Guide.*

*4. Minutier central* (Central Minute Book). This refers to the 144 surveys by notaries of Paris mentioned above. The earliest date in this series is 1452. For the period 1780–1830 there is a *fichier* of more than 1,000,000 names. If the researcher knows the name of the notary and the date of the document, the matter is easy. Otherwise, a long and laborious search may be necessary.

*5. Sceaux* (Seals). This is a particularly valuable section for heraldic information.

## ARCHIVES DE LA SEINE

These cover, first, civil status before 1860—births, marriages, deaths, and so on—of Parisians as far as this has been reconstituted from the destruction in 1871. Then comes the civilian status after 1860 (Parisian); that of the suburbs; the deaths of soldiers in the military hospitals, 1792–1817; naturalizations, in some cases from the time of the Revolution; quinquennial census returns in Paris; electoral lists, 1848–1938; dossiers dealing with decorations, and so on. These are among the treasures of this departmental archive.

## LES ARCHIVES DEPARTEMENTALES

The archives of the *départements* include the archives of local administrations in the *département*. There is a guide to this called *Etat des Inventaires des Archives Nationales Départementales*. This is called the Supplement from 1937 to 1954, but in fact it is more of a Complement to the *Etat* of 1937, copies of which are, I understand, no longer available.

The first part of this work gives the additions to the National Archives under the five sections set out above. The second part gives additions in the archives of the *départements* in the list at the close of this section.

## ARCHIVES OFFICES

| Départements | Adresses |
|---|---|
| AIN: | Préfecture, Bourg-en-Bresse |
| AISNE: | Préfecture, Laon |
| ALLIER: | "Bellevue," Izeure |
| ALPES (BASSES): | Rue des Archives, Digne |
| ALPES (HAUTES): | Préfecture, Gap |
| ALPES-MARITIMES: | Avenue E. Cavell, Nice-Cimiez |
| ARDÈCHE: | Préfecture, Privas |
| ARDENNES: | Citadelle, Mézières |

| Départements | Adresses |
|---|---|
| ARIÈGE: | Avenue de Général de Gaulle, Foix |
| AUBE: | 21 Rue Etienne-Pedron, Troyes |
| AUDE: | 48 Rue Bringer, Carcassonne |
| AVEYRON: | Rue L. Oustry, Rodez |
| BELFORT: | Préfecture, Belfort |
| BOUCHES-DU-RHÔNE: | Préfecture, Marseille VIe. |

| *Départements* | *Adresses* |
|---|---|

CALVADOS: 1 Parvis Notre-Dame, Caen

CANTAL: Rue du 139e R.I., Aurillac

CHARENTE: 5 rue de la Préfecture, Angoulème

CHARENTE-MARITIME: Préfecture, La Rochelle

CHER: 9 Rue Fernault, Bourges

CORRÈZE: Rue Souham, Tulle

CORSE: Préfecture, Ajaccio

CÔTE-D'OR: 8 Rue Jeannin, Dijon

CÔTES-DU-NORD: 9 Rue du Parc, Saint-Brieuc

CREUSE: 4 Rue des Pommes, Guéret

DORDOGNE: 2 Place Hoche, Périguex

DOUBS: Préfecture, Besançon

DRÔME: Rue A. Lacroix, Valence

EURE: 2 Rue de La Préfecture, Evreux

EURE-ET-LOIR: 9 Rue du Cardinal Pie, Chartres

FINISTÈRE: Préfecture, Quimper

GARD: 20 Rue des Chassaintes, Nîmes

GARONNE: (HAUTE): 11 Boulevard Griffoul Dorval, Toulouse

GERS: 6 Rue Ed. Quinet (B.P. No. 6) Auch

GIRONDE: 13–25 Rue d'Aviau, Bordeaux

HÉRAULT: 40 Rue Proud'hon, Montpellier

ILLE-ET-VILAINE: 2 Place St-Mélaine, Rennes

INDRE: 32 Rue Vieillie-Prison, Châteauroux

INDRE-ET-LOIRE: Rue des Ursulines, Tours.

ISÈRE: Préfecture, Grenoble

JURA: Préfecture, Lons-le-Saunier

LANDES: 26 Rue Victor Hugo, Mont-de-Marsan

LOIR-ET-CHER: 21 Rue d'Angleterre, Blois

LOIRE: Préfecture, Saint-Etienne

LOIRE (HAUTE): Boulevard Jules Vallès, Le Puy

LOIRE-ATLANTIQUE: 8 Rue de Bouillié, Nantes

LOIRET: 15 Rue Chappon, Orléans

LOT: 14 Rue des Cadourques, Cahors

LOT-ET-GARONNE: Place de Verdun, Agen

LOZÈRE: Préfecture, Mende

MAINE-ET-LOIRE: Préfecture, Angers

MANCHE: Préfecture, Saint-Lô

MARNE: 1 Rue des Buttes, Châlons-sur-Marne

MARNE (HAUTE): 1 Rue Dutailly, Chaumont

MAYENNE: Rue Noémie-Hamard, Laval

MEURTHE-ET-MOSELLE: 1 Rue de la Monnaie, Nancy

MEUSE: 44 Rue du Petit Bourg, Bar-le-Duc

MORBIHAN: 2 Rue Alain le Grand, Vannes

MOSELLE: Préfecture, Metz

NIÈVRE: 1 Rue Charles Roy, Nevers

NORD: 1 Rue du Pont-Neuf, Lille

OISE: Préfecture, Beauvais

ORNE: Préfecture, Alençon

PAS-DE-CALAIS: 14 Place de la Préfecture, Arras

PUY-DE-DÔME: Préfecture, Clermont-Ferrand

PYRÉNÈES (BASSES): Palais du Parlement, Pau

PYRÉNÈES (HAUTES): Rue des Ursulines, Tarbes

PYRÉNÈES-ORIENTALES: 11 Rue du Bastion Saint-Dominique, Perpignan

RHIN (BAS): 5–9 Rue Fischart, Strasbourg

RHIN (HAUT): Cité administrative, 3 Rue Fleischhauer, Colmar

RHÔNE: 2 Chemin de Montauban, Lyon

SAÔNE (HAUTE): Préfecture, Vesoul

SAÔNE-ET-LOIRE: Préfecture, Mâcon

SARTHE: Rue des Résistants Internés, Le Mans

SAVOIE: Préfecture, Chambéry

*Départements*               *Adresses*

SAVOIE (HAUTE): 4 Rue du 30° R.I.,
Annecy
SEINE: 30 Quai Henri IV, Paris
IVe.
SEINE-MARITIME: 21 Rue de
Crosne, Rouen
SEINE-ET-MARNE: Préfecture, Me-
lun
SEINE-ET-OISE: 12 Rue Neuve
Norte-Dame, Versailles
SÈVRES (DEUX): Préfecture, Niort
SOMME: 88 bis Rue Gaulthier de
Rumilly Amiens
TARN: Cité Administrative, Avenue
du Général Giraud, Albi
TARN-ET-GARONNE: 5 bis Cours
Foucault, Montauban
VAR: 1 Boulevard Foch, Draguig-
nan
VAUCLUSE: Palais des Papes, Avig-
non

*Départements*               *Adresses*

VENDÉE: Préfecture, La Roche-sur-
Yon
VIENNE: Rue Edouard Grimaux,
Poitiers
VIENNE (HAUTE): 2 Rue des
Combes, Limoges
VOSGES: 4 Rue de la Préfecture,
Epinal
YONNE: Préfecture, Auxerre
ALGER: Préfecture, Alger
CONSTANTINE: Préfecture, Constan-
tine
ORAN: Préfecture, Oran
MARTINIQUE: Préfecture, Fort-de-
France
GUADELOUPE
GAUYANE
RÉUNION: B.P. No. 289, Saint-
Denis-de-la-Réunion

# SPAIN

## CIVIL REGISTRATION

This was established in Spain by a law of June 17, 1870. It includes particulars of birth, marriage, and death. The Offices of Civil Registry function in Spanish territory under the direction of the Justices of municipalities, of districts, and of the peace, who are charged with the administration of these offices. They (that is, the Civil Registry Offices) come under Justices of Municipalities in provincial capitals and in municipalities which have more than 20,000 inhabitants. The District Justices have the offices in their charge in the principal municipality of the district where they reside, and the Justices of the Peace do likewise in each of the remaining municipalities of the nation.

Each Spanish consulate in foreign territory has the character of a Civil Registry Office for the entry of the facts (of birth, marriage, and death) relative to Spaniards under its jurisdiction.

Finally, there is a Central Registry, which is found in the establishment of the Director General of Registers and of Notaries in the Ministry of Justice. In the books of this Central Registry are inserted the duplicates of the consular entries, those referring to strangers or Spaniards who have no known domicile, and also those of privately celebrated marriages.

## PAROCHIAL, OR ECCLESIASTICAL, REGISTRATION

In this respect, Spain can claim a position far in advance of the rest of Europe.

Before the Council of Trent (1545–63), even in the fifteenth century, some parishes of the Catholic Church had registers of baptisms, marriages, and burials. Cardinal Cisneros, in the first Synod of Alcalá, held at the beginning of the sixteenth century, decided that this practice should be adopted throughout Spain. This occurred some years after the complete unification of Spain under Ferdinand and Isabella. The last Moorish kingdom, Granada, was conquered by the Spanish forces in 1492.

*The Guidebook of the Spanish Church,* published by the General Office of Information and Statistics of the Church in 1954, gives a list of all the parishes of Spain divided by dioceses. In each case, the date is given of the most ancient register book in each one of the three categories. The most ancient parochial register in Spain is that of the parish of Verdú, in the diocese of Solsona, the oldest document of which dates from 1394.

In the *Guidebook* referred to above, 37 other parochial registers are mentioned whose age goes back to the fifteenth century. From an examination of the same guide it can be deduced that, of the 19,000 parishes which exist in Spain, there are 1636 parishes whose registers are anterior in date to 1570, the period when most parochial records begin.

I do not know if the above-mentioned *Guidebook* is identical with a directory of parishes mentioned by one of my correspondents under the name *Guía Ecclesiástica y Civil de los Pueblos de España,* by J.V. This directory gives (not in all cases) the name of the parish when there is more than one in the locality, and the address in the important towns. Otherwise, it is sufficient to address the correspondence to: Revdo. Sr. Cura Párroco.

It should be noted that many registers were destroyed in the War of Independence against France (Napoleonic invasion of Spain, 1808) and others in the struggle between the present government and the Communists (1936–39). There is no Central Register from which one can learn whether a particular register exists. The branch of the International Institute (see below) known as El Instituto Luis de Salazar intended to accomplish this task but has desisted from the attempt.

## WILLS

In the Spanish civil legislation, three kinds of wills are recognized as valid: (1) open, (2) closed, and (3) holograph. These are the three most important species of wills, which can be considered as normal.

*1. The open will* is that which is made by the testator personally before a notary and three witnesses. This is the most usual form. There are variations of it—for the will of a lunatic (the will being made in a lucid moment), for that of a deaf or blind person, and for a will made in a foreign language and translated. There are likewise arrangements whereby an open will can be made without a notary, but these details concern the student of Spanish law rather than the genealogist.

*2. The closed will* is that written by the testator, or by some other person at his request, and delivered to the notary in a sealed envelope before five witnesses.

*3. The holograph will* is that which is written completely by the testator, sealed by him, and kept by him. The person who finds it after the testator's death must deliver it to the Justice. Arrangements exist for the making of wills by military and maritime personnel in consideration of their peculiar circumstances.

Limited to certain regions and reminiscent of the ancient Foral Law, there exists a form of will made before the parish priest. This is called a sacramental will and can occur in Catalonia, Aragon, and Navarre.

Testaments made before or deposited with a notary are obviously the best for both the testator and the genealogist, since these satisfy the most exacting legal requirements and are therefore more easily preserved. But other kinds of wills pass a rigorous scrutiny before the Justice of First Instance before they are admitted to protocol (that is, probate) and entered into the registries of the notary in the country seat or district.

Wills admitted to probate in the last twenty-five years are kept by the notary in his dwelling and are his care and responsibility. Those which are more than twenty-five years old go to the general archives of probate in the charge of a notary.

The archives of the notarial protocols (probate), of which there is one in each notarial district, are situated in the following capitals, which are the same as those which exist for the Territorial Audiences (that is, High Courts): Albacete, Palma de Mallorca, Barcelona, Burgos, Cáceres, La Coruña, Granada, Madrid, Pamplona, Oviedo, Las Palmas de Gran Canaria, Seville, Valencia, Valladolid y Zaragoza.

By a decree of the President of the government of March 2, 1945, there was created, in each archive of the protocols, a Historical Section. In this are kept all the wills older than 100 years. These sections are open to scientific investigation, and the examination of the documents there preserved is free. The Historical Sections correspond to the provincial capitals; they form part, but as independent sections, of the respective provincial historical archives. The keeping and preserving of these Historical Sections is entrusted to the notaries, archivists, and others, of the Staff of Archivists, Librarians, and Archaeologists.

There exists, also, in the Ministry of Justice, a Registry of Last Deeds. In this are kept, in alphabetical order and indexed, wills in extracts authorized by the notary. On the death of a person, those interested in his property request from this registry a certificate. From this, the last wishes of the deceased can be learned.

The Register of Wills exists only from the end of the nineteenth century. Today these archives do not belong to one single organization; some are under the care of the municipality or province, others belong to certain institutions of historical studies and may have been lost. The reason for this dispersion is that formerly these protocols were the private property of the notary, and on his death, his heirs either sold them to another notary or allowed them to get lost.

## PUBLIC RECORD OFFICE

There is nothing corresponding to the Public Record Office in London. At present there is, however, in each of the government ministries a Historical Administrative Archive. The establishment of a Central Archive is projected.

Official regulations are published in the *Official Bulletin of the State* (corresponding to the London *Gazette*), but if they have a general character they appear in the legislative collection, which is published by the Ministry of Justice.

## HERALDRY

It would appear that there does not exist in Spain any official entity analogous to the College of Arms in England. In olden times there were persons known (as elsewhere in Europe) as Kings of Arms. They were authorized to issue certificates in matters of nobility, genealogy, and coats of arms. By a royal decree of July 29, 1915, of the Ministry of Grace and Justice, the examinations used to test the fitness of aspirants to the posts of Kings of Arms were regulated. By a decree of April 13, 1951, of the Ministry of Justice, this matter was regulated again. The title of Chronicler of Arms then superseded that of the old King of Arms. They are bound to be senior in age and graduates in law or philosophy and literature. They are appointed by a ministerial order after having passed an examination. Only those who have the title (of Chronicler of Arms–Cronista de Armas) approved by the Ministry of Justice can supply certificates on the matters mentioned. By a law of May 4, 1948, legislation anterior to April 14, 1931 (when the Republic was set up), was re-established for the recognition, transmission, and rehabilitation of noble titles; the subject comes under the control of the Ministry of Justice.

The following archives contain documents dealing with nobility:

*The Historical National Archives of Madrid, which contain documents of the four Military Orders of Chivalry—those of Santiago, Alcántara, Calatrava, and Montesa.*

*Archives of Simancas (Valladolid).*

*Archives of the Indies (Seville).*

*Archives of the Crown of Aragon (Barcelona).*

*Archives of the chancelleries of Valladolid and Granada.*

*Regional archives of Valencia, Galicia, and Mallorca.*

*Private archives of the nobility.*

*The National Library (Biblioteca Nacional), Madrid.*

*University libraries.*

There are some useful bibliographies which can be mentioned in the above collection:

*Benito Municio y García Cuver,* Bibliografía Genealógica de la Biblioteca Nacional.

*Zazo y Rosillo,* Alfabeto General de Apellidos (*that is, surnames*).

*García Caraffa,* Enciclopedia Genealógica y Heráldica.

*Atienza,* Diccionario de Apellidos.

*Montoto,* Nobiliario de Conquistadores.

## PUBLICATIONS

1. *Armory and Nobility of the Spanish Kingdoms* (*Armería y Nobiliario de los Reinos Españoles*). This work has been published by the International Institute (see below). It contains the arms and genealogies of many Spanish families with indication of the documents where their dates can be found. One volume has been published; the second is in course of publication (as of 1957).

2. *Nobiliary Dictionary* (*Diccionario Nobiliario*), by Julio Atienza. Arms of a large number of Spanish families, also with their nobiliary titles. Published by Aguilar.

3. *Heraldic and Genealogical Encyclopedia; Spanish-American* (*Enciclopedia Heráldica y Genealógica; Hispano-Americana*), by Alberto and Arturo García Caraffa. More than fifty-five volumes have been published; according to one statement, up to seventy-nine, as far as the letter *R.* It contains the arms and genealogies of a multitude of families in Spain and Latin America. This work can be found in every library of any importance in Spain; probably in the Library of Congress.

4. There exist also numerous nobiliary studies of particular regions in Spain. Details of particular regions can be obtained from the International Institute.

5. Sala de los Hijosdalgo (literally Hall of the Sons of the Nobles). There is a catalogue of all the documents brought forward and proved, by Alfredo Basanta; new edition by *Hidalguía* (kept in the Archives of the Royal Chancellery in Valladolid). To be recognized as belonging to the *hidalguía* (nobles, or gentry), it is necessary to prove this condition in a plea brought before the

Royal Chancellery (Valladolid, Oviedo, Granada, and Pamplona) in the corresponding Sala de los Hijosdalgo. The whole of the lesser gentry of Spain base their genealogies on these pleas. The present state of the archives in each case is as follows:

*Valladolid*. The whole is preserved; catalogued (see above).

*Oviedo*. The records were burned by the Communists in the war of 1936. There is a catalogue published by J. de Rujula.

*Granada*. Records partly preserved, no published catalogue, but information can be obtained in the archives.

*Pamplona*. Almost all preserved. A catalogue has been published by J. M. Huarte Jauregui.

In the kingdom of Aragon, the equivalent to the Sala is the Court of Justice. The archives are preserved at Zaragoza, but there is no published catalogue.

6. The *Index of the Salazar Collection* (*Indice de la Colección Salazar*), by B. Cuartero and El Marqués de Siete Iglesias. Of this, nineteen volumes have been published, and genealogical information begins chiefly with Vol. X. The documents are kept in the Royal Academy of History in Madrid. Address: Real Academia de la Historia, Calle de León 21, Madrid.

7. Genealogical documents and manuscripts in the National Library (Biblioteca Nacional, Madrid). Catalogue by M. Santiago.

It should also be noted that there are catalogues of particular organizations which have a bearing on genealogical information; for example, the Spanish Military Orders, the Titles of the Kingdom, The Royal Company of the Marine Guards, and others. In this connection may be mentioned the *General Military Archive of Segovia*. (See below.)

Finally may be mentioned many works of extraordinary merit which were published in the seventeenth and eighteenth centuries, among which must be cited those of Don Luis de Salazar y Castro, which study mainly the families of the first nobility in Spain.


## INTERNATIONAL INSTITUTE

Instituto Internacional de Genealogía y Heráldica. Address: Apartado de Correas 7.077, Madrid. This institute is valuable not only for Spanish archives but also as a center of genealogical information on a large scale. Through the Institute, conferences are organized in various European capitals, which are very useful as gatherings for genealogical and heraldic scholars. See the Introduction to the present work for more information.

## "GENERAL MILITARY ARCHIVE OF SEGOVIA: INDEX OF PERSONAL DOCUMENTS"

At Segovia are the archives of the Spanish state as regards military personnel. I have visited this place myself and seen some of the records. The above title shows the extent of the work which has been produced by Luis de Salazar y Castro, under the direction of the Colonel Director of the Archive. "In this monumental work there will be made known the names and Christian names, quality, matter, and year of entrance of those who have served Spain during the seventeenth, eighteenth, and nineteenth centuries and whose complete documents [personal, decorations, matrimonial, pensions, etc.] are conserved in the Military Archive of Segovia." There are said to be 850,000 entries in the Archive. The book can be obtained from the periodical *Hidalguía*, Calle de Atocha 91, Madrid. The whole work will run to ten or twelve volumes. Price per volume is 400 pesetas (approximately $6.65).

# PORTUGAL

Portugal is a country with a great and glorious history. Its Orders of Chivalry alone are deserving of close study. The country remains a great colonial power with large territories in Africa and Asia. In view of all this, it may be expected that records of genealogical value would be found there, and this is the case.

## CIVIL REGISTRATION

Civil registration appeared in Portugal for the first time on May 16, 1832. It appears that it was recognized by legislation in the civil code of May 28, 1878, and the regulation for those Portuguese who were not Catholics became obligatory by the Code of Civil Registration in 1911. Normally the registers are preserved with the *conservadors,* and information can be obtained from them. Records over 100 years old are sent to the archives under the control of the Inspector Superior of Libraries and Archives. There is one in every *conselho* (county) and various ones in Lisbon and Oporto. The address of the Director General is:

> *Direccão-Geral do Registo e Notariado*
> *Do Ministério da Justiça*
> *Lisbon, Portugal*

## PARISH REGISTERS

These go back in some cases to a period before the Council of Trent (1545–63). Portugal was, in fact, one of the first countries to introduce parish registers. For the past hundred years they have been kept in their respective civil registries. The latter are kept partly in a Central Archive in Lisbon and partly in the various district archives. The Central Archive in Lisbon has the following address:

> *The Director, Arquivo dos Registos Paroquinais*
> *Rua dos Prazeres*
> *Lisbon, Portugal*

This archive contains books of parish registers from parts of the country from the second half of the sixteenth century. It may be noted that a study of parochial registers has been published in the review *Archivum* by the present Inspector Superior of the Libraries and Archives of Portugal (Senhor Dr. Luis Silveira). There is also a valuable work called *História da Igreja em Portugal,* by Fortunato de Almeida (Coimbra, 1917). It should be observed that not all parish registers over the past hundred years have been incorporated in their respective civil archives. Some are even kept in municipal libraries. Efforts to centralize these registers have not met with success, largely due to local politics.

## NATIONAL ARCHIVES

These are held in the Arquivo Nacional da Tôrre do Tombo, and inquiries should be addressed to the Director, putting the address simply as Lisbon.

Among other contents of the National Archives are registrations of armorial bearings. All old armorial bearings were registered there. Requests for certificates regarding these should be made to the Director. Unfortunately, the greater part of these registers before 1755 were lost in the famous Lisbon earthquake of that year. A full account of the surviving registers was published in the last century by the Viscount Sanches de Baena. With the exception of arms for counties, arms are no longer granted.

Wills are also concentrated partly in the National Archives and partly in the district archives. Certificated copies can be obtained from the directors in each case, but fees have to be paid.

In connection with heraldry, two other bodies may be mentioned:

*1. Conselho de Nobreza* (The Council of Nobility). This is under the direction or authority of the Duke of Braganza, the pretender to the throne of Portugal, and has a commission dealing with heraldry and also genealogy. The address is: Praça Luis de Camões 46, 2°, Lisbon.

*2. Instituto Português de Heráldica.* Address: Largo do Carmo, Lisbon. The president of this institute is El Marquês de São Payo, to whom I am obliged for much assistance in compiling these notes on Portugal. This institute is a private academy, legally incorporated, and is the only body in Portugal thus dedicated to the study of genealogy, heraldry, and nobility. The Institute is associated with the official archaeological society, the Associação dos Arqueólogos Portuguêses. The Institute has no special records but possesses a small library; it publishes a review, *Armas e Tropeos.* Inquiries of a genealogical or heraldic nature can be considered by the Institute.

There is a wealth of historical information in Portugal, but it is not easy to extract details of it from official sources. This is a common failing with Portuguese government departments, and it is the more unfortunate in view of the very fine publications which are produced in Portugal. I have had some very splendid books in my hands dealing with the numerous Orders of Chivalry in Portugal. Below, I give a note on some historical works which could be of assistance to anyone whose family was among the ancient nobility of Portugal who took part in the colonization of Brazil and other parts of the Portuguese Empire.

NOTE: *História da Colonização Portuguêsa do Brazil* (3 vols., 1921–26). This is a magnificent work, beautifully illustrated, as the monumental edition commemorative of the first centenary of Brazil.

*História da Expansão Portuguêsa no Mundo* (3 vols., 1937). This again is a splendidly produced work, beautifully illustrated.

The value of the above works lies in their general historical information, but the genealogical value is very slight, being limited to details about individuals who may have left descendants and to the illustrations of their coats of arms.

## ARCHIVES IN THE DIRECCAO-GERAL DOS REGISTOS E DO NOTARIADO

These contain: (1) particulars of birth, (2) filial descent, (3) marriage, (4) prenuptial contracts, (5) deaths, (6) emancipation, (7)the care or guardianship of minors or criminal persons, and (8) cases of mental trouble judicially verified. These matters cover every item in respect not only of Portuguese citizens but also of foreigners should they occur in Portuguese territory. An exception occurs in the case of prenuptial arrangements which came about before the beginning of the operation of the civil code of 1878. These details cannot be recalled or examined except by relatives of those whom they concern or by their agents.

## WILLS

These fall into the following categories: public, sealed, military, maritime, foreign, or made in foreign countries. The will which is made by the notary is published in his book of records. The sealed or private will can be written or signed by the testator or by other persons at his request. The will can be presented to the notary and held by him. On the death of the testator, the notary will register the will in his records.

# ITALY

## PARISH REGISTERS

These originated in the seventeenth century. Some of the oldest registers have been taken in custody by the diocesan episcopal archives (*archivio vescovile della diocesi*). Otherwise, the parish registers are supposed to be kept by the local parish priests. As an Italian authority puts it, "Some of these may happen to be quite intelligent and learned persons and prove therefore very helpful if *personally* asked for the information wanted. The records of some parishes contain regular entries since the seventeenth century."

An example of the keeping of ecclesiastical records is given under

Rome. Apply to:

> *The Secretary*
> *Vicariato di Roma, Archivio*
> *Via della Pigna 13/a*
> *Rome*

In this last case, records cover Rome only.

## STATE REGISTERS

*Archivi anagrafici municipali*. These were begun in 1860–70. Since then they have been kept in good order by local officials (*sindaci,* or mayors). Extracts from these registers can easily be obtained for a nominal fee.

Particulars regarding civil registration are derived from:

> *Istituto Centrale di Statistica*
> *Via Cesare Balbo 16*
> *Rome*

The latter organization has published a number of booklets on the subject of the registers. These are:

*1. Movimento Anagrafico.* This describes the general scheme for obtaining information about the movement of the population, and it gives a survey of the conditions which prevail in other countries, at least as regards the date when state registers begin.

*2. Nascite (Births).* It is pointed out that different conditions prevailed in different parts of Italy. In Parma and Piacenza, the Code Napoléon (which was brought in during the French conquest after the French Revolution) was still in force, and also in Umbria. In other places in Italy the system was much less exact in 1860. In this booklet details are given of the forms required to be completed when giving particulars of birth.

*3. Matrimoni.* Examples of the forms to be completed are given, and similarly in (4) *Morti (Deaths).*


## CENSUS RECORDS

These were established in Italy about 1600, but many have been lost or destroyed. Some may be found in the Archivi di Stato. In the South, they are called *libri dei fuochi,* or books of the hearths (recalling the hearth tax in the seventeenth century in England). In the North, they are known as *libri degli estimi.* Here again, recourse for information may be made to the Istituto Centrale di Statistica.


## AMORIAL BEARINGS

Sources of information are:

Mannucci, *Nobiliario e Blasonario del Regno d'Italia,* 5 vols. This was edited about 1928 by the Collgio Araldico. Price: 30,000 lire.

Marquis Vittorio Spreti, *Enciclopedia Storico Nobiliare Italiano,* 8 vols. It was edited in Milan in 1928–36 with the help of the government. Unfortunately it is impossible to consult this book outside Italy.

There is in Rome the Collegio Araldico. This is the Istituto Araldico Romano, which was founded in 1853. It issues the *Rivista Araldica* and the *Libro d'Oro della Nobiltà Italiana.* This last was founded in 1910. It contains over 1200 pages of details concerning noble Italian families. The arrangement of the book is similar to that of the *Almanach de Gotha,* that is, there is a short account of the family followed by the name of the head with his immediate line. There are numerous illustrations of arms in black and sepia in the text, and in addition there are some full-page armorial illustrations in full color.

NOTES: The noblest names of Italy—Colonna, Orsini, Caracciolo —are often borne by peasants, shopkeepers, and other quite unarmigerous persons, not related in any way to their noble namesakes.

The present position in Italy is that, under the Republic, which was set up after the Second World War, noble titles are not recognized. They may be used as part of the person's name. But titles of nobility are not abolished.

## WILLS

Wills (*testamenti*) are generally kept in the *archivi notarili* existing in the offices (*studii*) of the notaries (*notai*). The office of notary is often hereditary, and thus ancient records of some interest may be traced in these offices. When notarial offices are sold or cease to function, their files and documents are deposited as a rule (when not dispersed) at the Archivio di Stato of the province.

Information on wills is obtainable from:

> *Archivio Notarile, Ispettatore Generale*
> *Via Flaminia 160*
> *Rome*

## PUBLIC RECORDS AND NATIONAL ARCHIVES

The source here is:

*Archivio Centrale della Stato*
*Corso Rinascimento 40*
*Rome*

The following information can be given with regard to the great Archives of State. These exist at Torino, Genoa, Milan, Venice, Parma, Mantua, Modena, Bologna, Florence, Rome, Naples, Palermo, Siena, Lucca. If the research has a reference to the establishment of descent from a noble family, then there are fixed dues to be paid to the Archives. If, on the otherhand, the scope of the inquiry is purely scientific, research is free. I am obliged for this last piece of information to the Rassegna degli Archivi di Stato, Redazione, Ministerio Interno, Ufficio Centrale Archivi di Stato, Rome.

# SWITZERLAND

## INTRODUCTION

The Swiss Confederation began in 1848, although as far back as 1291, in the days of the Holy Roman Empire, three communities—Uri, Schwyz, and Nidwalden—formed an alliance in defense of their independence.* Before 1848, civil registration had been a purely cantonal matter, and the date of the first civil records varies from canton to canton. Since 1876, registrations of births, marriages, and deaths have been made by secular clerks; before that time, registrations were made in the church records. Protestant cantons had a civil registration before 1848.

All records of birth, marriage, and death for the period of 1834–75 were handed over to the Registrar's Offices of the different communities.

In Switzerland, civil registration is always made in the Registrar's Office of the community in which the birth, marriage, or death took place. There is no central organization in Switzerland corresponding to the Public Record Office in England. The official documents of the federal administration are kept in the Bundesarchiv in Berne. Also, there is no central organization of returns of vital statistics similar to Somerset House in London. It is to be noted that the Swiss system of registration records all the vital facts about each Swiss citizen in the place where he was born. There are recorded not only the date of birth but also particulars of marriage, death,

---

* There are four national languages—German, French, Italian, and Romansch. The last is used only by a small minority.

divorce, nullity of marriage, details of children, change of place of origin, and so on. The Registrar can, on request, make extracts from these different records.

## WILLS

Wills are not preserved in any special place.

## HERALDRY

In Switzerland, there is no institution which corresponds to the College of Arms in England. There is, in fact, no official heraldic institution, nor does a state Herald exist. The Confederation, the cantons, and most of the towns and villages have a coat of arms or other heraldic emblems. There is a Swiss Heraldic Society, under the name of Schweizerische Heraldische Gesellschaft (Société Suisse d'Héraldique). The address of the secretary of the Society is:

*Verena Sigrist*
*Zwinglistrasse 28*
*St.-Gall*

This society was founded about seventy years ago. It publishes the *Archives Héraldiques Suisses* and the *Archivum Heraldicum;* it collects copies of all the heraldic monuments in Switzerland as well as copies of the coats of arms of Swiss families. The Society owns a fine library and is ready to supply any information about Swiss heraldry. The Society does its best to prevent the incorrect use of arms. Members pay a subscription of twenty Swiss francs; they have the right to borrow books from the Society's library and meet once a year in a general assembly.

## CANTONAL RECORDS AND ARRANGEMENTS

In conformity with the federalist structure of Switzerland, all the Swiss offices of the civil state are subordinate to the supervisory authority in the matter of the civil state in their respective cantons. The supervisory authorities are given below.

The initial letters in front of the following are as follows: *D* indicates Deutsch (German); *F*, French; and *I*, Italian.

| D | Direction de l'Intérieur du canton de Zurich | Zurich |
|---|---|---|
| D/F | Direction de la Police du canton de Berne | Berne |
| D | Departement des Affaires Communales du canton de Lucerne | Lucerne |
| D | Direction de la Justice du canton d'Uri | Altdorf |
| D | Departement de l'Intérieur du canton de Schwyz | Schwyz |
| D | Chancellerie d'Etat du canton d'Obwald | Sarnen |
| D | Chancellerie d'Etat du canton de Nidwald | Stans |
| D | Chancellerie d'Etat du canton de Glaris | Glaris |
| D | Direction de l'Intérieur du canton de Zoug | Zoug |
| D/F | Departement de la Justice du canton de Fribourg | Fribourg |
| D | Departement de la Justice du canton de Soleure | Soleure |
| D | Departement de la Justice du canton de Bâle-Ville | Bâle |
| D | Direction de la Justice du canton de Bâle-Campagne | Liestal |
| D | Direction des Affaires Communales du canton de Schaffhouse | Schaffhouse |
| D | Chancellerie d'Etat du canton d'Appenzell R. Ext. | Herisau |
| D | Gouvernement du canton d'Appenzell R. Ext. | Appenzell |
| D | Departement de l'Intérieur du canton de St.-Gall | St.-Gall |
| D/I | Departement de l'Intérieur du canton des Grisons | Coire |
| D | Direction de la Justice du canton d'Argovie | Aarau |
| D | Inspectorat de l'Etat Civil du canton de Thurgovie | Frauenfeld |
| F | Departement de la Justice et Police du canton de Vaud | Lausanne |
| D/F | Departement de la Justice du canton du Valais | Sion |
| I | Departement de l'Intérieur du canton du Tessin | Bellinzone |

| | | |
|---|---|---|
| F | Departement de la Justice du canton de Neuchâtel | Neuchâtel |
| F | Departement de la Justice et Police du canton de Genève | Genève |

These supervisory authorities give to their subordinate offices the authority to supply information when they do not possess the competence independently to give the information, and to deliver the documents of the civil state. The two following articles of the federal ordinance on the civil status (state) of June 1, 1953, lay down how far this independence can go and in what circumstances an authorization is required.

ART. 29. Private persons have no right to consult the registers of the civil state. The supervisory authorities and the tribunals have the right to consult them. The cantonal authority of overseeing can, if it considers the request justified, grant the right to other authorities, and sometimes to private persons.

The official delivers the extracts of the entries in the registers, or, lacking these, certifies that they do not exist. Certifications, and communications which under another form are incumbent on the official, in virtue of special dispositions, are reserved.

Cantonal rights permit the publication of legitimate births, of deaths, of announcements and celebrations of marriage. Exceptions can be made only with the authority of the supervisory authority.

ART. 138. The official of the civil state delivers the following extract of the entries in his registers:

1. *Special registers:* birth, death, marriage, legitimation, and recognition.

2. *Registers of families:* family deeds and, for single persons, certificates of their civil state. Abbreviated documents can be supplied for birth, death, and marriage.

Anyone can obtain extracts of those registers which concern him personally. Apart from this, extracts are given only to relatives by blood or adoption, or to private persons who can justify a direct interest, to a guardian or mandatory of such a person, or to the authorities set out in Art. 29. Extracts or copies of a register which has been erased cannot be given to private persons.

As regards ecclesiastical records, many still exist. In 1876, civil registers were introduced for the whole of Switzerland. Ecclesiastical records were passed over to the civil officials, and they are to be regarded as the forerunners of the registers of the present civil state. In certain cantons and even in some communes, some old ecclesiastical registers (since 1850 at least) are kept at the office of the civil state. Elsewhere they are found in the cantonal archives or in other places designated by the canton.

The Federal Service of the civil state does not grant any authorization to consult the registers, to give information, or to deliver documents of the civil state. This belongs to the cantonal authorities, who superintend the civil state. Application should be made to the authorities listed above.

The above account may seem very unrewarding for the inquirer who is of Swiss origin, but as a stimulus to inquiry, I can tell him that there are cases in which a Swiss pedigree is traceable, with armorial bearings, back to the fifteenth century. One in particular which I remember is that of Sir Eric Miéville, G. C. I. E., a former private secretary to King George VI, whose pedigree I have seen in book form.

# MONACO

Monaco is one of those tiny states which exist in Europe as relics of a distant past and as a result of the forbearance of the great powers. Putting aside the various legends which give Monaco a past contemporary with the famous Hercules, we can trace eight centuries of history from 1191. In that year the emperor Henry VI ceded Monaco to the Republic of Genoa. The Grimaldis were a powerful family in Genoa, and in 1297 Francis Grimaldi founded the dynasty which still reigns in Monaco. The present prince is His Serene Highness Rainier III, who succeeded his grandfather in 1949. He married at Monaco, on April 18, 1956, Grace Patricia Kelly, daughter of John Brendan Kelly. Princess Grace's beauty and charm are famous throughout the world. The Kelly family in Ireland goes back to a princely origin (see the chapter on the Republic of Ireland).

In the territory of the Monagesques is the famous Monte Carlo with its Casino. The Monagesques are a tiny nation, the population of Monaco being not much more than 20,000, but as one would expect from such an ancient principality, its records are very old. I cannot refrain from telling the story of my inquiries in Monaco. I referred at first to the Consul General of Monaco in London, where I would normally go for information. Here I was advised to inquire concerning genealogical records of the Office National au Tourisme et à l'Information, 2a Boulevarde des Moulins, Monte Carlo, Monaco. From this office I received a courteous response which stated simply that they were pleased to inform me that the archives held at the Mairie de Monaco dated from the year 1600. To this I replied with my original questions put in another form. Did the archives to which the Office referred include particulars of births, marriages and deaths or baptisms and burials of all classes of society in Monaco from 1600, or did they refer only to the families of the upper class? Another courteous short reply: The archives which were held at the Mairie de Monaco were for all classes of society. There the matter rested save for one other item. This last was in respect of wills, about which I had made the usual inquiries with regard to their preservation. The office gave me the names and addresses of the following three notaries, who would be able to advise me.

NOTAIRES, PRINCIPAUTÉ DE MONACO

*M. Louis Aureglia, 2 Boulevard des Moulins, Monte Carlo.*
*M. Jean-Charles Rey, 2 Rue Bellando de Castro, Monaco-Ville.*
*M. Auguste Settimo, 26 Avenue de la Costa, Monte Carlo.*

Three kinds of will are known in Monaco.

*1. The authentic will.* This is received by the notary himself, who writes it entirely in his own hand in the presence of the testator and four witnesses. It is kept by the notary. After the testator's death, this will is not submitted to any judicial formality and can be executed without the intervention of the Tribunal. It is necessary only to present it to the fiscal administration of registration in the three months set aside for the receipt of rights of registration and the verification of declaration of succession which are made by the beneficiaries.

*2. The holograph will.* This kind of will is written directly by the testator and is kept by him or confided to the notary at the time of death. When the death is known, this will is presented by the notary to the president of the Civil Tribunal, who verifies it if the necessary conditions have been observed and puts his visa upon it before restoring it to the notary. The latter then puts it with his files, and the original will stays there. A holograph will has to be the subject of a judicial formality, *l'envoi en possession,* which is solicited by the universal legatee from the President of the Civil Tribunal, at least provided that the legatee is not one of the legitimate beneficiaries provided for by the legal code; in this last case the judicial formality is dispensed with.

*3. The mystical will.* This is a typewritten will, signed by the testator and deposited by him with the notary in a sealed envelope, on which the notary puts a mark in the presence of witnesses. The subsequent formalities are the same as for the holograph will.

Wills are thus kept by the notaries, and information should be sought from them on the subject of wills which may have a genealogical bearing.

# LIECHTENSTEIN

Liechtenstein is an independent state on the north bank of the Rhine between Switzerland and Austria. Its history goes back to the fourteenth century, and it has had its own independent sovereign monarchy since 1806, when the Holy Roman Empire came to an end. There are some 14,000 inhabitants. Church registration of marriages and deaths (presumably also of births and baptisms) began in the different parishes between 1640 and 1647. The records are preserved in the parsonages. Civil registration was introduced on January 1, 1878. The work of keeping civil registers devolved upon the Catholic clergy, so that the civil records are also preserved in the parsonages. There is no Public Record Office in Liechtenstein.

With regard to wills, they can be deposited with the court; they may also be retained at home and must then be written by hand and signed by the testator. If the will is typewritten, the testator must sign it and it must be certified by three witnesses.

There is no College of Arms (see chapter on England) in Liechtenstein.

Inquiries should be addressed to the Chancellery of the Liechtenstein government at Vaduz (Kanzlei der Regierung des Fürstentums Liechtenstein).

# POLAND

## CIVIL REGISTRATION

Civil registration of the whole population began on January 1, 1946. Before that date it was nonuniform and as follows:

*1. Exclusively civil registration was compulsory in the western and northern voivodships (see below) and in the northern part of the Katowice voivodship.*

*2. Ecclesiastical registration was compulsory in the eastern part of the Białystok voivodship and in the former eastern voivodships.*

*3. Mixed registrations—that is, either ecclesiastical or civil according to the denomination of the person registered—was compulsory in the central and Silesian voivodships and in Cieszyn Silesia.*

## PRESERVATION OF CIVIL REGISTERS

Civil registration records are now, as before 1946, entered in the Civil Registration Offices, which are under the authority of the Presidiums of the local People's Councils (see below). Before the unification and general secularization of the law relating to civil registration in Poland, in the former Russian-governed areas (that is, before the First World War) the persons authorized to keep civil registration records were the parish priests; in the former Austrian-governed part, the parish priests were state officials of civil status and as such kept the statistical records; in the former Prussian-governed part, the records were kept by secular bodies. For those not adhering to any religious denomination, the civil registration records for all of Poland were kept by the administrative organs of the government.

*Voivodship.* This is roughly of the same concept and status as an English county but is a good deal bigger.

*The People's Councils* are the machinery of local government corresponding somewhat to the English rural and urban district councils, city and borough councils, and the county councils. The Presidium of a Council corresponds roughly to a Parliamentary and General Purposes Committee in Britain. (N.B. These comparisons have been made by the Polish Cultural Institute in London.)

## ECCLESIASTICAL RECORDS

Under this heading I can only reproduce the information given to me by the Polish Cultural Institute, which is as follows:

"It is impossible to say when ecclesiastical records begin; where they exist, such records are presumably more or less as old as the church and parish, as with parish records in England, and similarly vary from place to place. Moreover, in Old Poland, owing to the country's troubled history, there can have been few places where consistent records were kept over any long period."

(Author's notes: While accepting the probability of wide variation in the keeping of parish records and in their preservation, it must surely be possible to know at least the approximate date at which the keeping of parish records began. Poland is the only Slavonic country to be within the fold of the Latin (Roman Catholic) Church and should therefore be within the same movement to keep parish registers which appears in other parts of western Europe. But Iron Curtain countries are always reluctant to give information about church records, possibly for fear that Western folk may open communication with the natives.)

## WILLS

These are deposited in the local courts or with a notary. They have never been the property of ecclesiastical bodies, although these had and have the right of inspection if they were or are legatees or beneficiaries, and wills remain private property.

## HERALDRY

There is no special heraldic archive in Poland. The records of the former heraldry of the Polish Kingdom were destroyed by fire during the 1939–45 war. Certain information on noble families and their coats of arms can be found in old Polish records kept in voivodship archives or in the main Historical Records Archive (Archiwum Głownym Akt Dawnych, Warsaw, ul. Długa 7).

## CENTRAL ARCHIVES

There is a Central Archive of Old and Modern Records in Warsaw, corresponding to the Public Record Office in London. Their names and addresses are as follows: Old Records—Archiwum Glowne Akt Dawnych, Warsaw, Długa 7. New Records—Archiwum Akt Nowych, Warsaw, Długa 7.

There are also local archives, a list of which follows.

## LOCAL ARCHIVES

Wojewodzkie Archiwum Państwowe w Białymstoku, Białystok, Kilinskiego 16.
    Public records to 1945 and from 1945.
Wojewodzkie Archiwum Państwowe w Bydgoszczy, Bydgoszcz, Dworcowa 65.
    Public records, archives of educational institutions and political bodies, private collections, maps.
Oddział Terenowy w Toruniu, Torun, Ratusz.
    Archives of Torun, 1252–1945. Archives of the Prussian lands

from Old Polish era, archives of various institutions and organizations (guilds, churches, etc.), modern documents.

Wojewodzkie Archiwum Państwowe w Gdańsku, Gdańsk, Waly Piastowskie 5.

Gdańsk municipal archives, Elblag municipal archive, cessions of the Prussian States, archives of Gdańsk for 1919–39, documents from 1939 to 1945, and from 1945 onward.

Wojewodzkie Archiwum Państwowe w Katowicach, Katowice, Jagiellońska, 25.

Public records, industrial records, private archives, modern records (after 1945).

Oddział Terenowy w Cieszynie, Cieszyn, Regera 6.

Local records from 1388 to beginning of twentieth century.

Oddział Terenowy w Częstochowie, Częstochowa, Narutowicza 16.

Records of the Częstochowa municipality guild, industrial, local legal, etc., documents.

Oddział Terenowy w Gliwacach, Gliwice, Zygmunta Starego 6.

Local records.

Oddział Terenowy w Pszczynie, Pszczyna, Zamek.

Local records.

Wojewodzkie Archiwum Państwowe w Kielcach, Kielce, Rewolucju Październikowej 17.

Public records to 1918 and from 1918, records of denominational, social, cultural bodies, private archives.

Oddział Terenowy w Radomiu, Radom, Zeromskiego 53.

Local records (1789–1918). Documents from 1918 to 1939 and for 1939–45 and postwar periods.

Archiwum Państwowe M. Krakowa I Wojewodztwa Krakowskiego, Kraków, Sienna 16.

Public records to 1795 and from nineteenth and twentieth centuries. Records of denominational, educational, and sociocultural bodies. Guild and trade records, private archives, cartographical collections.

Wojewodzkie Archiwum Państwowe w Lublinie, Lublin, Narutowicza 10. Old Polish records. Documents of Polish and Russian administration of nineteenth century. Documents relating to peasant affairs and to land reform of 1864. Records from 1918 to 1939. Municipal archives and guild records. Private archives. School records for nineteenth and twentieth centuries.

Archiwum Państwowe M. Lodzi i Wojewodztwa Lodzkiego, Lodź, Pl. Wolności 1.

Public records to 1918, and from 1918 to 1945. Postwar documents, municipal records of Lodź from 1794 to 1949. Industrial documents from 1834 to 1945. Records of banking and financial houses, private archives. Cartographical, iconographical, and local-press collections.

Oddział Terenowy w Piotrkowie, Piotrków, Torunska 4.
Local records.
Wojewodzkie Archiwum Państwowe w Olsztynie, Olsztyn, Zamek.
Public records to 1945. Legal records and land registers from
eighteenth to twentieth century. Private archives, public records,
1945 onward.
Wojewodzkie Archiwum Państwowe w Opolu, Opole, Zamkowa 2.
Public records from nineteenth and early twentieth centuries.
Municipal documents, including parchments from thirteenth
century. Records of social institutions and organizations. Public
records from postwar period.
Oddział Terenowy w Brzegu, Brzeg, Chrobrego 17.
Local records.
Archiwum Państwowe M. Poznania i Wojewodztwa Poznańskiego,
Poznań, 23 Lutego 41/43.
Documents, 1215–1813. Legal records, 1390–1794. General
administrative records, municipal and guild records, 1405–1939.
Economic records, 1850–1954. Records of institutions and
organizations (educational, legal, ecclesiastical), private archives.
Cartographical collections, modern public records.
Oddzial Terenowy w Rzeszowie, Rzeszów, Rynek 6.
Public records, municipal, private, and denominational records.
Industrial documents.
Wojewodzkie Archiwum Państwowe w Szczecinie, Szczecin, Sw.
Wojciecha 13.
Feudal records. Documents of Prussian administration. Munici-
pal records from fifteenth to twentieth century. Private archives.
Postwar public records.
Archiwum Państwowe M. St. Warszawy i Wojewodztwa Warszawskiego,
Warsaw, Nowomiejska 12.
Municipal and voivodship records from nineteenth century.
Postwar public records. Cartographical collections. Library of
local history.
Oddział Terenowy w Płocku, Płock, Tumska 2.
Local records.
Archiwum Państwowe M. Wrocławia i Wojewodztwa Wrocławskiego,
Wroclaw, Pomorska 2.
Public records to 1943. Records of socio-cultural, denomi-
national, etc., institutions. Private archives, cartographical
collection. Public records from 1945.
Oddział Terenowy w Jeleniej Górze, Jelenia Góra, Podwale 27.
Local records (municipal, guild, economic, factory, legal,
ecclesiastical).

# THE FORMER BALTIC STATES

The three countries mentioned in the present section—
Estonia, Latvia, and Lithuania—were formerly provinces
of the Russian Empire, into which they have been incorporated by force. In 1918, following the outbreak of the Russian
Revolution, they proclaimed their independence and continued as
the independent republics of Estonia, Latvia, and Lithuania, until
their occupation by the Russian Army in June 1940, under the
Russo-German agreement of August 23, 1939. During World War
II they were under German occupation from 1941 until 1944. The
three republics were forcibly incorporated into the U.S.S.R. in
August 1940. *De facto* recognition of the incorporation has been
accorded by the British Government, but not by the United States
Government, which continues to recognize diplomatic and consular
representatives from the three republics in the United States.

The information given below relates to the state of affairs before
1940 unless otherwise stated.

## ESTONIA

From 1721 to 1918 the laws of Imperial Russia applied to the
territory of Estonia. The independence of the Republic of Estonia
was proclaimed on February 24, 1918.

### Registration of Births, Marriages, and Deaths

A law relating to civil registration of births, marriages, and deaths was adopted on June 29, 1920, by the Constituent Assembly convened to elaborate the constitution of the Republic of Estonia. According to this law—the implementation of which was deferred until the passing of further legislation—the registration of births, marriages, and deaths was to be transferred from the pastors of the various parishes to local municipal and rural councils. However, it is not possible to establish from records now available whether or when the law of 1920 was actually applied.

In independent Estonia, registers of vital statistics were kept by civil Registrars of family status in all towns, townships, and rural communes. Information relating to persons and families could be obtained from the Registrars of the towns or rural communes where the persons were domiciled.

Subsequently, a law was passed in 1925 known as the Law Relating to Family Status (this is a literal translation from the Estonian), which provided for Registrars-Ecclesiastic, who by special authorization of the government of the Republic could keep relevant family registers at their parish churches. The law of 1925, which came into force on July 1, 1926, replaced the law of 1920. From then onward civil registration took place. The Law Relating to Family Status means the "law relating to registration of births, marriages, and deaths."

### Wills

Probate of wills was granted by the relevant courts in Estonia, but there was no central Public Record Office, as in England.

### Titles

All hereditary titles and privileges were abolished in Estonia by the Constitution of June 15, 1920.

## LATVIA

### Civil Registration

The law of civil registration came into force in 1919 or 1920, and with it the offices of the Registry of Births, Deaths, and Marriages started to function. They were established at each government body, that is, parish or town council.

Under Par. 51 of the Latvian Civil Law, the pastors of the various confessions—that is, religions—had the right to make civil registrations. One copy of each entry in the register had by law to be sent to the Ministry of the Interior, where all entries in the civil registers were collected, and interested persons could at any time get copies of these entries. After the Soviet Communist military occupation of Latvia, to the best of our information, all registers of births, deaths, and marriages, and also the former archives of the parishes, were sent to Moscow and concentrated in the Chief Council of Militia (Glavnoye Upravleniye Milicii, Archiv Zapisei Grazhdanskovo Sostoyaniya). Copies of respective entries in the civil registers can be requested at the local Soviet embassy, for which purpose a questionnaire must be filled in at the embassy.

Before the introduction of the Registry of Births, Deaths, and Marriages, these registrations were made by the parish pastors, each in his own parish, and the registers were kept in the parish.

### Wills

According to Latvian civil law, wills came into force only after their confirmation by the respective district court—at Riga, Jelgava, Liepaja, or Daugavpils. In the district courts, copies of proved wills were also kept. After ten years, the district court passed all documents to the State Archives.

### State Archives

The documents of all public organizations and institutions were, after ten years, passed to the State Archives, where they were put in order and kept. Interested persons could request and receive copies of the documents.

### Heraldry

There was a Heraldic Committee under the auspices of the President, which dealt with the state, municipal, etc., coats of arms. Latvian independence in modern times was of comparatively short duration, but there were indications that, with time, the use and regulation of family crests and coats of arms would have come, though this is rather a matter of conjecture.

The Baltic German families who formed the "nobility" in Latvia in the past centuries (a status which the formation of the independent Republic of Latvia brought to an end) had their family emblems. Reference should be made to the body which exists now in Germany under the title of Union of Members of the Baltic Knighthoods, the address of which is: Verband der Angehorigen der Baltischen Ritterschaften, c/o Munchen 13, Elisabethstrasse 5/1, Germany.

## LITHUANIA

### Registration of Births, Marriages, and Deaths

Before proclamation of the independence of the Republic of Lithuania in 1918, registration was regulated by the laws of the Czarist Russian Empire, of which Lithuania was then a part. There was no civil registration in its proper sense.

After proclamation of independence, the registration of births, marriages, and deaths was entrusted to the parishes of various religious denominations, and the heads of such parishes were acting as state functionaries, properly authorized and paid by the state for performing the acts of registration and for keeping records. Thus, the religious ceremony coincided with a civil registration. The records of registration were kept in the said parishes and copies were sent at regular intervals to the central authorities; very old original certificates, usually entered into official books, were transferred to the State Central Archives in Kaunas.

During the Second World War, while Lithuania was for some years under the German occupation (1941–44), the same order of registration was observed. During the Soviet-Russian occupation (1940–41) and from 1944 to the present time, the above system was abolished and special offices of civil registration were established. No details of this new system are available, but it is believed that new offices of registration were established in every district of the country.

### Wills

Before Lithuania was occupied by Soviet Russia in 1944, the wills were proved in the courts of the justices of the peace. After the reform of the court system in Lithuania in 1933, the wills were proved in the district courts. The entire text of the will was incorporated into the court's decision, and thus the copy of a will became a part of the court's official record. The official copy of the court's decision could be issued to the interested party or parties. All documents relating to the proving of wills were kept in the court's archives. There was no central depository of these documents. There is no reliable information available at the present time as to the procedure under the Soviet occupation, but it would seem that the proving of wills is done by notaries public.

### Public Records

The public records were kept in the appropriate institutions as stated above. After ten years the old records passed to the Central State Archives, where they were permanently kept. Copies could be issued to interested parties. Thus, the Central State Archives performed the function of a Public Record Office.

### Coats of Arms

The use of coats of arms in the grand duchy of Lithuania, in a form and style prevalent at that time in western Europe, dates from 1413. *The Lithuanian Encyclopedia* (Vol. VIII) indicates that the Lithuanian nobility (*bajorai*)—which originally came, in Lithuania as it did everywhere else, from the ranks of eminent warriors—were using coats of arms even before the date mentioned above. Thus the personal escutcheon of the Lithuanian grand duke Gediminas (1316–41)—a knight of the white horse, charging and known as Vytis—in due time became the coat of arms of the famous Lithuanian dynasty of Gediminas (1316–1572) and of the grand duchy of Lithuania itself (up to 1796, when Lithuania became a prey of Czarist Russia). One result of this Russian conquest was that most of the state records of Lithuania, including records and material pertaining to heraldry, were confiscated and removed to St. Petersburg (Leningrad), where they became part of a general office of heraldry of the Russian Empire.

Upon re-establishment of the independence of Lithuania in 1918, a new constitution proclaimed a new basic law, according to which all citizens of the Republic were declared equal before the law, and thus all formerly existing classes and privileges based on a class, religion, etc., were formally abolished.

It is to be noted, however, that the newly promulgated constitution of the land—and subsequently promulgated new editions thereof—does not explicitly mention abrogation of titles or family crests, etc. It confines itself to abolition of the privileges based on class or religion. As a matter of fact, the ancient coats of arms of various provinces of Lithuania and of her cities continued to be publicly recognized and formally used during all the time of independence of the Republic (1918–40). It was maintained therefore —not without good reason, it would seem—that various titles of nobility as well as coats of arms and family crests could be used privately, although no privileges could be claimed as conferred by them, and they were not recognized in official documents.

In view of the above, there was no practical necessity for a College of Arms in modern Lithuania. However, it may be of interest to mention here that on April 26, 1928, there came into existence an organization named the Association of the Lithuanian Nobility, which was duly registered in the State Register of Associations and which interested itself in matters pertaining to Lithuanian heraldry. This organization existed until the occupation of Lithuania by Soviet Russia at the beginning of World War II, when it was forcibly closed by the invader, thus meeting the same fate as all other Lithuanian national institutions.

# ALBANIA

## CIVIL REGISTRATION

This dates from 1929 but is best considered on the lines of the whole record system of the country, such as it is. Albania formed part of the former Turkish Empire (see introduction to the Balkan countries) until 1912. The Orthodox and the Roman Catholic churches kept complete records of their respective parishes. There is a considerable Moslem part of the population, and for them records of a sort were kept by the authorities as they then were. Deaths were recorded in the mosques, but not marriages or births. The records kept by the Christian churches were considered official.

After the country became independent of the Turks and until 1929, the ecclesiastical records continued to be kept, and these records were regarded by the new state as valid and reliable. The Moslem records continued to be incomplete. In 1921 there was a general census, at which these records were checked, finally legalized, and new information was required with regard to the Moslems.

In 1929 a new civil code came into force based on the French and Belgian models. According to this, a new office was created for each municipality, which was to deal mainly with the records of birth, marriage, and death. These offices were empowered to solemnize civil marriages, on the lines of a Registrar's Office in England or America. In addition, these offices absorbed all the records kept by church and mosque until the information was completed. During the last war the practice continued the same. After the war the Communist regime also continued on the same lines but attached the Record Office to the Executive Council of each locality.

Until 1929 there were only religious marriages, that is, marriages could be celebrated only in church or mosque. After 1929 there was also civil marriage as in England and America. A religious marriage had to be registered at the Record Office in order to be valid, but it was not necessary for the couple to undergo a civil ceremony in addition to their religious one. Since the setting up of the Communist regime there is no religious marriage which is recognized by the state. For any marriage to be valid, it must be civil. The couple can, of course, marry in the building of their religious denomination, but by itself that does not count.

## RELIGIOUS RECORDS

Such religious records as existed until the early years of Second World War have now been destroyed by the Communists. The Registrar's Offices, to which reference is made above, are permanent fixtures of the administrative apparatus, and not offices whose purpose is to absorb information from the old church records. The process of absorption began and was completed long before 1939. The Communist regime after the war began to use the existing state files and continued to keep them up to date with regard to population changes. Complete indifference reigns as regards the various ecclesiastical records. All Executive Councils are directly responsible to the Prime Minister's Office. Inquiries should therefore be addressed to the latter.

This, however, is purely theoretical, because in the prevailing atmosphere in Albania any request for genealogical information or details from the old church records would be viewed with suspicion and thrown into the wastepaper basket. Inquiries from America or other parts of the free world are at once suspect.

# BULGARIA

It is very difficult to obtain information of any sort from Bulgaria, and it is to be hoped that few Americans of Bulgarian stock will seek to trace their ancestry, as they are likely to find it more difficult than it is in the majority of Communist countries. The information set out below does also indicate what a late starter Bulgaria has been in record keeping. It must, however, be remembered that Bulgaria as an independent modern state dates only from 1878.

## CIVIL REGISTRATION

Civil registration of births, marriages, and deaths began on January 1, 1893. The records are kept in the respective District People's Councils, which act as Public Record Offices.

## PAROCHIAL REGISTRATION

Parochial registration began in 1860, and the registers are kept in the respective churches, if they have not been destroyed.

## WILLS

Wills, if made officially, are deposited with the notary public of the state. Wills made privately are taken by interested persons, after the death of the testator, to the notary public of the People's Court. Old archives are kept at the Ministry of Justice, and current archives at the Court of Justice.

## HERALDRY

During the many centuries of Greek and Turkish rule in Bulgaria (see Historical Introduction), there was no body resembling the College of Arms in England, and there has been none since.

## ADDITIONAL NOTE

To approach the District People's Council, it would be necessary to go through the official channels. For example, British subjects would have to go through the Foreign Office, or the British Legation in Sofia. Bulgarian nationals could apply through the Bulgarian Legation in their country of domicile. Americans should make their application through the State Department.

It appears that no records were kept by the Greek Church and that the parochial records mentioned above as begun in 1860 were kept by the Bulgarian Church when it broke away, about that date, from the Greek Orthodox Church.

# GREECE

## CIVIL REGISTRATION

Civil registration in the largest towns began in 1856, but these registers were not well kept and are therefore incomplete. The systematic organization of registration offices began in 1925, and since 1931 register keeping has been extended to the whole of Greece.

Register keeping is regulated by the Registration Legislation of 1931, being basically as follows: Each municipality and community constitutes an individual registration area. The Registrar is the mayor or the president of the community, assisted in his task by a secretary. There are, however, special registration offices in the three large towns—Athens, Piraeus, and Salonika. The main registers kept by each Registrar are: births, marriages, and deaths, and these are registered according to reports by the responsible persons.

## CHURCH REGISTERS

In most parishes of Greece, church registers were traditionally kept, but since 1912 church-register keeping has become obligatory in all parishes. Thus, each parish keeps three books in the form of lists: marriages, births and baptisms, and deaths. These books constitute a list in which is recorded data about persons for whom marriage, baptismal, or funeral rites have been held. There may be, however, small parishes in which the said lists are not strictly kept.

## ARCHIVES OF LOCAL AND STATE COMMUNITIES

In each municipality and community of Greece, there is a book containing the names of all Greek citizens (males and females). Archives in municipalities had been kept since 1833, but incompletely. Since 1954, however, these books have been recompiled in accordance with a more recent law, but in some large towns this recompilation is not yet completed.

The name of a Greek citizen is registered at his birth in the archives of the municipality or community where his father is registered. The citizen is not obliged to make a new registration when changing his residence. It is at his option to register himself in the new municipality or community.

## WILLS

There are three kinds of wills.

*1. Written wills.* These must be dated and signed by the testator himself in his own handwriting. Otherwise they are considered null and void.

*2. Secret wills,* which are handed over by the testator to a notary public, in the presence of three witnesses or of a second notary public and one witness. The secret will is a sealed document, and at the handing over an oral statement is made asserting that it is the last will and testament of the testator.

*3. Public wills* are written by a notary public in the presence of three witnesses or of another notary public and one witness. It is written after an oral statement made by the testator concerning his will.

As soon as he is informed about the death of a testator, the notary public who holds the will sends a copy of it to the secretary of the Court of the First Instance, in order that it may be published.

Also, any person holding a will written by a testator in his own handwriting, on hearing of the testator's death, forwards the will to the Court of the First Instance for publication.

A written statement is prepared about the publication of a will, and copies of this are sent to the Attorney General and also to the secretary of the Court of the First Instance in Athens.

Copies of written statements about wills of Greeks who have died abroad, and whose wills are brought before the Greek consular authorities, are treated in the same way.

Thus, the secretary of the Athens Court of the First Instance keeps copies of the written statements of the publication of all wills, whether published in Greece or abroad, and is thus able to issue certificates, copies, and information on request.

## HERALDRY

There are no coats of arms in Greece. No titles of nobility are conferred, and there is no institution which deals with the pedigrees of Greek families. To this should be added, in the words of the Greek government department concerned, "No official archives of Hellenic family pedigrees are kept in Greece since no titles of nobility exist here. Our *Golden Book* was kept at the Ionian Islands during the Venetian occupation."

In this latter connection, it is of interest to note the pedigrees of some Greek or Levantine families which have been entered in *Burke's Landed Gentry* (see the Chapter on England). The Argenti family is of Italian origin, hailing from Genoa. They settled in the Byzantine Empire at Constantinople and held properties on the island of Chios and other places near to or in Asia Minor. In the fifteenth and sixteenth centuries, the Genoese and Venetians dominated part of the Levant, and as the Argentis intermarried with noble Genoese families, their names were inscribed in the *Libro d'Oro* of Genoa in 1532. Eventually the family left Chios, after several terrible massacres by the Turks in 1882, came through France, and settled in England. Here they are connected with the Rallis, the head of which family is Sir Strati Ralli, second baronet. The Rallis descend from Stephen John Ralli of Marseilles, who was born on the island of Chios in 1755 but who escaped during the Turkish massacre there and settled in Marseilles. Another family of Levantine origin is that of Ionides, the founder of which in England was Alexander Constantine Ionides, who became a naturalized British subject in 1837.

Two other very interesting families from the pedigree point of view are Scaramanga and Schilizzi. I mention these cases as they may be of service to Americans whose origins are Hellenic. It is clear that in ordinary cases—that is, with families which are not noble—tracing a pedigree before 1856 is going to be extremely hard, if possible at all. The five noble families which I have mentioned are of the order referred to by the Greek government authorities as being mentioned in various genealogical sources such as the *Libro d'Oro* of Venice or Genoa. If, therefore, any American inquirer comes of these or similar families, these few notes may be of considerable use to him.

The Scaramangas were of Byzantine origin, and they settled in Chios (then under Genoese rule) in the fifteenth century. According to *Burke's Landed Gentry,* "In the register of the Roman Catholic Cathedral in Chios it is recorded that in 1602 the Church dedicated to St. Isidore, and in 1617 that dedicated to the Holy Virgin, belonged to the Scaramangas. After the Massacres of 1822, when the family suffered severely, they settled in Russia, Austria, France, and England."

The Schilizzis, again, are a family of Byzantine origin, traceable to the ninth century, who followed the fortunes of the Byzantine emperors. After 1204, when the Western crusaders took Constantinople, the Schilizzis went to Nicea but later settled in Chios. Here they figured among the other nobility of Genoa. They suffered as did others in the Massacre of 1822, but many of them settled in Italy, France, and England.

The moral is clear. If you can settle yourself into a family of Byzantine or other ancient Greek origin, you have a good chance of going back to the sixteenth century at least.

# RUSSIA

In dealing with genealogical inquiries in Russia, we are up against the most difficult of all propositions, if only because the Soviet regime is extremely suspicious of any attempt to obtain information on any subject, however apparently harmless, about the U.S.S.R. Such details as I can give direct from Soviet sources are derived from the *Soviet Encyclopedia,* via the Russian Embassy in London, and also from Russian émigré sources.

## REGISTRATION OF BIRTHS, MARRIAGES, AND DEATHS

What is known as civic status and the facts bearing on it was first introduced into Russia in 1722. By "civic status" is meant the facts of birth, marriage, divorce, and death. Before the Bolshevik Revolution it was in the hands of the church authorities of the various denominations. Civil registration of births, marriages, and deaths did not exist in Russia as we understand it in America or Britain, save for persons who had no definite religion or who belonged to one of the forbidden sects, such as the Baptists. Details for such persons were made by the police. The principal religions— Greek Orthodox, Roman Catholic, Lutheran, Moslem, and Jewish —each had their own system of records, handled by their own clergy. In the case of the Orthodox, which was the state Church of

Russia, the clergy of every parish transmitted every year a copy of their records of births, marriages, and deaths to the regional consistory, from which official copies could be obtained. This system was introduced in Russia about 1820, though parochial record books existed long before. They are of great value in establishing genealogical facts, especially dates of death. It should be noted that up to about 1820 the Orthodox priests received a new family name on their ordination by the bishop. The serfs had no family names (only baptismal names) before their emancipation in 1860.

After the Soviet Revolution (referred to among the Russians as the Great October Socialist Revolution), the Church was separated from the State. Civil registration of births, marriages, and deaths then began for all, and the first code of laws regarding records of civic status was issued in 1918.

Registration of births, deaths, marriages, divorces, and adoptions in the towns and district centers is conducted by the urban and district offices for registering records of civic status (*zags*), and in rural localities and workers' settlements by the village or settlement soviets. The work of all these offices for registering records of civic status is directed by the U. S. S. R. Ministry of Internal Affairs' department of civic status records.

· The entry in the register is read out to the notifier and signed by the official performing the act, and by the notifiers. Entries may be disputed by interested parties through the courts.

Registrations of births must be made within a month of the date of birth. Notification may be made by the parents (or by one parent) or by relatives, neighbors, or others. The birth entry records time and place of birth, sex, and first name of the child, also the surname, first names, patronymics, home address, occupations, and ages of the parents.

In the register of death is recorded the death and the recognition (by notarial act or judicial act) that the person has died. Notifications of death must be made within three days of the death, and in the case of death by violence, suicide, or accident, not later than twenty-four hours after death. The notification must be made by persons residing with the deceased, or the house managment, neighbors, or others. Facts of decease must be verified by medical certificate.

Marriages are registered according to the residence of either of the applicants. Entry recording the marriage registered is entered

in the passports (identity cards) of the husband and wife. The breakup of a marriage (divorce) is registered on the basis of judicial decree, after which a certificate of divorce is issued. When this is issued, the identity papers of each party are endorsed accordingly.

Other records of civic status which may be mentioned are adoptions and changes of name.

Registrations of births, deaths, and adoptions, and the issue of first certificates regarding the registrations made, are carried out free of charge and free of all duty. Special duty is levied for the registration of marriages, divorces, and changes of name.

## PRE-BOLSHEVIK RECORDS

The above are mainly the particulars of records since the Russian Bolshevik Revolution. Most Americans of Russian descent will want information regarding records which relate to the period before 1918. The Bolshevik Revolution caused the dispersion of thousands of Russians of the upper classes. Many of these have reached the United States. They are the very class who in old Russia were well recorded, but of course in the great majority of cases they had to leave their records behind. What are the chances of tracing anything in the nature of genealogical records before 1918?

As far as inquiry in Russia is concerned, very little. For several years I have had instances in which I have wanted to secure details of the period before the Revolution. I have never been successful in getting anything. At first—say, eight or nine years ago—I did not expect to get any information. One might write to a Russian official, but the most one ever received was a brief acknowledgment. On one occasion I made my request for information through the British Embassy in Moscow. One inquiry concerned a lady in Istanbul (Constantinople) who thought that her family was connected with that of the English admiral Nelson and whose forebears for two or three generations had lived in Russia. No answer was ever obtained to my inquiry.

In another case, a British subject of Russian descent was anxious to use his coat of arms, and for this purpose wanted to establish to the satisfaction of the English College of Arms that he had a coat of arms. There was no chance of getting information from Russia, and we were reduced to using a design on some old note paper—

which might have been mistaken for a watermark—as proof of the inquirer's family coat of arms.

In the last few years, the Soviet authorities have become much more reasonable on the supply of information regarding industry and statistics, but this has not yet extended to genealogical details. I have sought information from the Ministry of Home Affairs, Moscow, but have not been favored with a reply.

The White Russians (the name given to the Russian émigrés) have to some extent endeavored to redress this difficulty in tracing pre-Bolshevik information. There is a Union de la Noblesse Russe, and the President of the Bureau Généalogique of this union is Nicolas Ikonnikov. His address is: 8 Rue Gabrielle d'Estrées, Vanves (Seine), France. He has produced a series of Multigraphed books running into some two dozen volumes under the title *La Noblesse de Russie*. The subtitle of this work is—*Elements to serve for the reconstitution of the genealogical records of the Nobility, from the available records and documents, completed, thanks to the devoted assistance of Russian nobles.* In these volumes there are genealogies of many Russian families, with such particulars as they have been able to obtain. Thus, the family of Arapov is given from the early seventeenth century. The principal sources are given as being certain printed genealogies, presumably preserved outside Russia, and living persons who have contributed details.

## THE NOBILITY

In the Introduction to the series of volumes, M. Ikonnikov gives some notes regarding the nature of nobility, and in particular of Russian nobility. The history of Russia is the history of the nobility. It was not the nobles who governed the country, but those who governed the country were nobles. The old nobility of Russia were the boyars. Under Vasili I, the principle was established that those who occupied the posts of government should become nobles. This tradition was continued by the dynasty of the Romanovs, who succeeded to the throne in 1613. As the Russian Empire grew, fresh classes of nobles were brought in from various territories. Thus the family of Bagration were a branch of an old dynasty and were kings of Georgia until 1801.

To understand Russian nobility, one must understand something of Russian history. A Viking, Ruric by name, founded the Russian state in the ninth century. The country was divided into principalities under his descendants. In the thirteenth century the Tatars, Mongol savages, overran Russia. The princes of Moscow retained a servile independence as the taxgatherers of the Tatars. Ivan III (1440–1505), Grand Duke of Moscow, rebelled, and in 1547 the grand duke Ivan IV proclaimed himself Czar of all the Russias. The nobles of Moscow were known as the boyars, a term which included officials of the court. The princes of Russia were compelled by the Czar to come to the level of the boyars, and all were inscribed in a register (*rodoslovnoia knega*). This record was copied in the reign of Ivan IV (1533–84), when two families, those of Adasheff and Guedemine, were added. It was also decided that the rank of the nobility should be regulated by the position held, in either civil or military employment, by the father or other ancestors of each nobleman. This decree was known as Mestnichestvo and remained in force until 1682. Under Czar Theodore III (1676–82), the Mestnichestvo was abolished, and under a new decree all Russian noblemen were given the same rights irrespective of their origins. The old register was copied for the last time, and it came to be called the *Velvet Book* (*Barhatnaia Knega*), from its binding in red velvet. Families which had become prominent since the previous copying were unable to get their names into the record.

Titles were introduced by Peter the Great (1689–1725), who created princes, counts (1706), and barons (1710). In 1722 he decreed that all officers of the armed forces and civilian officials who had attained a certain rank should acquire hereditary nobility. Peter the Great also began the use of armorial bearings in Russia. He established (1722) a House of Nobles under a Herald-Marshal. The *Velvet Book* was preserved in the Heraldic Office of the Senate at St. Petersburg, at least until the Revolution. An official record of armorial bearings for the arms of the nobility was begun by the emperor Paul. Of this armorial ten volumes were published; fourteen more were ready for printing, but were never published. Many coats of arms for those who had acquired nobility by tenure of military or civil positions were established but never printed. Under Catherine II, about 1790, more stringent regulations were made. An Assembly of the Deputies of the Nobility was instituted in each province. A deputy from each district was present in this assembly, over which a Marshal of the Province presided. The Marshal's duty was to keep a book, which was divided into six parts. In these six sections were entered:

1. *Gentlemen without title who had been ennobled by diploma or letters patent.*
2. *Military nobility, as mentioned above.*
3. *Civil nobility, as mentioned above.*
4. *Nobility of foreign origin and having foreign titles.*
5. *Princes, counts, and barons created by letters patent.*
6. *The old princes and nobles, whose ancestors were in the* Velvet Book.

The five classes of Russian nobility were: (1) princes, (2) counts, (3) barons, (4) gentlemen ennobled before the reign of Peter I, and (5) gentlemen ennobled after the reign of Peter I. All the Russian nobles had equal privileges, however.

It can be understood that the particulars of the Russian nobles as outlined above are not quite the type of facts which would commend themselves to the present rulers of Russia. For this reason alone, the work of M. Ikonnikov will be increasingly valuable, for it will provide the information concerning the families of the nobility who are now dispersed throughout the world.

When the Czarist empire was at its height and included many European territories which are now satellite states, the nobilities of Poland, Lithuania, Livonia, Courland, Estonia, Georgia, Astrakhan, and the Crimea were included in the Russian Empire.

Apart from M. Ikonnikov's work, the following references may be useful to anyone concerned with Russian noble ancestry.

*Annuaire de la Noblesse de Russie* (various editions, nineteenth and early twentieth centuries. *La Noblesse Titrée de l'Empire de Russie,* by Dr. R. J. Ermerin (1892). *Les Principales Familles de la Russie,* by Prince Peter Dolgorauby (1859).

## WILLS

So far as is known, there was no central deposit for wills as in England. A will was examined and confirmed by a regional tribunal of justice, in whose archives it was kept.

# CZECHOSLOVAKIA

## CIVIL REGISTRATION OF BIRTHS, MARRIAGES, AND DEATHS

This did not start until 1918, when Czechoslovakia regained her independence. Even then it was compulsory only for those who were not "members" of any church, that is, what is called in Czechoslovakia "without confession." The children of these people were not baptized, their marriages were concluded at the district office, or town hall, and they were buried at a state- and not church-owned cemetery. Since 1950, however, all the registers have been taken over by the state, and they are the only legal form of registering these events, although the churches still keep their registers, for those who wish to baptize their children or to hold a marriage ceremony in the church after the official one at the town hall. These registers are kept at the town halls, and in the case of villages, there is usually one register for two or more places. There is a printed list of the existing registry offices.

All information regarding civil registration, but not actual copies of the records, is obtainable from the Archivni Sprava, at Prague 6, Trida Obrancu miru 133, or, in the case of Slovakia, through the Slovenaska Archivni Sprava, at Bratislava, Vajanskeho Nabrezi 8.

All certificates in respect of births, marriages, and deaths previous to December 31, 1949, whether issued by the civil authorities or by church and religious bodies, are obtainable through the relevant organs of the National Committees in the district towns and some of the larger villages. Foreign applicants should, however, apply to the Ministry of Foreign Affairs. In the event of application being made to the local National Committee, the document required will be forwarded through the Ministry of Foreign Affairs.

## CHURCH REGISTRATION

Before 1950 the registers kept by the different churches were official records, and every parish office was entitled to issue appropriate certificates. From 1918 to 1950 these registers included only those who considered themselves as members of their respective churches, Catholic or Protestant. Church registers began as far back as 1620 in some places, and there is a reasonable chance of finding register books in almost every parish. Before the reign of Emperor Joseph II (1741–90) there were only the Catholic registers, which were written mostly in Czech but, later, sometimes in Latin. After the time of Joseph II, Protestant registers were kept. He was a great reformer and was keen to have religious toleration in his dominions. He prescribed a certain form to be followed in making the register entries. Before his time, the church registers were very much concerned with the last confession of the deceased, while ignoring the actual cause of death. The reforms of Joseph II stopped this. Also, after his reign, the full names of parents and grandparents were entered in the registers of birth.

Joseph II ordered the registers to be kept in German or Latin, and not in Czech. Many priests preferred Latin to avoid using German. All these registers were taken over by the state in 1950. The books containing entries after 1870 are kept at the town halls together with the new registers, while the older ones are kept at one place for each of the nineteen regions of Czechoslovakia (usually a castle). They are open to the public and are arranged according to the former parishes. Czech began to be used in church registers again after 1848. The old parish registers are kept in the state archives. The new register offices are called *matricni urad*.

Parish registers are no longer used, having been closed by the end of 1949 and passed over to state register offices. They are now kept, starting with entries about 1860, at these offices. The older parochial records are in the state archives. There are, however, about 7000 parishes in Czechoslovakia, the number being uncertain, as there are Catholic parishes and Protestant parishes, which vary greatly in size and cover different places. The Catholic parishes are administered by four bishoprics in Bohemia and two in Moravia. State archives keeping the old parish registers are situated in each of the nineteen regions. In Bohemia and Moravia, they are not, however, in the chief city of the region, but usually in a castle, and only the registers of the whole Prague region are actually in Prague. The other places where similar archives are kept are as follows: Trebon (for Ceske Budejovice), Klasterec nad Ohri (for Karlovy Vary), Litomerice (for Usti nad Laben), Lemberk (for Liberec), Kuks (for Hradee Kralove), Telc (for Jihlava), Kunstat (for Brno), Janovice u Rymarova (for Olomouc), and Opava (for Ostrava).

Wills are not kept in any central depository, but with the state notaries, who are the proper persons to register them. The state notary has an office in each town with district administration, altogether 270 in the whole country. The Czech name for this office is *statni notarstvi.* Wills can also be kept at the People's Courts, also in district towns. They can be proved by the notary or the People's Court.

## HERALDRY

Coats of arms were registered in Vienna for the whole Austro-Hungarian monarchy prior to 1918. After that date the use of arms was no longer protected by the law, new arms have not been granted, and no registers kept. Before Czechoslovakia lost its independence in 1621, all the coats of arms were registered in Prague, at the royal court.

## GENERAL NOTE

Family archives of outstanding persons are kept at their respective state archives, apart from a few which are kept at the Archives of the National Museum. All inquiries concerning these and also inquiries regarding heraldry and genealogy should be addressed to the relevant state archive.

The various state, district, and town archives publish literature containing information as to the funds they administer. A list of all such literature so far published is given below. These publications can be ordered from Artia, Ltd., Prague. (Artia is the name of the Czechoslovak state publishing house in Prague.)

Martin Kolar, *Ceskomoravska Heraldika I* (Prague, 1902).

————, *Ceskomoravska Heraldika II* (Prague, 1925) (upravil Aug. Sedlacek).

Kral z Dobré Vody, *Heraldika* (Prague, 1900).

Ant. Schimon, *Der Adler von Böhmen, Mähren und Schlesien* (Ceska Lipa, 1859).

J. Siebmacher, *Grosses und Allgemeines Wappenbuch einer Neuen Auflage mit Heraldischen und Historisch-Genealogischen Erlauterungen;* IV Bd., 9 Abt.: "Der Böhmische Adler"; 10 Abt.: "Der Mährische Adler" (Norimberk, 1886–89).

Also, the following give lists of publications on heraldry and the old nobility of Bohemia and Moravia:

*Dodatek K Seznamu Archivnich Publikaci* (za Rok, 1957–58).

*Seznam Archivnich Publikaci.*

# YUGOSLAVIA

## CIVIL REGISTRATION

1. State registers of births, marriages, and deaths have been kept in the territory of Yugoslavia since May 9, 1946. Earlier, state registers were kept only in the territory of Voivodina, and that since 1895. Uniform state registers have been introduced in the whole of Yugoslavia. This means that these registers are exclusively kept by the state bodies.

2. Before May 9, 1946, registers were kept by church authorities according to the regulations of religious organizations. Registers were kept according to state regulations only for the Moslems.

3. State registers are kept by the People's Committees of the communes. In the People's Committee of the commune, the registers are kept by an official specially appointed for the purpose— the Registrar. The general management of the service of the civil status in the whole of Yugoslavia is the responsibility of the State Secretariat for Internal Affairs.

4. The following facts are entered in the state registers: birth, marriage, dissolution of marriage, annulment of marriage, death, proclamation of death, adoption, admission or denial of parentage, establishment of parentage, extension of parental custody and guardianship, and changes of family and other names. Separate registers are kept for births, marriages, and deaths. The state registers are public.

## HERALDRY

The following note is given at length because of the interest shown in matters heraldic in this Communist state; also because it denotes a historical interest in medieval coats of arms.

Coats of arms, blazons, and emblems of rulers, states, the Church, aristocratic families, and especially knights and military persons were most current in the Middle Ages, when rulers had them on their seals and knights on their shields. These bearings probably originated from ancient belief in magic means for combating spells (two-headed eagles, winged lions, dragons, and the like). The Slavs had taken them from their Western neighbors and from Byzantium. Among the South Slavs, they came into use during the twelfth and thirteenth centuries, upon the formation of South Slav states in the present-day regions. Actually, the old Slav coats of arms have not been sufficiently studied yet, and even some older manuals with lists and drawings of heraldic devices are unreliable. Such manuals date only from the sixteenth and seventeenth centuries and are all more or less the product of arbitrary combinations.

After the victory of the Entente powers in the First World War, on whose side the kingdom of Serbia had fought, the kingdom of the Serbs, Croats, and Slovenes was created in December 1918. From 1921 this has been called the kingdom of Yugoslavia. The state coat of arms had been determined under the Vidovdan Constitution of 1921, being composed of the coat of arms of the kingdom of Serbia, the coat of arms of Croatia, and the Illyrian-Slovenian-Celje coat of arms. The composite coat of arms had the following appearance: a white eagle poised for flight on a red shield. Both heads of the white two-headed eagle were topped by the royal crown. Superimposed on the eagle's breast was a shield with these coats of arms: Serbian—a white cross on a red shield with one ocellus in each arm (quarter) of the shield; Croatia—a checkered shield with twenty-five alternate red and silver squares; Slovenia—three golden six-pointed stars on a blue shield. Below this there was a white crescent.

The Constitution of the Federal People's Republic of Yugoslavia from January 31, 1946, determined the appearance of the coat of arms as follows:

"The state coat of arms of the Federal People's Republic of Yugoslavia represents a field encircled by sheaves of wheat. At the base the sheaves are tied with a ribbon on which is inscribed the date 29–XI–1943. Between the tops of the ears is a five-pointed star. In the center of the field five torches are laid obliquely, their several flames merging into a single flame."

The ribbon on the coat of arms bears the date November 29, 1943. Further details are given of the arms of other constituent parts of Yugoslavia.

## WILLS

Little information can be obtained from Yugoslavia regarding wills in that country, but I was advised that inquirers should apply to the Lawyers' Association: Udruzenje Pravnika FNRJ, Belgrade, Proleterskih Brigada 74.

# HUNGARY

## CIVIL REGISTRATION

The civil registration of births, marriages, and deaths in Hungary began on October 1, 1895. The records are kept in the National Center of Archives (Leveltarak Orszagos Kozpontja, Budapest I, Uri Utca 54–56). Relatives may send their applications to this address.

## PARISH REGISTERS

Registration of baptized persons was prescribed by the Diocesan Council of Veszprém in 1515. Obligatory registration was decreed by the Diocesan Council of Györ in 1579, and laid down in the Agendarius of the Diocese of Esztergom in 1583. It was again prescribed by the Provincial Council of Nagyszombat in 1611, and by the Diocesan Council of Esztergom in 1629. Registration of marriages, effective for the whole of the Church, was decreed by the Council of Trent (1545–63). This is where the registers of birth were first mentioned. Registration of deaths was decreed by Pope Paul V with his Roman Ritual issued in 1614. These ecclesiastical records were formerly kept in the parsonages of the parishes, but it is said that the older records have now been deposited with the National Archives in Budapest.

## WILLS

In Hungary there is no central registry for wills. According to the rules of probate, authorities or any other persons are obliged—as soon as they have been authentically informed about the death of the testator—to send the will in their possession to the notary public who is competent in probate. In the Hungarian law of succession the form of will may be either public or private. A public will must be made before a notary public or, if he is unable to assist, in court. To make a private will, neither the signature nor the assistance of the notary public is required.

## NATIONAL ARCHIVES

By far the largest collection of old documents is that in the state archives at Budapest. It is really a conglomeration of different archives. There are the Hungarian National Archives, which keep documents of the main government offices. There are also the Central Economic Archives, in which records of the most important economic organs are kept. Both these function in Budapest.

The documents preserved in the state archives have generally been calendared, and the inventories are registered with the National Center of Archives, the address of which has been given above.

In addition, there are twenty-one state archives organized on the geographical principle, each of them covering the territory of approximately one county. These provincial archives almost without exception function in provincial centers.

Another large group of Hungarian archives is composed of the private archives of national interest. The bulk of them are church archives (those of archbishoprics, bishoprics, and more important monastic orders). The overwhelming majority of their records have generally been calendared, a copy of their inventories being also kept in the National Center of Archives. With regard to foreign inquiries, all the Hungarian archives are exclusively represented by the National Center of Archives, which is ready to answer requests.

## HERALDRY AND NOBILITY

Law IV of 1947 abolished all noble and aristocratic ranks and prohibited the use of titles of nobility, coats of arms, and similar badges. Thus, dealing with such coats of arms is out of the question today. Nor did any authorities or bodies exist earlier to deal with and register coats of arms. The superior authority of the nobility was the Minister of the Interior; accordingly, it was he who—if need arose—authenticated the coats of arms on the basis of data kept in the National Archives. To this may be added the following. There has never been a College of Arms in Hungary. Letters patent given under the great seal were promulgated at the general assembly of the county in which the grantee lived. After 1526, these grants were, with changing regularity, matriculated in the so-called *Libri Regii*. A sort of central register was kept separately for Hungary and for Transylvania—before 1867 in Vienna and after that date in the International Archives in Budapest. Hungarian nationals, wishing to bear arms legally or use their titles of nobility (including territorial designation) in the kingdom of Hungary, were obliged to matriculate in the public register of arms and titles, kept and conducted by the Ministry of the Interior in Budapest. The National Archives acted in these cases as experts for the Ministry. The *Libri Regii* and this register have been published.

In addition to the deed issued by the Ministry of the Interior, the sheriff of every county had the right to issue similar certificates for persons living in his shrievalty. Both officers, that is, the Minister of the Interior and the sheriff of the county, were authorized to endorse birth briefs.

# JEWRY

## INTRODUCTION

In dealing with the problem of tracing Jewish ancestry in
Europe, I think that the way most likely to assist my readers
is to retrace my steps in securing such information as I can
give.

First of all, it is necessary to get the number of Jewish citizens of
the United States in proper proportion. There are, according to the
best estimates, about 5,200,000 Jews in America out of a total population of about 170,000,000; that is, Jews constitute about 3.1 per
cent of the whole U.S. population. Further, Jewish immigration into
the American continent did not really begin until the enactment of
the May Laws in Russia in the 1880s.

Second, research into the genealogy of Jews in Europe, and especially in eastern Europe, is likely to prove a very difficult task. I
now quote from the Secretary to the Board of Deputies of British
Jews (London): "In the first place, records of births, marriages,
etc., as we know them in this country were hardly brought into use
in the East European countries until at the earliest a century ago.
[Author's note: This can easily be seen by a reading of the entries
for Balkan countries in this book.] In the second place, such records
as existed in Poland, the Baltic countries, etc., have been wiped
out as a result of the extermination of the Jews by the Nazis. In connection with compensation by the Germans to the survivors of the
Jews who were persecuted by the Nazis, it has been necessary to try
and trace origins, and I can only tell you that this has been one of the

most difficult tasks ever undertaken and there has been no certainty about it throughout. The only suggestion I can make is that perhaps you or your correspondents in the U.S.A. might refer to the American Jewish Committee, which publishes an American Jewish Year Book, which gives much statistical information about Jews, but in the main these statistics are estimates and not based upon anything like a definite census. As far as we in this country [Britain] are concerned, I am afraid that we cannot help you, nor is there any source of information in this country to which I can refer you."

## SOCIETIES

I have quoted the above at length because it so fairly sets out the difficulties. I then turned to the American Jewish Committee. The address of this body is:

> *165 East Fifty-sixth Street*
> *New York 22, New York*

Communications should be sent to the Librarian. The Librarian stated that records of Jewish communities in Europe in connection with genealogical research on Americans of Jewish descent was a subject completely outside the field of competence of Committee. The Librarian, however, made some very useful suggestions regarding (*a*) the use of Jewish encyclopedias in this matter of research and (*b*) communication with two American Jewish organizations whose particulars are set out below.

The American Jewish Historical Society. *Address: 3080 Broadway, New York 27, New York. Communications should be addressed to Librarian Editor.*

*The Yivo Institute for Jewish Research (devoted to the social sciences and the humanities), 1048 Fifth Avenue, New York 28, New York. Address letters to the Secretary, Commission on Research, etc.*

From the last-named body I gained the following information: "In Poland the Jewish communities kept their own records. Registries of births, marriages, and deaths were known in Poland as *metryka,* and the Jewish community organization had a special department by that name." The Yivo Institute carries on the work that it began originally in Vilna before World War II, under the name of the Yiddish Scientific Institute. It is now working jointly with Yad Washem in Jerusalem on the history of the Jewish communities which were destroyed by the Nazis.

From the American Jewish Historical Society the following information was obtained, among other items. A list was prepared several years ago, by the Conference on Jewish Social Studies, of European Jewish libraries or libraries specializing in Jewish history and in Judaica and Hebraica. Accordingly, I referred to the Conference on Jewish Social Studies, Inc., 1841 Broadway, New York 23, New York. I was told by the Administrative Secretary that the reference must be to the list of Jewish cultural treasures in Axis-occupied countries published in the January 1946 issue of *Jewish Social Studies,* the latter being a quarterly published by the Conference.

## ENCYCLOPEDIAS

There are several standard Jewish encyclopedias which contain biographies of well-known Jews, whose families may still be flourishing.

*Jewish Encyclopedia:* a descriptive record of the history, religion, literature, and customs of the Jewish people from the earliest times to the present day—prepared under the direction of Cyrus Adler and others; Isidore Singer, managing editor (New York: Funk, 1901–6; 12 vols., illustrated). This is described by the American Jewish Committee as an excellent source for the genealogies of prominent older American Jewish families.

*The Standard Jewish Encyclopedia,* edited by Cecil Roth, published in London by W. H. Allen and in New York by Doubleday & Co., Inc. (1959). This is described as the most up-to-date, comprehensive, and authoritative single reference book on Jewish life, literature, and thought ever published. Over 8000 articles, 600 illustrations and maps, and 12 plates in full color. Many biographies are included.

*Valentine's Jewish Encyclopedia,* edited by Albert M. Hyamson and Dr. A. M. Silbermann (London: Shapiro, Valentine & Co., 1938). Contains numerous biographies.

## OTHER SOURCES OF INFORMATION

With regard to eastern European Jewish history and research resources, the following are described as authorities: (1) Prof. Ben Zion Dinur, Hebrew University, Jerusalem, Israel. (2) Prof. Israel Halpern, same address. (3) Prof. Bernard D. Weinryb, Yeshiva University, Amsterdam Avenue and 186th Street, New York 33, New York. (4) Prof. Cecil Roth, Chalbury Road, Oxford, England.

I would point out to the American inquirer the value of seeking information from the Yeshiva University. I was in communication with Professor Bernard D. Weinryb. In answer to my inquiries he informed me that "of the [Jewish] archives, those in Soviet Russia —including those of the former Baltic States—are so far inaccessible. Polish archives are accessible under certain conditions (I do not know the situation in Rumania). West German archives— including the Archivlager in Göttingen, which harbors parts of the former Berlin archives—are generally accessible. It is more difficult, however, to reach the archives in East Germany." The reader who studies the chapters on the various countries referred to will be able to confirm the above information for himself. From Professor Weinryb I have also gathered the following information: "In the inter-war years a periodical appeared in Germany (1924–34) dealing with Jewish genealogy, entitled *Jüdische Familienforschung.* In *Essays in American Jewish History,* published in Cincinnati, Ohio, by the *American Jewish Archives* (1958), an article by Malcolm H. Stern is printed, 'The Function of Genealogy in American Jewish History.' A note by the editor informs [us] that Mr. Stern has finished a compendium of genealogy, *Americans of Jewish Descent,* which will be published soon." It is suggested that Mr. Stern may be contacted through the Hebrew Union College, Cincinnati, which publishes the *American Jewish Archives.*

From the Israel Archives Association I have received a pamphlet entitled *Archives in Israel, Surveys on the Institutional Members of the Israel Archives Association.* The portion of this which is of great interest is that under the heading "The Jewish Historical General Archives." Address: Jerusalem, Yad Washem Building, Har Hazicaron, P.O.B. 1062. From this I quote the following account:

"With the ingathering of the exiles a growing need was felt for creating a central institution in Jerusalem to serve as a national repository for Jewish historical research, which is increasingly concentrated in Jerusalem. This need was filled by the Jewish Historical General Archives—an organ of the Historical Society of Israel—which since their foundation in 1939 methodically collect archives of Jewish communities, institutions, and organizations, public and private records as well as odd historical documents from the Diaspora. After the extermination of European Jewry the Archives concentrated their efforts in post-war years on recovering the archival remnants of destroyed Jewish communities. On the initiative of the Archives, special missions and local experts conduct a systematic survey of Jewish records in various European countries in order to register and microfilm the material if unable to acquire the original documents and files. This also applies to relevant material which is found in non-Jewish Archives and will complete the Archives transferred to Jerusalem or replace lost Jewish records. So far the Archives or remnants thereof of about 1000 Jewish communities from dozens of countries are kept at the General Archives as well as more than 700,000 frames of microfilm. Reports on current activities of the General Archives are published regularly in *Zion, A Quarterly for Research in Jewish History,* published by the Historical Society of Israel. The General Archives supply photographs and microfilms for research purposes against payment of expenses. Director: D. J. Cohen, M.A."

Of even greater importance is the following information derived from the Jewish Historical General Archives, the address of which is:

> Jerusalem
> 9 Shlomzion Hamalka Street
> P.O.B. 1062

From this source it is stated: "A collective research work on the registration of Jewish births, deaths, and marriages in European countries has lately been carried out in our archives. The survey contains an introduction, which covers several European countries and refers to the internal registration made by Jewish communities mostly before the time the Jews were included in the general instructions given by the authorities. In the survey itself exact data and details on registration are given on Germany. The survey will be printed in *Archivum,* Vol. IX, which is to appear in 1960."

In the Israel Archives Association there are the following sections:

*1. The State Archives,* Jerusalem, Hakirya. This was founded in 1949. Its information is mostly concerned with the administration of Palestine under the British Mandate and the hand-over to the new state of Israel.

*2. The Central Zionist Archives.* This was founded in Berlin in 1919. It was transferred to Jerusalem in 1933–34. It consists of the historical archives of the Zionist movement which led up to the settlement of the Jews in Palestine. Address: Jerusalem, 1 Rehov Ibn Gavirol, P.O.B. 92.

*3. The Archives of Religious Zionism,* Jerusalem, Rabbi Kook Foundation, Shehunat Maimon, P.O.B. 642. These archives were established in 1953.

*4. The Jewish Historical General Archives,* Jerusalem, Yad Washem Building, Har Hazicaron, P.O.B. 1062. (See above.)

*5. The Central Archives of Yad Washem,* Jerusalem, Yad Washem Building, Har Hazicaron, P.O.B. 84. "Among the most important collections are to be mentioned the archives of the Munich Historical Commission, which include thousands of German documents dealing mainly with the extermination of German Jews, as well as testimonies given by survivors of the massacre; a great deal of documentary material on war criminals amassed in the two archival groups of the 'Historical Committees' in Vienna and Linz, and the 'Archives of the Underground Movement in Białystok Ghetto.' Great importance is attached to many millions of microfilmed documents, which include the secret archives of the Warsaw Ghetto, etc."

*6. The Archives of the Israel Defense Army,* Tel Aviv, 4 Rehov Esther H. Hamalka.

*7. Archives and Museum of the Jewish Labor Movement,* Tel Aviv, Beit Lessin, 26 Rehov Hanassi Ch. Weizmann, P.O.B. 303. Founded in 1932.

*8. The Jabotinsky Institute in Israel,* Tel Aviv, 38 Rehov King George, P.O.B. 2171. Founded in 1934, contains material bearing on the national liberation movement.

*9. The General Archives of the Tel Aviv–Jaffa Municipality,* Tel Aviv, Municipal Building, 27 Bialik Street.

*10. The Weizmann Archives,* Rehovoth, Weizmann House.

*11. Archives of the Kibbutz Arzi Hashomer Hazair Movement,* Merchavia.

*12. Ghetto Fighters' House in Memory of Yizhak Katznelson,* Kibbutz Lohamei Haghettaot, Post Office, Haifa.

From the above account it will be seen that to trace Jewish ancestry in Europe is a difficult task. The reasons for this are to be found in the circumstances of the last war and the Nazi persecutions. What of European countries like Italy, or Britain? Within the last century or 120 years, the details would be found, as regards birth, etc., in the public registers; before that date, in the separate records of the Jewish community.

Curiously enough, although I have seen many Jewish pedigrees, I have rarely found them going back a long way. In Britain the Jews have been settled in peace since 1655, and some of the Jewish pedigrees which are now found in *Burke's Peerage* and other books cover the past 300 years. In other cases, like that of the famous Benjamin Disraeli, Earl of Beaconsfield, where the origin of the family was in Italy, only a few generations are given. It is possible that the anti-Jewish persecutions which have often occurred in Europe, long before the time of Hitler, have prevented the preservation of Jewish records. The longest Jewish pedigree which has come my way was that of an English Jew whose forebears had lived for several centuries in Vienna. This pedigree covered 500 to 600 years.

It would be advisable for the American Jewish inquirer to begin with the American sources I have indicated above. After he has ascertained the rudimentary details, everything will turn on the part of Europe from which his forebears came.